MISSING CONNECTIONS

CHALLENGING THE CONSENSUS

The search for hidden truths,
obscured patterns, and unseen realities

edited by
J. DOUGLAS KENYON

FROM THE ATLANTIS RISING® MAGAZINE LIBRARY

Published in 2016 by Atlantis Rising
Distributed to the trade by Red Wheel/Weiser, LLC
65 Parker St., Unit 7 • Newburyport, MA 01950-4600
www.redwheelweiser.com

ISBN: 978-0-9906904-2-9 (pbk)

Cover and text design by Kathryn Sky-Peck
Photos and Illustrations @ *Atlantis Rising* Magazine

PRINTED IN CANADA
10 9 8 7 6 5 4 3 2 1
MAR

CONTENTS

PART THREE:
SECRET SOCIETIES, LOST RELIGIONS

PART FOUR:
THE UNKNOWN JESUS

Help for the Color-Blind

BY J. DOUGLAS KENYON

T his is a book for those who suspect there may be more to our collective human history than what they've learned from mainstream academia. This is a tome for those who go against the grain of "accepted" fact, those who dare to doubt the truth of the truthmakers, for those who recognize the looming realities that go unseen and unheeded by the established academic/scientific order. Over hundreds of years, human consensus has passed down its legacy without question. But there are missing connections, giant question marks, and links that cannot be ignored. What if Columbus didn't discover America? What if Egyptians visited the grand canyon? What if the Knights Templar and the Aztecs had a common history? What if Jesus and Horus were one and the same? What if history was much more colorful than just the accepted black and white? There are those who would shun such questions, those who are color-blind in a potentially more colorful world. For those in search of missing connections, we offer this collection of 30 essays by some of the most forward-thinking, critical researchers of our time.

Since *Atlantis Rising* first saw print, we have made it our business to challenge the abuses of the prevailing scientific and historical authorities. Indeed, we have tried not to miss an opportunity to point out the shortcomings of orthodoxy wherever we found them. The pervasive corruption, materialism, mediocrity, and so forth—to say nothing of the suppression of contrary points of view—have not inspired our confidence.

Nevertheless, having said that, we don't want to give the impression that we are blind to problems at the other end of the spectrum.

Alas, what might be called the "new age," with its emphasis on impulse, intuition, and the like, suffers itself, we fear, from a lack of objectivity, self-discipline, depth and even integrity and fosters many practices which, we feel, might well lead us all by a short route to destruction. Most pundits today seem to be in one camp or the other, but what matters most, we think, is not so much the politics of left and right, as the challenge of uniting left brain and right brain.

The point has been made before in *Atlantis Rising*, but it is worth repeating: We need balance. Without it there is no transcendence. As anyone knows who has ever worn those red and green plastic glasses at a 3-D movie, both eyes when operating alone see only a two-dimensional world; but when teamed up, they reveal a third dimension (depth). Similarly, the balanced union of the left and right hemispheres of the brain opens the doorway to previously unseen or unrealized dimensions. The failure to unite the two different modes of knowing—objective and subjective, linear and holistic, scientific and artistic, masculine and feminine, etc.— keeps us trapped between poles, bound to the present plane of conflict. Like crippled foot travelers lost in a snowstorm, we circle forever with our stronger side dominating. The successful tightrope walker, however, allows neither left nor right to rule but, instead, masters both.

Recently, in a couple of arguments with a pair of self-styled experts on the revealed wisdom of the current order, we were told in no uncertain terms that the writers of this publication were not qualified, academically speaking, to discuss the topics presented in these pages. Since both gentlemen seemed somewhat irate, in the interest of peace, we referred one of them to those among our ranks who hold high degrees from such exalted institutions as the University of Chicago, M.I.T., Cambridge, etc., but before we tried that approach with the other, we paused to reflect on just what was going on here.

It seemed clear that we were being bullied into accepting the appeal to authority as a standard for argument, which is separate from, and unrelated to, the actual logical merits of the cases being considered. Any debate over credentials would be changing the subject from the actual issues that we believe need to be covered and that we believe become perfectly clear to any reasonably intelligent person, expert or not, when the case is properly and honestly made.

The real question, which should be answered by the custodians of the current conventional wisdom, is: What exactly has them so upset? If they are so certain of the plausibility of their case, what possible concern can they have over the rantings and railings of a little book like this?

On any debated point—whether it is the reality of the afterlife or the evidence of extraterrestrial existence—the general argument between the skeptic and the defender of the consensus seems to go like this: "I don't know that it doesn't exist, but you don't know that it does." And the academic elite pursue their stance with a rhetoric that approaches emotional fervor. What should be inferred from such behavior? Is it possible that their zeal serves to mask their doubt of the actual truth? Or does it betray an insecurity that their cherished consensus might actually be fallible?

We have observed before in *Atlantis Rising* that the following analogy holds true: there are those who are color-blind in a more colorful world. Truth is not either/or; it is not black and white. We wish to promote awareness of the many hues that fill the world—some of which cannot be seen until properly pointed out. The academic consensus may be that the sky is blue, but look deeply enough and soon we are discussing the sky in hues of purple, green, and yellow—a myriad of color that opens a door to deeper understanding.

PART ONE

UNSOLVED CRIMES

"The departure of John and Sebastian Cabot from Bristol
on their first voyage of discovery, 1497."
(Ernest Board, 1906)

1

THE MURDER OF JOHN CABOT

How Did the Great Genoese Explorer Really Meet His End? And How Did America Really Get Its Name?

BY STEVEN SORA

Homicide detectives know that after 48 hours the trail to the perpetrator starts getting cold. After five hundred years the odds of solving a murder are small, making the violent murder of John Cabot a true cold case. It involves a Genoese merchant, a Spanish soldier, and an English sheriff whose name came to grace the North and South American continents.

John Cabot, born Giovanni Caboto, was a Genoese navigator sailing for the British. He was a businessman who had accumulated enough money to settle anywhere, and for a brief time lived in Venice where he received citizenship. At heart he remained an adventurer. He was sailing for cod and a route to China and became the first European to get credit for reaching North America.

Alonso de Hojeda was the epitome of the brutal conquistador of the Americas and was sailing for the king and queen of Spain. He had a reputation as a brute and a cutthroat, but in the eyes of Isabella and Ferdinand, this added up to the efficient sergeant that they needed to control Columbus.

By the time Columbus had set sail for America, he had been a mapmaker fortunate enough to marry into the wealthy Perestrello family. Just after his wedding he was given a gift of the maps and charts of the Knights of Christ, the reincarnated Portuguese Knights Templar. He had sailed to Bristol in England where the citizens regularly sent out ships to find cod in the remote waters of the western Atlantic. And he sailed possibly as far as Iceland where the Norse had also known of the rich fishing grounds we know as the Grand Banks.

When Columbus returned from the New World, John Cabot was in Spain, and made the decision to find employment elsewhere. He headed

Alonso de Hojeda

to Bristol in England. Already wealthy, he had to conceal his affluence as Bristol and Venice (Cabot's adopted city) were often at odds in trade suits. To further his connections to the powers-that-be, Cabot quickly made the right friends.

One of his new friends was Richard Ameryk. Ameryk was a merchant who wore many hats, including that of sheriff and customs agent for the port. He regularly invested in ships sailing south to Spain and Portugal and west toward the rich fishing grounds. He also exercised a certain amount of control on local trade and benevolently looked out for his fellow merchants.

As a newcomer, Cabot quickly realized one was either with this Bristol "mafia" or one might as well find another port. Cabot and Ameryk became quick friends.

Bristol had been sending out ships for cod for decades, but the Hanseatic league, an alliance of traders, claimed the sea around Iceland as their own and regularly warred against interlopers. Bristol's merchants devised a plot to throw up a smoke screen around their fishing trade. They claimed each year to be sending ships to search for an island known as Hy-Brasil. This oddly named island may have been one of those isles that had once sunk into the Atlantic. Or it could have been a subterfuge. The outgoing ships were always packed with salt, a necessary ingredient in drying cod.

In 1497, Cabot made a real voyage of exploration for the English king and left from Bristol. Sheriff Ameryk was one of his investors. Instead of discovering China, Cabot cruised the waters of what would become Canada's Maritime Provinces. He brought home a map that has not survived the centuries in good condition, but most likely he coasted Newfoundland and Nova Scotia and possibly even Maine. The place names he left on his first map of the New World can barely be read and others did not survive the effects of age on the chart.

Around the same time Cabot reached the New World, the king and queen of Spain were getting impatient with their explorer Columbus. He may have found a New World, but he didn't find Cathay or Cipangu, China or Japan, nor did he bring home gold and silver. To make the voyage pay, the Spanish did kidnap a handful of Arawak natives, but they proved unsuitable for labor as slaves, inconveniently dying.

The Spanish royals decided to send a more efficient agent. They picked Alonso de Hojeda. The Spaniard was more a pirate than an explorer. With little time to waste on moral issues or legal niceties, he actually attacked other ships on the way to the Americas. Next he stopped at the island of Lanzarote in the Canary chain where he plundered the house of the daughter of Columbus, Dona Beatriz! One of the men who would regret taking passage on Hojeda's ship was Amerigo Vespucci. He was one of the bankers who worked for the Medici family and as a merchant outfitted the expedition. Along for the journey was another man who would play an important role, Juan de la Cosa.

John Cabot's first expedition was to be followed by a much longer voyage of exploration. He was a given a charter by King Henry to explore the New World, although it specifically dictated that Cabot not travel into the land claimed by Spain. There is reason to believe that the king knew exactly where he would be traveling but didn't want to risk alienating the Spanish. Cabot left England in 1498 and never returned. There is evidence that he may have started from his southernmost point of his first voyage and headed further south. He would have coasted the still "undiscovered" Virginias and Florida and finally reached the coast of what would become South America.

There, in South America, the first country name that would remain on the map of the America's was Venezuela. Meaning "Little Venice," it had reminded European travelers of the Italian Venice because of houses built out into the coastal waters. Was it John Cabot who named it after his adopted city of Venice? Or was it the brute Hojeda or someone who had appreciated the beauty of the South American coastal villages?

The year was now 1499. Hojeda, who was a favorite of the crown because of his ruthlessness and daring, took his more controversial orders through an intermediary. This man was the Bishop Juan de Fonseca who advised him to kill any Englishmen he came across. Fonseca was a capable administrator whose spy network had tentacles that reached as far as London and Bristol. A letter from the Spanish envoy stationed in London, Pedro de Ayala, claimed that Cabot had already sailed into waters claimed by Columbus. It also declared he was going to be heading again toward Spanish waters.

Through the de Ayala communication, and through information by John Day of Bristol, the Spanish understood that not only was Cabot looking for Cipangu—the outermost island of Asia—but that he was provisioned for a full year. This was much unlike the quick first voyage. To the Spanish it was a threat. The orders to kill were unfortunately typical as other English and French colonists would later find out. The cruelty of the Spaniards did not end with the Native Americans.

Cabot's expedition had set out with a "king's ship," that is, a ship provided by the English king, and four merchant-owned ships. One had problems and quickly returned to England; the other four headed west.

Hojeda's ship sailed from Cadiz in May of 1499. They reached South America around modern-day Surinam and then coasted to the island of Curaçao. Their next landfall was at Coquibacoa in August of that year. Here Hojeda killed a handful of natives and raided their village in search of gold. He reported in his journal that they had indeed come across "certain Englishmen." He didn't state that he had killed them, but his orders had been explicit. Since there were no other English expeditions to the Americas at this point, it is highly likely that the Englishmen he encountered were none other than Cabot and his crew.

The reason for keeping a low profile in reporting his actions is that England and Spain were not at war. It was an act of piracy. It would actually be an offense that not only deserved hanging but could be the catalyst for a declaration of war. No other witness among the Spanish produced any written record that detailed his encounter with the English. And none of the English survived to tell their side of the encounter.

Most likely, he first attacked Cabot's ships, then killed his men, and finally looted and sunk his ships. Immediately after this encounter at Coquibacoa, Hojeda's ships were in need of substantial repairs, so it is possible that Cabot's crew put up some resistance. After repairs in Hispaniola, Hojeda returned home as a hero and was rewarded with the title of governor of the Province of Coquibacoa. The document granting him the title specifically mentions the discovery of English exploration that he thwarted.

Did the English king find out? There is no record of it, yet Cabot's pension stopped being paid in September of 1499. Neither the Spanish royalty nor the English king wanted war, so if this brutal act of piracy did take place, it might have been best left behind. What happened in Venezuela stayed in Venezuela.

But one man was clearly upset with whatever crimes were committed when he was part of the expedition. The Italian Vespucci decided not

Cosa's Map

to return with Hojeda. In fact, Vespucci would write two or more letters regarding the voyage with Hojeda but never mention his name. He most likely refused to be a part of the atrocities, which included wantonly murdering Europeans and Native Americans alike. He refused to go on slaving expeditions that Hojeda planned in the Bahamas. And finally upon landing in Hispaniola, he took another ship to Europe. Was it a moral issue for Vespucci or did he fear being hung as a pirate along with the Spanish marauder? He even refused to remain an agent to the Spanish after this voyage and switched to the competition, Portugal.

Juan de la Cosa did stay loyal to Hojeda. Cosa would put together a map that not only showed the coastline of Guyana and Venezuela; it also showed the coast from at least Maine on down to Florida as well as islands of the Caribbean. Since there were no Spanish ships that far north, and it was still fifteen years before Ponce de Leon would map Florida, where was the source for Cosa's map? Hojeda's ship is accounted for day by day and had not departed from the southern Caribbean Sea.

Letters and certain charts of the expedition fell into the hands of Martin Waldsemuller, a cartographer in the employ of Rene II, the Duke of Lorraine. On the first Waldsemuller map was depicted the name Amerigo Vespucci, in letters twice as large as other names. Did he intend to name the New World after the banker? He knew Columbus was the discoverer of the new lands. If he had intended to name it after Vespucci, possibly because of a relationship between the Vespucci family and Rene II, why would the land be named America?

Why not call the New Land "Vespucci"? One reason might be that the word was derived from the Italian word for "wasp" (Vespa), not an appealing name for a country, yet there are few place names named for a first name outside of those named for royalty.

There is evidence to bear that Vespucci was not considered as a name for the new lands. When Waldsemuller revised the maps, the next two additions did not mention Vespucci by first name or last.

Then how did the New World become America? Consider the possibility that it was John Cabot's map that became the basis for the Cosa map and the other charts sent back to Europe. Historians, including James Williamson, point out that the coast of Venezuela on the Cosa map is highly accurate and that it was not explored fully by the Spanish in the year 1500. Cosa himself has five flags that are noted as places explored by the English, again in 1500, when no English (outside of Cabot) sailed that far south. In fact, no part of Cosa's map is more accurately drawn than the coast between Trinidad and Maracaibo. Cabot, like many Italian explorers, would have bestowed upon the new lands names of his sponsors, his partners, and possibly his own family. The name America could have come from his good friend and occasional partner Richard Ameryk.

While spelling in the fifteenth and sixteenth centuries was not an exact art, the incorrect spelling of a name is not enough to disqualify it. A letter to Henry spells Cabot's name as "Kabotto." The surname Ameryk is actually derived from the Welsh surname Ap Meryke. The sheriff's family had additional alternative spellings including Amyreke. Last, the Sheriff's merchant seal is the most telling, spelling his name in a circular form, A-M-E-R-I-C and finally returning to the A.

The map drawn by Cabot may have extended from the point of his first voyage south to Venezuela. It may have included the names he left as acknowledgments of his partners and sponsors. It may have then been part of the booty taken by Hojeda who mentions his encounter with the English, but leaves out the details. Cosa, an inferior in terms of cartography, was then able to give details even on lands far away from those navigated by the Spanish. Charts and letters from Cosa, Vespucci, and others were sorted out by the mapmakers of St. Die, and somehow a name Cabot left on his map became the name for the New World.

2

SHAKESPEARE
AND THE BERMUDA TRIANGLE

Following the Strange and Tragic Saga
of the Good Ship "Sea Venture"

BY STEVEN SORA

T he survivors of a wrecked craft find themselves on an impossibly remote island. They salvage what they can from the craft and make camp on the beach. On this island, compasses don't work, strange lights appear and disappear, boars crush through the forest. At least one man would find the new island the clean slate he so badly needed. Most would later regret leaving the island. Sound familiar?

Actually, this is not the crash of Oceanic 815 (from the popular ABC series *Lost*). It is the story of a shipwreck that occurred nearly four hundred years earlier at the eastern edge of the mysterious Bermuda Triangle. On this island, then known as the Isle of Devils, the strange phenomenon of St. Elmo's fire was recorded, as were bizarre compass bearings.

The story of the wreck of the *Sea Venture* also became pivotal in the debate of just who wrote the works of Shakespeare.

On July 24, 1609, a storm brewed in the Atlantic. Before the seas would calm, the Bermuda Triangle claimed one of its many victims. The *Sea Venture* was part of a small fleet heading for the Jamestown colony in Virginia. Supplies and reinforcements were badly needed and the Virginia Company had sent 800 people aboard a flotilla to the desperate colony. Two of the fleet did not survive the passage thanks to the Tainos God of Destruction, Huracan. One disappeared, most likely to the bottom of the sea; the other broke up on the deadly reef that surrounded the island of Bermuda.

The *Sea Venture* survived just long enough for the 150 passengers to launch a life boat and get everyone as well as a great deal of supplies to safety. Among the survivors were Sir Thomas Gates, destined to be the governor of Virginia, Sir George Somers, the admiral of the fleet who would have served with Sir Francis Drake, and Robert Devereaux, the Earl of Essex, and a failed civil servant, William Strachey, so deeply in debt that the New World was the only refuge from his creditors.

The survivors quickly found their island to be both a hell and a heaven. Most of them had never been laborers, nor had any experience living in the wild. The cries of large birds, the crashing of wild boars in the brush, and the noise of the sea crushing their ship into splinters all served to send fear into the hearts of the castaways.

Before the wreck of the *Sea Venture,* there were few who had seen the islands of Bermuda. One was Columbus, who wrote in his log of strange lights and bizarre compass bearings. Another was Juan Bermudez, who called the tiny islands the Isle of Devils. After his visit in 1503, he advised the king that the island chain might serve as a supply station for Spain, but the pounding surf and the dangerous reef allowed few visitors. A Portuguese vessel had wrecked on the dangerous reefs in 1543 and a French vessel was grounded in 1594. Both were able to rebuild and sail on to safety.

The *Sea Venture* survivors quickly organized themselves and began working on a ship to complete the trip to Virginia. They built this ship from the wreckage of the *Sea Venture*. Hastily patched together, it may not have been ready for the hundreds of miles of ocean between Bermuda and the coast of the Virginias. Before they received word if their first rescue attempt was successful (it wasn't), they built two more ships, the *Deliverance* and the *Patience*, that would safely reach Virginia. There they found the colony in terrible shape. The fort was run down, attempts at agriculture had failed, and after a series of dishonest encounters, the native population refused to trade with them. While the river was rich with fish, native archers made attempts at fishing deadly. The Bermuda survivors were sorry that they had left the island behind.

THE SOURCE OF SHAKESPEARE'S TEMPEST

Many of the Bermuda survivors headed back to England, although William Strachey stayed in Virginia. He could barely share a drink with friends at the Mermaid Tavern without the fear of being arrested for his debts. His circle of friends once included Henry Wriothesley, the Earl of Southampton, Sir Francis Drake, the writer Ben Jonson, the poet Michael Drayton, Sir

The Sea Venture (artist's rendition)

Philip Sidney, and Sir Francis Bacon. Many of these friends had shared schooling at Gray's Inn and enjoyed London's literary scene. Strachey had dropped out of Gray's and begun a life of failed endeavors.

In the first days ashore in Virginia, he composed a letter describing the adventure of being shipwrecked in Bermuda. Addressed to a Lady Sara, the wife of Sir Thomas Smythe, it was actually more than a letter—before he was done his text was 25,000 words long. While the letter would not be published until 1625, within two years of the shipwreck someone writing under the name of William Shakespeare produced a play called *The Tempest*. Generally considered to be written around 1611, *The Tempest* was the last drama written by the bard, but was not published until 1623.

For those who debate the authorship of Shakespeare's works, *The Tempest*, because of its date and other references became pivotal. (See *Atlantis Rising* #54)

The Tempest tells the story of a shipwreck in the Mediterranean that strands Prospero, the Duke of Milan, with his daughter on an island, along with the passengers who survive. There are passages from the Golding translation of Ovid as well as Florio's *Montaigne* that are found in several works attributed to Shakespeare; however, the most remarkable passage of *The Tempest* is in Act 1 when Ariel visits the "still vexed Bermoothes."

SECRETS SOCIETIES

In England there were several intellectual circles that strove to change the system of state and church. Two institutions ran the world, bringing twin evils of taxation and war while stifling the development of learning. Advances in the sciences including astronomy, chemistry, medicine, and navigation all were conducted under the threat of excommunication and death. Two of the most influential players were Sir Walter Raleigh and his "School of Night," and Sir Francis Bacon's London-based group. Both pushed for an agenda of creating a new world in the colonies that would incorporate democratic principles and a lessening of the state and church authority. Bacon is often credited with being the founder of Rosicrucianism. Raleigh called himself the Red Cross Knight. These both implied a commonality with the Knights Templar, who wore the Red Cross and used it for the design of the masts on their ships.

The meeting houses of these societies served as the lodges did for craft masonry. The intellectual circle was considered speculative masonry. In 1600, the masons were still a secret society. Finally, in 1717 they came out in public and met in publicly recognized lodges.

Members of both Raleigh's and Bacon's groups were active in writing plays, including comedies and historical recreations. The plays often contained opinions that might be dangerous if expressed in the England of Queen Elizabeth I and later King James. It was not uncommon to hire a "beard" to produce such controversial works as one's own. In the 17th century, the reference for someone who fronted for the writings of others was known as a "Terence." One contemporary writer, John Davies, dedicated a poem to their shared English "Terence," Will Shakespeare.

PLAYERS AND PLAYWRIGHTS

Edward De Vere (the Earl of Oxford) is someone who often gets the credit for writing the works of Shakespeare. He could not publish under his own name because of the tenuous political climate, but that would not stop him completely. The problem with De Vere and *The Tempest* is that De Vere was already dead when the wreck occurred. Others claim he wrote *The Tempest* not based on the *Sea Venture* but on a ship of Sir Walter Raleigh's in the Bermuda triangle before De Vere's death, and another wreck that included a Bacon relative, Bartholomew Gosnold in 1602. All three voyages shared the same backer, Henry Wriothesley, the Earl of Southampton.

It is more than coincidence that Wriothesley was Shakespeare's principal patron, in fact providing him with the funds to buy his first home in Stratford. Wriothesely's close circle included Sir Francis Bacon, Edward de Vere, Roger Manners (Earl of Rutland), and others who are all suspects as the true authors. As the political situation had no opportunity for the upper class to threaten Queen Elizabeth with their literary pleasures, a scapegoat was needed. Then Shakespeare came along. The Earl of South-ampton immediately saw an opportunity. Wriothesley and a family member would become Shakespeare's most important patrons. Shakespeare, in dire need of funds, would gladly take the chance of playing the "bard." Wriothesley thus became the conduit that had published the writings of a handful of men under the byline of someone who was considered "an illiterate butcher's apprentice turned actor." Beginning in 1592, a singularly large amount of money passed from Wriothesley to Shakespeare allowing the newly minted "bard" to buy property.

Between 1598 and 1604 thirteen plays of "Shakespeare" appeared. When De Vere died in 1604, these plays were staged as a memorial to him. After his death, no plays appeared for four years. Did someone else take up the pen? Christopher Marlowe is another suspect, but he was also believed dead at this time. A study of Marlowe's vocabulary and Shakespeare's by Thomas Mendenhall convinced him that they matched each other like a fingerprint. Mendenhall, a physicist and statistician, had been hired to back the Francis Bacon as Shakespeare case. But many rationalize this as the true Shakespeare author simply improving Marlowe's work. Marlowe's *Jew of Malta* becomes new and improved as Shakespeare's *Merchant of Venice*.

If *The Tempest* with its "Bermoothes" reference was written after the death of both De Vere and Christopher Marlowe (d. 1593), are there other authorial suspects? Sir Francis Bacon is the best choice. In *Players*, by Bertram Fields, there is a list of several lines that are similar or exact between *Promus*, known to be a Baconian text, and Shakespeare. At least one Baconian proverb "Thought is Free" is exactly mirrored in *The Tempest*.

William Stanley, another suspect, was the Earl of Derby. In *The Tempest* there is a character, Ferdinand, the son of the king of Naples, who may have been named for Stanley's brother. He had a habit of signing as W. S. One of his ancestors had betrayed Richard III, resulting in the coronation of Henry VII, who was part of Stanley's family tree. He went to the right schools, traveled and played the sports of the wealthy. A Jesuit priest once wrote that Stanley was writing comedies, although nothing appeared under his own name.

The likeliest candidate for being the author of many of Shakespeare's works is Francis Bacon. Like patron Henry Wriothesley, Bacon was very much involved in the New World. When Bacon studied at Grey's Inn he was the driving force behind an invisible knighthood, The Order of the Helmet. The "helmet" was the one worn by the goddess Pallas Athena who is depicted with both helmet and spear. The influence of Bacon and others who promoted the Virginia colony is evident in the way that their goddess remains on the Virginia State flag four hundred years later.

Virginia played a most important role in forming the democracy that became America; Bermuda played a parallel role. Friends of Bacon and members of his intellectual circle decided the Isle of Devils was not so bad after all. The crest of Sir Francis Bacon contains a wild boar, which is identical to the heraldic device of Bermuda. In fact, in the first years of the Virginia colony—run by a handful of Bacon supporters and friends—they coined "Hog Money." Bacon's role in creating a democracy was of course not approved by King James I who would forbid the circulation of Hog Money.

FRIENDS OF BACON AND BERMUDA

Bermuda, like New Orleans, is divided into parishes. Evidence of Bacon's circle is reflected in nearly every parish. Henry Wriothesley, Earl of Southampton, the backer of Shakespeare, would have Southampton Parish named for him.

Pembroke Parish was named for the Third Earl of Pembroke. This is the man to whom Shakespeare's 1623 *Folio* is dedicated. He was a Knight of the Garter and actively involved in the Bermuda Company. Through marriage, the Pembroke family was related to Philip Sydney, author of *Arcadia*. The Third Earl was also a close friend of Bacon's. Another Knight of the Garter, James Hamilton, would lend his name to Hamilton Parish.

Devonshire Parish is named for the uncle of the Earl of Pembroke. Paget Parish was named for the Fourth Lord, William Paget, who served in the military with Essex.

St. George's Parish is named for George Somers, who was a friend of Raleigh's. He died in Bermuda in 1610. He had taken Spanish treasure ships and warships alike. His heart remains in St. George Parish while his body was returned home.

Warwick Parish was named for Robert Rich, the second Earl of Warwick. He had his own troupe of actors, known as "the Earl of Warwick's men," later managed by Edward de Vere (Earl of Oxford). The company put on plays that were later attributed to Shakespeare. Robert Green would call Shakespeare "Shakes Scenes" and accused him of both buying plays and stealing scenes. Like Bacon, the Earl of Warwick would not agree with the capricious royalty and was once imprisoned for condemning illegal taxation. Like others favored in the Elizabethan court, including Drake and Raleigh, he would send privateers to the Caribbean to disrupt Spanish shipping.

Bermuda was given little attention by the Crown as it had no gold or resources. It survived on the edges of legitimate trade. In the research for my book, *Secret Societies of America's Elite*, I found that at least one third of all trade in Bermuda was illegal smuggling. The tiny island chain served as a conduit for goods needed by the Virginia revolutionaries against the armies and navies of King George III of England. Virginia needed guns, Bermuda needed food. Freemasonry was the glue that allowed such trade to be kept secret and when exposed, to go unpunished. The center of trade was the St. George Custom House. The Lodge of St. George met at the Custom House. This building also serves as a government building, yet the design might be called Early-Freemasonry. All the trappings of Masonry are in plain sight.

While the New World failed to become Bacon's utopia, an island ruled by an intellectual elite, Bermuda might serve as the closest to his concept of a New Atlantis.

3

Bacon, Shakespeare & the Spear of Athena

Was the "Bard of Avon" Really from Avon,
or Some Place More Intriguing?

BY STEVEN SORA

William Shakespeare, we are told, was born of illiterate parents, schooled only to around the age of 14, and apprenticed as a butcher's boy. Five years after getting married, and saddled with three children, he decided to leave his family and hometown of Stratford-upon-Avon for London. Once in the great city he began writing plays, and joined an established acting company that would perform them. His plays displayed knowledge of English, French, Greek, and Roman history, legal and medical principles, military and naval terms, falconry, horsemanship, and terms only used on the Cambridge campus. In short, the plays exhibited everything outside of his realm of experience.

After a long career, he headed home where he put the sixth and last signature of his life on his will. His will left household items, including a bed, but no books, and notably no folio of work. His death received no notice either in Stratford or London until years later.

While writers are generally voracious readers, book lovers, diary keepers, and keepers of correspondence, the individual known as William Shakespeare was actually the opposite. He most likely couldn't read or write, never owned a book, never kept a diary, and it wasn't until long after his death that anyone got the idea to celebrate the "playwright." It was also years after his death that a "folio" of his work was put together. This was not an original folio (that is, original manuscripts from the time of authorship) since none of those are known to exist.

Certainly the original plays were written, and copied, yet none have ever surfaced. With such a large body of work, this is at least suspicious.

Trying to put William Shakespeare in the role of the writer of "his" plays has been, and is, impossible, and soon the effort attracted detractors who believed Shakespeare himself could NOT have been the author. Among them were Walt Whitman, Mark Twain, John Greenleaf Whittier, Benjamin Disraeli, and Ralph Waldo Emerson.

The man believed to be the "bard" was born in 1564. Queen Elizabeth I had been on the throne since January 15, 1559, and ruled with a capricious but iron hand. On a whim she could arrest or execute anyone from her court to her countryside. Her court included Sir Francis Bacon, born in 1561, Christopher Marlowe, born in 1564, Edward de Vere, the Earl of Oxford, born in 1550, and Henry Wriothesley, the Earl of Southampton, born in 1573. It was a full-time job keeping Elizabeth happy. Sir Walter Raleigh was sent to the Tower for impregnating one of her ladies-in-waiting. Robert Devereaux, the Earl of Essex was punished for getting married a second time and soon after, for his role in putting on the play *Richard II,* was beheaded. Her physician, Ruy Lopez, was suspected of plotting against her and was drawn and quartered.

Speaking freely had its price.

None of William Shakespeare's plays included his name until 1598, although they would after that year. If producing *Richard II* was treason, then why was the writer allowed to go unpunished? It may have been that Essex was actually considered the author. Edward de Vere, Earl of Oxford, was also a candidate. He wrote plays, owned a theatre, and had been to Italy. De Vere, some believe, faked his death on June 24, 1604. It was the feast day of St. John the Baptist, a sort of patron saint to esoteric knowledge. James I had eight Shakespearean plays performed as a tribute to De Vere.

While both Essex and Oxford are suitable candidates, with education and worldly knowledge, the most accepted candidate for the bard's works is Sir Francis Bacon.

The prolific Bacon could not have written *Richard II* without fear of the chopping block. He did have the knowledge that had been oddly attributed to a young butcher's apprentice. He studied at Cambridge, studied law at Grey's Inn, was fluent in languages, the law, loved cryptology, and invented his own sophisticated code. He was also, many believe, a quiet homosexual who surrounded himself with handsome young men. One of these was Henry Wriothesley.

In 1592, the first recorded "Shakespearean" play was dedicated to Wriothesley. The sonnets, in which the poet speaks of his love for "the youth," were also dedicated to Wriothesley. Coincidentally it was in 1592 that Henry Wriothesley became a patron of William Shakespeare. More likely this is the year that Shakespeare and Bacon made a deal. In 1592, Shakespeare received a large amount of money and bought the second largest house in Stratford. He bought other property as well, traded commodities, was party to lawsuits, and collected taxes.

A deal, if made by Shakespeare and Bacon, served them both well. Sir Francis Bacon avoided the executioner's axe and William Shakespeare became a landowner. The two men could not be more different.

Francis Bacon

Bacon was educated, worldly, sensitive, and genuinely interested in changing his world. Shakespeare could barely sign his name, was brash, greedy, and had few qualms about leaving his wife and children. A typical Stratford man might have a working vocabulary of 400 words, while a Cambridge graduate might have one of 4,000 words. The author of the works attributed to Shakespeare had a vocabulary of 20,000 words.

A Poet by Any Other Name

Why did Bacon pick Shakespeare to "front" his work?

When Bacon studied at Grey's Inn, he was the driving force behind an invisible Knighthood called the Order of the Helmet. The members dedicated themselves to an ancient goddess, Pallas Athena, who was depicted with helmet and spear. Her nickname was "the Shaker-of-the-Spear." Meeting a country bumpkin by the name of Shakes-spear might have seemed almost divine intervention. Bacon's motto was *Occulta Veritas Tempore Patet,* meaning "Hidden truth comes to light in time." In the last five years of his life, notably after the death of Elizabeth, he could be more open in his writings. Notably he penned his *New Atlantis,* searching for a peaceful world where royalty ruled as a result of wisdom. Under King James I he also translated what would be called the King James version of the Bible. In Psalm 46, the forty-sixth word down from the first verse is "Shake" while the forty-sixth word from the end is "Spear." He also authored the *Sylva Sylvarum,* which discusses numerous scientific experiments including one to preserve documents in mercury and another on creating artificial springs.

FINDING AVALON

England was a latecomer in the rush to colonize the Americas. It was Elizabeth's astrologer, Dr. John Dee, who convinced her she had rights in the New World. While the illustrious John Dee would serve well as a model for a character in *The Hobbit*, he did convince her of the need of a strong navy, as well as the "fact" that Arthur's Avalon was indeed America. Intellectually she lived vicariously through her wizard. Dee, a magician and an alchemist, wrote on Rosicrucianism and Navigation. His estate held 4,000 books and a "magic mirror" to tell of the future.

The queen's adventurous side was lived through the likes of Sir Francis Drake and Sir Walter Raleigh. She sent them to conquer lands, steal treasures, and explore the seven seas.

Jamestown

MISSING CONNECTIONS

When Elizabeth's life and reign expired, Bacon's status was elevated. He was able to get King James to be more serious in efforts across the ocean. Bacon made sure that he and his circle were granted lands in the New World. They shared grants in Newfoundland and Nova Scotia, and further powers as part of the Virginia Company. With Bacon as Lord Chancellor, the Jamestown settlement was planted in Virginia. Named for the "Virgin" queen Elizabeth, the seal of Virginia that has survived to modern times depicts Athena. She is the ruler, complete with helmet and spear, of the land where her wisdom will prevail.

In Bacon's New Atlantis?

There was a great deal of secrecy in the settling of the colonies. The American "New Atlantis" was chosen to allow people to grow intellectually without fear of state and church repression. It would also serve as the repository of knowledge of those secret societies that grew around Bacon. In an era where Copernicus was afraid to publish his theory of the sun as the center of the universe, there was much that Bacon and his circle kept secret. The original texts of the plays attributed to Shakespeare might have been just a small part of a secret Masonic/Rosicrucian library.

In 1911, Doctor Orville W. Owen, who had spent years decoding Bacon's ciphers, mounted an expedition to England. Under the Wye River he expected to find such a secret library. A secret vault was found. It, however, was unfortunately empty. Someone had stopped the river's flow long enough to build the vault, conceivably fill it in, and empty it again. Employing such hydraulic abilities was nothing new. The body of King Lear had similarly been placed in a vault under the river Soar. The body of Attilla was safe under the Busento River in Italy. Nine years later, Burrell Ruth, who had followed Dr. Owen's work, believed the original folio of Bacon's Shakespearean works had been moved to Nova Scotia in the New World. In Mahone Bay, Nova Scotia, underwater booby traps had been placed by builders adept at the science of hydraulics. Mercury flasks had been found on Oak Island•, where the longest treasure search in history has been underway—a search now in progress for two hundred years.

In recent years, the owners of half of Oak Island have broadened their search to other islands in the bay. Tunnels are believed to connect more

See chapter 7, "Return to Oak Island," on page 52.

than one island and a spiral staircase leading underground has been said to be on an island nearby to Oak Island.

NATIONAL TREASURE

The Virginia Company, established in 1606, was made up of Bacon and his inner circle. Interestingly enough, it included both Virginia and a new colony called Bermuda. The first mention of Bermuda is in *The Tempest,* a Shakespeare play about a shipwreck on a small island. The Virginia Company would also engineer a place to house its own secrets. Among the first jobs completed at Jamestown was the construction of an underground repository and, over this vault, the first Jamestown church. The vault was used to house documents brought over in 1635 until Jamestown itself was seen as less in need of a defensive position. In 1676, the documents were moved to a new vault located in Bruton parish. The area was known as the Middletown Plantation and later would become Williamsburg. A brick church was built and 20 feet underneath, the vault was placed. This church did not survive, and a newer church, which survives today, is on Duke of Gloucester Street; it is both a tourist attraction and an Episcopal Church. Somewhere under the churchyard lies a spiral staircase leading to the vault.

In the 1920s, the Rockefeller Foundation bought much of Williamsburg to create a tourist destination. Oddly enough they also bought Stratford-on-Avon, which had already become such a destination. The actual site of the Bruton vault was owned by the Anglican church and could not be bought; instead it was given to the United States government.

In recent years a group called Sir Francis Bacon's Sages of the Seventh Seal has sought permission to excavate the site, particularly under a pyramid-shaped structure known as the Bray monument. Fletcher Richman, a Baconian scholar, believes that beneath the monument, accessed by the underground spiral stairway, is a vault containing both the writings of Bacon and others that can have significant implications for the future. Permission so far has not been granted. Richman says this is just one of many hidden libraries.

For now, they remain hidden.

PART TWO

AMERICA'S SECRET ORIGINS

Ancient Egyptians in the Grand Canyon?

4

ANCIENT EGYPTIANS IN THE GRAND CANYON

Is a Century-Old Newspaper Story to Be Believed?

BY DAVID H. CHILDRESS

Did an Egyptian navy cross the Pacific or Atlantic and come to Arizona? Could they have left an Egyptian tomb in the Grand Canyon, something similar to those found in the Valley of Kings near Luxor, Egypt? Strangely, an article published on the front page of the Phoenix *Gazette* on April 5, 1909, claimed that just such an Egyptian rock-cut cave was found.

While many mummies have been discovered in Egypt, very few were in pyramids—and those that were found have been dated from the later historical periods. The older pyramids dating from the early dynasties (or before!) show no signs of funerary use. Mummies in Egypt are most often found in rock-cut tombs in desert canyons, which often feature tunnels going deep underground with various rooms and passageways along the way. Multiple mummies are often found in one tomb, and the crypts of the wealthy and royalty were filled with precious items and everyday necessities to ease the dead person's continued existence in the afterlife.

According to the Phoenix *Gazette* story, a necropolis of mummies and artifacts similar to an Egyptian tomb was found in the Grand Canyon. An explorer named G. E. Kinkaid, it was reported, uncovered a series of catacombs complete with statues, swords, vessels, and mummies in 1908 (the exact date of the discovery is not given). As we shall see, Kinkaid may not have been the first explorer to have seen this "cave." The account of Kinkaid's adventure was reproduced as a chapter entitled "Citadel of the Grand Canyon" in Joseph Miller's 1962 book *Arizona Cavalcade*.

The Phoenix *Gazette* article starts with four headlines and then continues through a most amazing account:

The entrance is 1,486 feet down the sheer canyon wall. . . . Over a hundred feet from the entrance is the cross-hall, several hundred feet long, in which are found the idol, or image, or the people's god, sitting cross-legged, with a lotus flower or lily in each hand. . . . Among the other finds are vases or urns and cups of copper and gold . . . enameled ware and glazed vessels . . . articles which have never been known as native to this country, and doubtless had their origin in the orient. . . . The tomb or crypt in which the mummies were found is one of the largest of the chambers . . . tiers of mummies, each one occupying a separate hewn shelf.

So what became of the artifacts described in the article? What became of Jordan? Did he return to the Smithsonian in Washington D.C. and disappear with all the records of his discovery? Has there been some archaeological cover-up reminiscent of the last scene in the movie *Raiders of the Lost Ark*, where the Ark of the Covenant is placed inside a crate in a giant warehouse never to be seen again?

It has also been suggested that while the discovery perhaps was real, the archaeologists working for the Smithsonian were not. These men may

Mummies in the Crypt (artist's conjecture)

not have been working for the Smithsonian Institution out of Washington D.C. at all, but merely claiming to do so. Could this have been a cover-up for an illegal archaeological dig that was raiding the ancient site and claiming legitimacy from a very distant institution? It would have been very difficult indeed, in 1909, to check on the credentials of the archaeologists.

THE SECRET CATACOMBS OF MUMMIES ON THE LITTLE COLORADO

In the small town museum of Springerville, Colorado, I came across several intriguing newspaper clippings, including one of particular interest from the *Los Angeles Times-Washington Post* news service. It describes how the archaeologist John Hohmann, now closely associated with the Casa Malpais site, had rappelled down a rope into a fissure of basalt in July of 1990 and had discovered an intricate series of passages and rooms that had been modified by the mysterious "Mogollon culture" into underground tombs for the internment of the dead. The remains of these people were apparently mummified, possibly naturally by the dry climate.

This curious discovery made national news in the early 1990s, but otherwise has been largely forgotten. The catacombs inside the Casa Malpais are described as a burial ground for hundreds of skeletons. However, nowhere in the article does it say that the dead are "mummies." But were they? Ritual mummification includes the removal of internal organs and the preservation of the skin and hair. Though we are given few details about these human remains, it would seem that they are mummies, rather than bare-bones skeletons.

It would not be unusual if the Casa Malpais remains were mummies. Rather, it would be unusual if they weren't. Mummified remains have been found at Mesa Verde in Colorado, at Hovenweep in Utah, and at locations in Arizona, including, apparently, Springerville.

SETH TANNER AND THE SECRET HOPI CAVE

In the 1966 film *Mackenna's Gold*, Omar Sharif plays the villain, a bandit named, in fact, Colorado. Early in the movie, Colorado has captured Sheriff Mackenna (Gregory Peck), who has seen a map of the route to the secret canyon. With his hands tied, Mackenna and the bandit gang cross a precarious rope-bridge over a narrow, but very deep, canyon. The group makes its way across the rickety bridge and ends up on the north side of what I believe to be the Little Colorado River Gorge. Today this area is a largely off-limits and roadless part of the Kaibab National Forest, and part of it lies in the Navaho Reservation.

It is somewhere beyond this crossing that Mackenna and Colorado find a secret canyon with a rich vein of gold along one of its walls and ruins high up on a cliff, which must have been part of an ancient mining operation. It is an exciting and imaginative western that claims to be based on fact—but is it? Perhaps the facts in this case are even more bizarre than the fictional movie itself.

One of the most important books (in fact, one of the only books) on the Grand Canyon and secret mines and tunnels is *Quest for the Pillar of Gold* (1997). This compilation of scholarly papers on ancient mines, mineral wealth, and modern-historical mining ventures in the Grand Canyon gives us the tantalizing reality behind all the fantastic stories. One would think that a geological wonderland such as the Grand Canyon would offer a wealth of minerals, including gold. There is definitely an ancient salt mine and other sites that are sacred to the Hopi. And tales of gold, such as in the John Lee gold mine, circulated around the Grand Canyon. Was one of the ancient mines in the Grand Canyon an Egyptian gold mine?

One celebrated gold prospector who apparently discovered a secret cave in the Grand Canyon or Little Colorado Canyon was Seth Tanner. Tanner (1828-1918) was a Mormon miner and trader who had gone west with Brigham Young in 1847 when the Mormons settled Salt Lake City. From Salt Lake City he was sent out to set up a small Mormon colony in San Bernardino, California, and it was rumored that he and his brother Myron had some luck in the California gold fields. Tanner also spent some time in San Diego, investing in a coal business that reportedly did not do too well. He returned to Utah and was married; later, he was sent on a scouting expedition to northern Arizona. In 1876, he moved his family to an isolated cabin on the Little Colorado River near Tuba City. The cabin was strategically located on old trade routes; Tanner, who got along well with both the Hopi and Navajo and spoke their languages, set up a trading post. Because of his burly countenance and extraordinary strength, the Navajos called him "Hosteen Shush" (Mr. Bear).

Tanner's final fate is told in *Grand Canyon Stories: Then and Now,* a book published by the famous magazine *Arizona Highways*. The brief story includes a photo that tantalizes us: Seth Tanner—a grizzly old man who is blind! According to the book, the Hopi blinded Tanner by throwing a potion in his eyes because he was "the discoverer of a cave containing sacred religious treasures of the Hopi tribe, which no white man was allowed to see." The book maintains that it would normally have meant death to see the secret cave, but Tanner was spared because his mother was Hopi. This is highly unlikely, since he was born in New York; it is much more likely he had taken a Hopi wife or had some other significant relationship to cause the tribe to debate his fate. He remained a prisoner of the Hopi, however, and was put in a cave and supplied with daily provisions for years. Supposedly, Tanner became accustomed to his blindness and began to venture out. But because of his alarming appearance, he frightened villagers around Cameron and Tuba City. To scare him off, they would throw water on him. Thinking it was more of the dreaded Hopi potion that had blinded him, he would run back to his cave.

At some point, he must have been released. The photo of him as a blind man is known to have been taken some time shortly after the year 1900. He died near Tuba City in 1918. He is still a famous character in the area, and visitors to the Grand Canyon can see Tanner Springs, Tanner Wash, and Tanner Crossing in addition to Tanner Trail. His children and grandchildren became wealthy trading post owners in the Tuba City

Kinkaid's discovery (artist's conjecture)

and Gallup areas. But part of Seth Tanner remains a mystery, and he never divulged the terrible secret or incredible treasure he had seen.

What did he see in the Grand Canyon or Little Colorado Canyon that meant death? Did Tanner discover in the early 1890s the caves full of statues and mummies that were to be reported years later in 1909 by the Phoenix *Gazette*—ancient caves filled with forgotten Egyptian artifacts, now sacred to the Hopi?

The similarities between the real-life Seth Tanner and the fictional Ed Adams in the film *Mackenna's Gold* are striking. As we have seen, Ed Adams was a real historical figure, but the fact that he was not blind and the description and location of the Adams Diggings make it seem unlikely that he was the real person upon whom the film character was based. That character, it appears, is actually Seth Tanner—a blind man who had seen the "Canyon of Gold."

If the Egyptians had sought out the Grand Canyon as some sacred spot where the River Styx disappeared into the underworld of Set, they may have built small outposts and forts for journeys to the Grand Canyon. Exactly such places exist, such as Wupatki and Tusayan, both ancient cities near the Grand Canyon. Wupatki and other nearby ruins are close to the Little Colorado River and are thought to have been built by the ancestors of the Hopi, though some archaeologists dispute this. Signs at the Wupatki Ruins Museum, run by the National Park Service, are ambiguous as to who the builders of this remarkable little town—complete with a ball court—really were.

But, if there was an Egyptian presence down deep inside the Grand Canyon, one would expect to find some sort of town or outpost on the canyon floor; and in fact, there is such a place. Excavations started in 1967 at an archaeological site known as Unkar, where the Unkar stream meets the Colorado River creating the Unkar Delta. Unkar Delta is just downstream (west) of where the Little Colorado meets the main Colorado River, deep inside the canyon.

After years of research and digging, the discoveries were published in a scholarly book called *Unkar Delta: Archaeology of the Grand Canyon*, by Douglas Schwartz of the School of American Research out of Santa Fe, New Mexico. His team cataloged building foundations, cut stone blocks, and broken pieces of pottery. Because of occasional super floods in the Grand Canyon, much of the Unkar Delta would have been periodically washed away. Schwartz concludes in his book that the Unkar Delta was inhabited circa AD 900.

One would think that if Unkar had originally been built by Egyptians, it would have been built around 500 BC, if not before. Perhaps earlier. dates will eventually come from Unkar; or perhaps this earlier city, if it ever existed, was washed away thousands of years ago, and the current Unkar—rebuilt, but now ruins—is from AD 900.

And what of the curious name Unkar? It could be an Egyptian word, perhaps a corruption of Ankh-Ka or Ankh-Ra. Is this a reference to the sun god Ra? One of the ancient Southwest legends held that the sun rose and set inside the Grand Canyon, and indeed, one could see the sun set into the canyon if one stood on the eastern rim looking west. Modern maps of the Grand Canyon indicate an Egyptian influence from somewhere—just look at all of the many Egyptian names (and some Hindu) given to the distinctive geological features of the Grand Canyon: Osiris Temple, Tower of Ra, Tower of Set, etc. Is it just a coincidence that the Grand Canyon has been given so many Egyptian names?

ANCIENT VOYAGES

Could the Egyptians have actually made voyages to Mexico and the American Southwest, such as a trans-Pacific voyage? According to an Associated Press story released on January 28, 2006, an Italian-American archaeological team announced that it had found the remains of well-preserved Egyptian ships in five caves along the Red Sea. The ships were dated to be about 4,000 years old.

An inscription on some wooden boxes indicated that the artifacts were from the land of Punt. The press release said that artifacts recovered included 80 coils of rope, and that Supreme Antiquity director Zahi Hawass said the remains showed the ancient Egyptians were "excellent ship builders" and that they had a fleet capable of sailing to remote lands.

It has been suggested that the Egyptians, and other seafarers, voyaged across the Indian Ocean to Australia and Indonesia and then out into the Pacific: to Fiji, Tonga, Samoa, Tahiti, and the Americas. Perhaps Punt was Australia or even Mexico or Peru. The mysterious Olmecs would have been part of this oceanic trade and fit into the time frame of 1000 to 2000 BC.

Amazingly, the 1909 story said that tunnel-vault system went for "nearly a mile underground… Several hundred rooms have been discovered... The recent finds include articles which have never been known as native to this country... War weapons, copper instruments, sharp-edged and hard as steel, indicate the high state of civilization reached by these strange people."

And what of Jordan and Kinkaid mentioned in the article? In a letter that I received in 2005, signed by a "Colin," I was told that there is a mention of an E. K. Kinkaid in correspondence archives for the Smithsonian Institution, Record Unit 189, Box 68 of 151, Folder 8. Said Colin, "These are records dating from 1860–1908, which is in the correct time frame for the Kinkaid mentioned in the Phoenix *Gazette*. It is a possibility that different first initials were used and that this is the folder that may contain the valuable information needed to locate the site." Perhaps Kinkaid had gone to Washington D.C. Was Jordan someone else, not actually from the Smithsonian, as he had claimed?

5

AVALON IN AMERICA?

Did King Arthur Cross the Atlantic?

BY STEVEN SORA

I n the late 16th century, Queen Elizabeth had watched as Spain and Portugal, the Netherlands and France established themselves in the New World. They all made legitimate claims to the Americas that England could not match. Then she consulted her advisor, Dr. John Dee. Dee and his ally Sir Francis Bacon told her that England had claims much older than all of Europe, indeed, said Dee, King Arthur himself had crossed the Atlantic and set foot in the new land.

Dr. Dee was Elizabeth's advisor, astrologer, and magician. He was also a deep student of the world's history and geography. His library may have been Britain's finest and his pioneering of science was an influence on many students and researchers to come. His interest in alchemy, his ability to conjure angels, and claims of ownership of a "magic mirror," as well as his whispered heresy, may have denied him a place among the ranks of English savants like Sir Isaac Newton and Robert Fludd; nevertheless, he was Elizabeth's Merlin.

Dee's influence is hard to overstate. He was, after all, the man who pushed Elizabeth to create a navy that would ultimately establish an empire for England. He coined the term "Britannia." And it is a fact that Dee based England's claim to America on the travels of Britain's most illustrious ancient king, Arthur.

THE ONCE AND FUTURE KING

King Arthur had spent a lifetime defending Britain. In twelve great battles Britain was victorious against foreign invaders, but one more remained to be fought at Camlann. Tragically, though victory came, the King had to be carried from the battlefield, whereupon he was taken west across the sea to recuperate, and in the belief that he would someday return. This is part of the legendary saga of King Arthur, and despite the fact that his life and battles are the subject of massive volumes, scholars cannot agree upon exact dates or exact places, and some deny that Arthur even existed.

There are several reasons for this lack of consensus. Historians in the 5th and 6th centuries were largely unreliable. Few could read and only a handful could write. What was actually written down and copied by hand came from oral tales told and retold. The printing press was centuries from being invented. These were the Dark Ages. There is, however, an overriding reason for the obscurity of the story of Arthur: politics. Arthur represented the Britons, the original and true inhabitants of the island we now know as England. The Angles, the Saxons, other Germanic tribes, and later the Plantagenet kings who made Britain into England had no room for a British hero; so Arthur was systematically edited, deleted, purged, and relegated to a medieval legend.

His last days in a faraway place called Avalon have provided great mystery and speculation. No one knows where or if such a place as Avalon existed. No final resting place for Briton's most beloved king was ever found; that is, until Britain's most influential wizard came along. John Dee had succeeded the original Merlin and provided evidence of Arthur's final resting place. It was in the newly rediscovered continent—the New World. Since the victors get to write the history, it often becomes difficult to establish the truth. There is little agreed upon among the various tales of the "once and future king." There is, however, some agreement on his background that can provide us clues as to where and when. When the Romans came to Briton they brought with them a system of government that resembled their home in the Italian peninsula. While battles are remembered, a long history of peaceful development is not. Britain enjoyed a *Pax Romana* that had many British families adopting the Italian economy. Many families intermarried with the occupiers, and this created a noble class of landowners who brought about peace and progress but still needed support from the Roman legions. Picts in the north, Irish to the west, and Germanic tribes to the east all looked for opportunities to invade this prosperous land.

The chance came in the early 5th century. Rome came under attack and military units were brought home to Italy. In the year AD 406, the Romans pulled out of the Isles completely, leaving behind a power vac-

Detail from "The last sleep of Arthur" (in Avalon) by the Pre-Raphaelite painter Edward Burne-Jones

uum. The Picts invaded and war raged for a decade around AD 450. The Briton king Vortigern, wishing to hold back the Picts and the Irish, invited the Saxons to England for help. It was a deal with the devil. The Saxons came, they saw, and they conquered—and they intended to stay. The Saxons had turned on Vortigern. Three hundred nobles were slain in an act of treachery that fatally weakened Britain. This was the first of the Briton-Saxon Wars, and the original history, written by the monk Gildas, does not mention Arthur. He does tell us that a series of battles were fought in the north, around Hadrian's Wall, which was built to keep out the invaders of the north. It is safe to say Arthur's enemies were first the Picts and then the Saxons.

BOOKS, LOST AND FOUND

Possibly a century afterward, Gildas, in a Welsh poem called "The Book of Aneiran," actually names Arthur and describes him as a great warrior. In the 9th century, another Welshman, Nennius, provides details that the monk Gildas left out. Arthur may not have actually been a king, but he was Welsh and so were his people, the true Britons.

Geoffrey of Monmouth who wrote *History of the Kings of Britain* (c. 12th century), claimed that a secret book was given to him with an expanded tale of Arthur. The book was the property of Walter the Archdeacon of Oxford and was written in Welsh. This work and many others are now lost to us.

Dr. Dee may have been privy to such texts, some of which have never known the light of day. He would have known of *The Voyage of Maelduin's Boat* (written c. AD 1000), in which a man named Máel Dúin (Merlin) sailed the North Atlantic to a place called Avalon, also known as Manannan after the Celtic Sea god. While many like to point to the isle of Man as Avalon, this nearby island, unlike the one in the story, required no passing of an island with fiery mountains (like Iceland), no columns or encounters with floating islands (icebergs) and did not need weeks at sea. Another choice is Manana Island off the coast of Maine.

Arthur and his Britons did their best to save their land, but the enemy was far greater. Britain became a country ruled by Anglo-Saxons, and later Normans. Many of the Briton families fled across the sea to Brittany, now part of France. The Britons who stayed moved west to Wales, but they were now second-class citizens in their own country. Subsequent texts took the story and placed it elsewhere since Wales had become a backwater and the relic of another era.

Missing from modern history is that Wales played a much greater role in the history of Britain. Also missing is that a great part of the British population are actually of Welsh descent. Wales, as Khymry, spread throughout the north of what is now England, separating Alban (Scotland) from England. Internal descent and external conquest had seriously hurt the Welsh culture, traditions, and self-knowledge. The low point may have seemed to come when Richard II (d. 1400) prohibited all writing in Welsh and suppressed the language. But it became even worse when successor King Henry IV (d. 1413) prohibited the importation into Wales of writing instruments. When the printing press was invented, it would not be allowed in Wales until the mid 17th century. Welsh texts were burned and, in effect, their history was nearly eradicated. Perhaps the final insult, though—even worse than erasing the story of King Arthur—was its re-creation as a story that robbed Arthur from the Britons.

Geoffrey of Monmouth took the 6th-century man and brought him into the 12th century, where he was invested with the tenets of chivalry. He was now more like a Templar Knight. There is nothing surprising in this as Geoffrey was a Cistercian monk. The Cistercians were a kinship order of the Templars. Geoffrey changed the geography as well, moving the important battle of Badon from the north of Britain, to Bath, in the south.

A strong possibility is that the original descriptions provide the closest relationship to the truth. One clue is that the wife of Arthur, Guinevere, was chosen because she was a Pict and of a royal family. Her real estate holdings were immense, as property among the Picts passed through the female line. She was, as were all her people, tattooed. While Arthur might have seen her as the way to unite the north of Briton with Pictish Scotland and the Orkneys, she might have seen him as a way to the same goal. The ships of the Saxons, after all, terrorized even those northern islands.

The marriage was not made in heaven, however, as the differences in custom were great. Pictish women often had more than one husband and saw no reason not to share them. They often did not live with their husband until their first child was born. They were not ready to give up their property to another if marriage didn't work out.

Later in the Christianized versions, Guinevere was found guilty of adultery. In Malory's *Death of Arthur* (*Le Morte d'Arthur,* 1485), she is nearly sent to the stake to be burned for her crimes. There was no such sin in the Pictish custom.

Author Norma Lorre Goodrich pointed out that even her name gives a better understanding of her identity. *Guin* actually meant "white" in the language of the Scots and Welsh. *Weure* meant "viper" or "dragon." Her title as the White Dragon makes her a priestess-queen of the highest order. Arthur's marriage was essentially political and later stories are simply an embellishment. Today it is custom that young women will not walk near her grave marker at Meigle. The seven-foot-tall slab with a dragon among the numerous symbols is more Pictish, less Christian, than other markers. Women believe it has the power to render them unable to bear children. The tiny town north of Dundee is the center of prominent Pictish burials.

WEST TO AVALON

Most tales of Arthur have him waging one final battle. It was the thirteenth battle, not a lucky number for Arthur or for the Knights Templar. Although his forces won the battle, he was badly wounded. He was then put aboard a ship and brought west to Avalon. Several locations have been suggested for Avalon. The best known is not an island at all. Monks at Glastonbury claimed that they held the grave of Arthur and erected a bogus gravestone. It was at the height of religious tourism, also known as pilgrimage. The greater the relic, the more the free-spending faithful were attracted. Others pick the small island of Bardsey off of Wales. It is in the right direction and known to have contained some important burials, but Arthur had not died. The bard Taliesin says the wounded king was put aboard a ship whose owner Barinthus knew how to navigate by the stars. This would not be necessary unless a much longer voyage was planned.

Celts and Norse had the ability to sail the Atlantic from early dates. What is referred to as the Nydam boat was found in Denmark and dated to the 4th century. It was capable of ocean travel, and there is evidence that deep-sea fishing had been practiced for centuries. A 17th century Norse ship was 75 feet long, capable of carrying more men than the ships of Columbus 800 years later. The sea god Manannan of the Celts may have been recognized on both sides of the Atlantic. Manannan, Manu, the Vedic Noah, and the North American Manitou share certain etymological aspects pointing to much wider contact than is recognized.

The Irish Saint Brendan also made his trip to the Americas in AD 510. At least one Welshman, Price Madoc, is on record as having made the crossing before Columbus. In 1170, Madoc is believed to have not only crossed the Atlantic but to have brought his people to settle in the new land. Author and 21st-century adventurer Tim Severin re-created his voyage to show at the least it was possible.

Author Graham Phillips wrote *Merlin and the Discovery of Avalon* (2005) after physically tracing the Merlin voyage to the Americas. On the small island of Manana, off the coast of Maine, are a handful of standing stones similar to those found on the western coast of Britain. Phillips and his research partner Glynn Davis connected the ancient history of Merlin and Arthur to an expedition, circa 1608, led by a prominent Rosicrucian, Pierre Dugua, who landed on Manana. It was actually a follow-up voyage after Martin Pring landed on Manana the year before. A prophecy foretold the discovery of Merlin's tomb in 1604. According to Phillips, Dugua, who was connected to both Dr. Dee and Sir Francis Bacon, actually found the tomb of Merlin, an event kept secret by that group.

Did John Dee share other information with Francis Bacon as to the final resting place of Arthur? The evidence might be lost to us today since suspicious neighbors of the wizard Dee burned down Mortlake, his home, along with his remarkable library of four thousand books. Among those numerous volumes,

Denmark's long-distance Nydam boat

could other Welsh texts have been lost in the fire? We may never know.

The efforts of Sir Francis Bacon to create his New Atlantis in the Americas led him to found more than one expedition. In 1607 Bristol's Society of Merchant Venturers, which included Bacon, formed the Newfoundland Company. The new company had 48 members and the Earl Northampton. They decided on a peninsula they would call the Province of Avalon to create a new colony. The name Avalon still graces the map of Newfoundland.

Does the rock-strewn coast of Avalon hide clues to the Avalon of Arthur? One text had Avalon "down from St. John's" and the peninsula in Newfoundland has as its largest town, St. John's. An older text has Avalon ruled by a queen Argantia. Similarly, Argentia is another Avalon placename in Newfoundland.

The province of Newfoundland, Canada, honored Bacon on the tercentenary of its foundation with a stamp of the visionary writer and philosopher. His writings, it is believed, were once hidden in a vault under the Wye River in England, which was uncovered in the 19th century and found to be empty. There is evidence that such documents were taken to America where they were concealed in numerous vaults. Someday the secrets of the author of New Atlantis may be revealed along with the final resting place of Britain's most beloved king.

6

THE HERETICS WHO LIT THE WAY
FOR AMERICA

Exploring Our Secret Debt to a Group
of Obscure Hermits

BY STEVEN SORA

When people think of Philadelphia's role in history, it most likely includes Benjamin Franklin and William Penn, the Liberty Bell, and the Continental Congress. The city's role in fashioning America begins nearly a century earlier however, in 1694, when a handful of "hermits" came to the city and moved into caves in what is now Fairmont Park. Their writings and their practices not only influenced William Penn but they also had an effect on George Washington and helped shape the birth of our constitutional government.

Known as the Hermits of Wissahickon Creek, they were actually Pietists, a sect often considered part of the numerous Protestant splinter factions that included Amish, Anabaptists, Brotherhood of Zion, Dunkards, Hutterites, Mennonites, Methodists, Moravians, Shakers, and Swiss Brethren. But they had little to do with the philosophy of Calvin and Zwingli and a great deal to do with the Rosicrucian Enlightenment.

The Rosicrucian movement was an export of England, brought across the channel to Germany through the efforts of Dr. John Dee and Sir Francis Bacon. Rosicrucian thought was soon active in both England and Germany. The Duke of Brunswick and Lunenburg, Augustus, came to London to study a philosophy attributed to Bacon and secretive societies. Friederich Count Palatine of the Rhine married the daughter of King James I, Elizabeth. Both were Rosicrucians. During the Thirty Years War, Rosicrucians and Freemasons were safe in England. Such protection would not last forever.

From Francis Bacon to William Penn to Benjamin Franklin a spiritual torch of enlightenment would be passed along. Bacon, through his New Atlantis, helped form the basis of a free society although he himself was born too early to see it come to fruition. Penn put the goals of such a society into action. The dark corners of European thought gave way to the Great Experiment, as Penn called it. The future Pennsylvania became the central location for creating a democratic nation. Franklin risked life and limb to ensure that it did.

THE LAND THAT PENN BUILT

William Penn is remembered as the founder of Pennsylvania. He was the son of Admiral William Penn and notably a Quaker. His famous statue, once the highest point in the skyline of Philadelphia, shows a content Pillsbury Oats face. Penn, however, was actually a radical. He was regularly imprisoned for his writings and four times his father interceded on his behalf to get him released from the Tower of London.

Notably, he was imprisoned for his work, *The Sandy Foundation Shaken* (1668), which dismisses the Catholic doctrine of the Trinity and the Calvinist theory of justification. He drew a daring line, and after frequent persecutions wrote a constitution for a colony in the New World. The coauthor was Algernon Sidney, who was the grand nephew of Sir Philip Sidney and heir to the philosophy of Francis Bacon. Sir Philip is best known as the author of *Arcadia*, but he spent of lifetime of esoteric study with a group that included Bacon, Dr. Dee, Sir Walter Raleigh, and Christopher Marlowe. The group called themselves the School of Night, although they were accused of being the School of Heretics.

William Penn's statue overlooks modern Philadelphia

Penn did not name his city "Philadelphia" because it meant "Brotherly Love" in Greek. Instead he had been influenced by the Book of Revelation, chapter 3. In it, the phrase "He that hath an ear," is used. Jesus used the same phrase numerous times and it meant those who were initiated, or those who could comprehend the lesson. The author was directing a letter to the "angel of the Church of

Philadelphia." In it the Holy One, the True One says that those who kept his word he will preserve from trial. Philadelphia was the city dedicated to those who kept the Word. And those who kept the Word were free from the persecution of the Church. This was Bacon's role in describing the city of "Bensalem," where all could worship and study freely. In City Hall today, the quote taken from the Book of Revelation is on the wall of the North portico. A Philadelphia suburb took the name Bensalem.

Penn's City became a refuge for free thinking in a way unequaled anywhere in the colonies. Philadelphia's Pietists were free to study astrology, astronomy, botany and music, medicine, and alchemy. At the time, alchemy, the art of transmuting metals, was treated as though it were kin to witchcraft. The Church's dominance over science was more powerful then than now. Opining on the placement of the Sun cost great thinkers like Giordano Bruno and Galileo everything. Galileo finished his life under house arrest. Bruno was burned at the stake. Today, transmuting metals through chemical reaction is more the work of men in white lab coats. Scientists replaced the magic wands, but the work is otherwise the same.

While the Church would never have allowed the Pietists their practice in Europe, in Philadelphia they were safe.

The story of Philadelphia's leading mystics begins with Penn who invited all to freely worship and practice. The Quaker doctrine was more genuine in its religious toleration than was Puritan society. The Society of Friends were Pacifist and even though Penn himself distinguished between wars of aggression and wars of defense, many in his community were against bearing arms at any cost. Through his efforts, many Germans from the continent were recruited. By the time of the American Revolution, Pennsylvania was only one third English-speaking.

The Pietists arrived in Philadelphia led by a young man by the name of Johannes Kelpius. Born Johann Kelp in Schassburg, Transylvania, he attended Bavaria's University of Altdorf where he Latinized his name. At the age of 16, he had his master's in theology and had published several works. Part Pietist and part Rosicrucian, his studies were steeped in what the Catholic Church would declare heretical. His master was Johann Jakob Zimmerman who wished to create his own Chapter of Perfection in America.

Zimmerman died the year before the trip was made and the 21 year old Kelpius took his mantle as leader. He quickly stepped up to the role of charismatic mystic who brought medicine, music, and magic to this break-off Protestant sect. He had met a woman by the name of Jane Leade in London, who was a prophetess and the cofounder of the Philadelphia movement in 1670. She was a medium who claimed the ability to channel the Virgin Sophia.

The brotherhood of Kelpius took passage to America in 1694 and landed in Philadelphia at the Blue Anchor Tavern on St. John's Eve. They lived as near-hermits in the wooded area known today as Fairmont Park on the banks of the Wissahickon Creek. Today, street names such as Hermit Terrace and Hermit Lane recall the reclusive mystics. They constructed a monastery of wood to await the fulfillment of the prophecy in the Book of Revelation. A great sign was to appear in the heavens: "A woman clothed with the sun, and the moon under her feet, and on her head a crown of twelve stars." (Rev. 12:1)

They called themselves the Society of the Woman of the Wilderness and blended a pagan Druidism with Rosicrucian theology.

Many have compared this to a doomsday cult awaiting the end. The "end" was supposed to happen in 1694, the year they arrived, and then again in 1700. But it was not an end as much as a second beginning they sought.

Near Hermit Lane is the cave where Kelpius meditated and sometimes gathered his brotherhood. They measured the skies, practiced astrology, experimented with alchemy, and studied numerology. On the eve of the feast of St. John the Baptist, they had a celebration that was said to cause visions of angels. It was understood as the anniversary of their arrival, but to members it was understood as the day the Sun enters Cancer. As had been done from most early pagan times, a bonfire was erected.

The brotherhood considered the number 40 to be sacred. It was a very important number in the Bible, both Old Testament and New. Kelpius' community generally numbered 40 members. His wooden monastery was 40 x 40 feet as was their burial ground.

In 1708, the end was actually near. Kelpius contracted pneumonia, no doubt from the rugged lifestyle. He is said to have placed some important artifacts in a box and instructed a follower, Daniel Giessler, to throw the box in the Schuylkill River. When Geissler returned, Kelpius knew he didn't complete his task. He instructed Geissler again and this time the job was done as assigned. When the box, called "the Arcanum," hit the water an explosion took place, complete with thunder and lightning coming out of the water. Legend has it that the box contained the Philosopher's Stone, a much-sought-after tool needed in alchemy.

Wissahickon, the creek, became the "Ganges of the Rosicrucians" in America. It may surprise many to learn that George Washington had connections to several in the Pennsylvania Rosicrucian movement. He is described in one text as "an Acolyte" of the sect. Those who influenced Washington included Peter Miller, who would translate the Declaration of Independence into European languages, and Conrad Beissel, who would lead the Pietists/Rosicrucians to the Ephrata Colony west of the city.

The community at Wissahickon dwindled after the death of Kelpius. Six holy men remained and one was Johann Seelig. At his death, his staff was thrown into the Schuylkill and it also exploded upon hitting the water. The Monks of the Ridge, as they became known, were regularly called upon for help in finding a spouse or casting a chart.

Kelpius and his group, though, were not an "end" but, in fact, a beginning for the philosophically like-minded colonies to follow. Wave after wave would come, escaping religious persecution or war. It soon became a time of birth for the numerous sects of what had been thinly disguised as "Protestant" religion. Many, like the Monks of the Ridge, derided such concepts like predestination and dualism as the limits of the human brain. They believed such philosophical points of division allowed religious men to fall into doing the devil's work. To what point would the True One have his children murdering each other over such concepts? He wouldn't. Love, faith, and good works were stressed.

Such ideals could have been proposed by Bacon himself for his New Atlantis.

The last surviving member of the six monks was an Englishman named Christopher Witt. Witt had studied anatomy and biology in his home country before sailing to America in 1704. He was adept in medicine and conferred the first medical degree in Pennsylvania. He was also adept in architecture, astrology, botany, and music. His healing powers mixed science and folk medicine and were prized by the community. The Germans regarded him as a *hexenmeister*, that is, one who can lift curses or, if one chose, place spells. The English equivalent would be a warlock. The Germans that settled further west, the Amish, are known for their hex signs to ward off evil.

In 1718, Witt bought 125 acres of Germantown, which allowed him to charge or not to charge for his medical services as he wished. He lived out his life with Daniel Giessler, and kept in touch with the other wizards. When he died in 1765 he was buried alongside Giessler and other monks in the community's High Street graveyard. Spectral blue flames were said to dance around his grave for weeks. The Hermits grave became known as Spook Hill until an Episcopal Church named St. Michael's was built over it in 1859. A black congregation later took over, and it is now known as the High Street Church of God. Giessler and Witt are said to lie directly under the altar.

By 1720 Rosicrucian chapters met in taverns throughout the city. According to Robert Hieronimus in *Founding Fathers, Secret Societies,* Benjamin Franklin had started his own lodge.

TO EPHRATA

Although the hermits were gone from Philadelphia, their influence remained in Pennsylvania. After Kelpius, one of the region's most charismatic leaders was Conrad Beissel. Born in the German Palatinate in 1691, he was initiated into Rosicrucianism and may have achieved its highest rank. He was knowledgeable as a mystic, familiar with Paracelsus and the Kabbalah. His teachings were described as "Rosicrucian doctrine pure and undefiled."

Beissel had a strong relationship to the Wissahickon Hermits but moved his group west. A great emphasis was placed on the sciences, on music, on astrology, and learning in general. A clock made by hermit Christopher Witt remains in a structure called the Saron that stands today. The clock still strikes the hours.

Under Beissel's direction, work began in 1738 on an unusual chapter house that, when completed, would be three stories high. The ground floor would be used for storage. The second floor was circular and was used for sleeping. The third floor would be 18 feet square and have four windows, each facing a cardinal direction. Secret rites of rejuvenation were practiced in this temple area. Thirteen members would spend 40 days, beginning on the first full moon in May, purging the body through fasting and laxatives, shedding blood, and partaking of the "grain of elixir." Whatever this substance was, it caused convulsions, sweating, and loss of speech.

The man-made cave where Kelpius and his followers met to practice their beliefs. The monument to the right was erected by the Rosicrucian brotherhood and declares that Kelpius was the first Rosicrucian master in America.

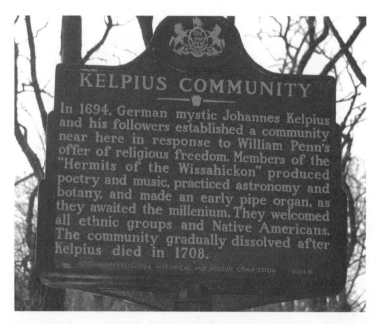

This recently erected historical marker is about 500 yards from the cave entrance.

They were called the White Brotherhood, not to distinguish themselves as a racial group, but in imitation of the Essenes of the Holy Land two thousand years before. Like the Essenes, the Brotherhood dressed in white, and walked barefoot. Such a band of 13 might draw comparisons to Jesus and his 12 apostles; however, whatever secrets were contained within the chapter house at Ephrata remained secret.

Today the Ephrata colony is a popular destination for those visiting the "Amish country" in Pennsylvania. Ten of the original medieval buildings have been restored to recreate the atmosphere of the community.

Back in Philadelphia, the group of hermits that once lived along the banks of the Schuylkill are mostly forgotten. Though Fairmont Park is described as the world's largest urban park, and is very popular with city residents, the Kelpius Cave is out of the way and hard to find. In 1961, the Rosicrucians put up a plaque to commemorate the Hermits of Wissahickon as the leading force in bringing their philosophy to America.

7

RETURN TO OAK ISLAND

The Search for Oak Island's Mysterious Treasure Begins Again

BY STEVEN SORA

The road stretches on from one small town to another along Nova Scotia's southern coast. Finally a sign indicates Oak Island, not a town, but a tiny island just over 100 acres in a bay that holds 300 islands. The turn-off from Route 3 leads past a few houses and finally to a causeway with a sign announcing that it is private property. There is little to indicate that this remote place, often shrouded in fog, is home to one of the world's greatest and longest treasure hunts. It began in 1795 and recently, new treasure hunts have begun again.

Over 200 years ago, three young men paddled out to tiny Oak Island. Pirates had been known to prey on traders in these waters and were believed to bury their treasure. Everyone's favorite story was Captain Kidd, who actually did bury a bit of treasure before being put under arrest. When these three young men saw a block and tackle hanging from a tree branch over a slight depression in the ground, visions of pirate treasure came to mind. They started digging.

At two feet they discovered flagstones, not indigenous to the island. They removed them and dug further. At 10 feet an oaken platform blocked their way. They removed it only to find another at 20 feet and a third one at the 30 foot level. Surely someone had gone out of their way to conceal something. While they were convinced they sat on a treasure, they were unable to go further.

Nine years later, one of the three, John Smith, was married and living on the island. The family doctor came to visit and was so intrigued by the treasure hunt story, he organized a company, called the Onslow Syndicate, to dig further. At 40 feet, a new oaken platform appeared and then again at ten foot intervals all the way down to 90 feet. A coded, inscribed stone described a treasure hidden 40 feet further, but just after the 90 foot mark, the shaft was flooded. It would hamper progress for years. The hole in the ground would soon become nicknamed the Money Pit as it would defy all attempts to uncover its secret, and a great cost in terms of dollars and lives was accrued in each pursuit.

As one crosses the causeway that didn't exist until 1967, the first thing one might notice is a memorial to six men that gave up their lives as part of the search. The first was in 1861. At that time, the treasure hunters knew that the shaft was being flooded by a booby trap. It was made up of water tunnels from both sides of the island. They attempted to stop the flow by building a coffer dam, by digging additional shafts, and by using pumps to prevent the seawater from stopping their efforts. A boiler explosion was the cause of the first casualty.

In the ensuing years, the work would stop and start, again and again. The list of investors grew to include Franklin D. Roosevelt, Errol Flynn, John Wayne, and Admiral Byrd. When the work stopped, the attention turned to research to narrow down the list of suspects. Evidently someone with a great treasure and a great amount of expertise went through quite a bit of trouble to create such a complex that is the Money Pit.

Suggestions that Micmac peoples, Huguenots and Acadians, even Vikings might have hidden some treasure underground are quickly shut down as they most likely did not have such treasure in the first place. Pirates were more likely candidates, as they were known to have buried treasure in vaults underground and a similar construction was uncovered on St. Mary's Island in Madagascar. British and French military payships might have had a large enough treasure and possibly the ability, but they more likely would have used forts constructed on the island.

David Tobias served in the Royal Air Force during the Second World War. He was stationed on Nova Scotia, heard of the dig, and later came back to buy most of the island. He controlled the dig until the late 1990s, and believed only Sir Francis Drake—the privateer who circumnavigated the world and preyed on Spanish shipping—would have had a treasure great enough to warrant such a construction as the Money Pit. But Drake was the favorite of Queen Elizabeth I. His proceeds funded the birth of English seapower while his personal fortune was immense. He had no motive to hide his treasure.

There was another organization that did have a motive, as well as the means, and most importantly, something of the greatest value—the Knights Templar.

Above: This fog-shrouded causeway leads to the site of one of North America's great mysteries. Below: The original Oak Island "Money Pit." The new dig may begin here. (Photos by Terry Sora)

By 1291 the Templars had retreated from the Holy Lands. The crusades were over and Europe had lost. The Templar organization had become the greatest multinational bank, the largest trading company, the most powerful navy, and an immense property owner rivaled by nothing Europe had seen before. They had, however, lost their reason to be. They were haughty, obeyed no king, and even though they were supposed to answer to the Pope, they didn't. King Phillip the Fair of France was living beyond his means, and even beyond the means of what he could gain through taxing his country. He expelled the Jews, confiscating their wealth; but still, he was in need of funds.

Knowing the Paris Temple, the central Templar bank, held the greatest amount of wealth in Europe, the king decided it was time to take the Templars by force.

On trumped up charges of heresy, he had the Pope condemn the order. Then on Friday, October 13, 1307, he ordered an attack on the Temple of Paris, the headquarters of the Templars. To the king's chagrin, the Templars also had the greatest intelligence force in the world and had been tipped off. Just days before, wagon trains were loaded with treasure and moved to the port of La Rochelle, where the treasure was placed on the Templar fleet, which then disappeared into history.

At Templar trials in England, testimony was given by two knights that the secret destination of the Templar fleet, along with its vast treasure, was Scotland. The excommunicated outlaws that were the Templars headed to an excommunicated country run by an excommunicated king. This was Scotland. The king, Robert the Bruce, earned his excommunication in 1306 by stabbing his rival on the altar of Greyfriars Monastery and declaring himself king just the year before.

His family was intermarried with the Sinclair family since the 11th century when both were part of the Norman power structure. Both families were prominent in France and Scotland, and the Sinclair family was notably prominent within the Knights Templar.

From there the treasure was stored in caves in the Esk Valley near the ancestral center of Sinclair power at Roslin.

The Templars repaid the favor of being allowed refuge by aiding in the Scottish war for Independence. At Bannockburn, the Scottish army was nearly defeated. The English army stretched on for two miles, a giant force. The Scots were in retreat when a fresh force of cavalry thundered onto the field and routed the English. It was June 24, the feast of St. John the Baptist, sacred to the Knights Templar and to modern Freemasons.

Later, the treasure of the order would be moved again.

While doing the research for my book, *The Lost Treasure of the Knights Templar,* I spoke to David Tobias and he believed it was possible; his partner Dan Blankenship didn't. In 2009, I visited the island twice to see the island as the next round of excavation was beginning. Blankenship hadn't changed his mind, and dismissed Drake, Capt. Kidd, pirates of any sort, as well as a Templar Treasure. Dan has four new partners from Traverse City, Michigan, who are continuing the attempt to get the island to give up its secrets.

Up to the present, the island had only tantalized treasure seekers with some gold chain, a parchment with a few letters, as well as medieval tools. What else could the Money Pit conceal? The Templars held, in their Paris bank, gold and silver as well as jewels that were pledged by royalty to fund Europe's near-constant wars. They may also have held treasures taken from Solomon's Temple in their earliest days of operation in Jerusalem. The Ark of the Covenant and the Holy Grail are among the greatest treasures, objects so great that a 100 foot pit, with hundreds of feet of interconnecting water tunnels, might be protecting them. Treasures so great that the years of construction were warranted.

In 1398, Henry Sinclair was the head of the family and the second most important man in Scotland. He was also Earl of Orkney, an island chain to the north of Scotland. It was here that he would meet Nicolo Zeno, a Venetian adventurer, and brother to the Admiral of that great city-state. Nicolo was shipwrecked and in great danger. Henry took him on as captain of his fleet. After hearing the story of an Orkney fisherman who had been to the Americas, Henry enlisted Nicolo's brother Antonio and led an expedition to this "new" world.

They landed on June 2, 1398, in Nova Scotia. Henry sent Antonio home and said he would explore this new territory in the hopes of establishing a colony. He left critical evidence in that future province, as well as in Massachusetts and Rhode Island. When he returned, Antonio sent letters and charts home that wouldn't see the light of day for over 100 years. The maps were later used by Mercator, Ortelius, and Martin Benhaim.

Sinclair's own papers went to his daughter Elizabeth. Sinclair's grandson William was the head of the family 50 years later when the English army threatened Scotland. The Sinclair castle at Roslin was destroyed, but if the English knew of the treasures the Sinclair's guarded, it was too late. William had moved them to Oak Island.

As Templars evolved into Freemasons, the Sinclair family was charged with being the Hereditary Guardians of Freemasonry. They held the power, the responsibility, and kept what might be the secret of Oak Island.

But the secret of lands in the west might have been shared. Elizabeth Sinclair married John Drummond. They would go to Madeira where the Knights of Christ held sway. The Knights of Christ was one of the reconstituted Templar orders that survived. Elizabeth's son, called John Escorcio, or John the Scot, married into the Perestrello family. The Perestrellos were from Genoa, sailing in the employ of the Knights of Christ with Templar crosses on their sails. They explored the Atlantic and discovered Madeira. As a reward, a Perestrello became the Capitano or Governor of Porto Santo on Madeira. As coincidence would have it, a young navigator met Felipa Perestrello at Sunday Mass in Lisbon.

They were soon married, and on the voyage to Madeira, Felipa's mother gave her young son-in-law a wedding present: the records and maps of her husband who had explored the Atlantic. It could not have been a better present for the young navigator, whose extended

Bust of Henry Sinclair

family now included the heirs of Henry Sinclair living on Madeira. The young groom's name was Christopher Columbus.

Since 2010, a new thundering force has rolled onto Oak Island. Not a cavalry, but a convoy of heavy construction trucks. And on January 5, 2014, the History Channel began airing a documentary series entitled *The Curse of Oak Island,* about a group of modern treasure hunters led and funded by two brothers, Rick and Marty Lagina of Michigan, who purchased the majority of Oak Island in 2006. We shall see what treasures lie in store.

8

LIVING UP TO THE
AMERICAN CONTRACT

Caroline Myss Thinks We Should Reconsider Our Obligations to the Founders

BY CYNTHIA LOGAN

"Not to know history," Caroline Myss tells me, "is not to have a compass on events; it's like being in the middle of an ongoing conversation and to not know what anybody has been saying." The well-known author, speaker and former medical intuitive (her book, Anatomy of the Spirit put her on the progressive map) deplores the fact that "Americans seem to disdain history." Only half jokingly, she remarks that she may have missed her calling. "I really should have been a historian; I just consume history." Yet she understands why most of us aren't the buffs she'd like us to be, since we're taught "here's the event, here's the date" *ad nauseam*. Instead, she feels history should be presented "as an evolution of thought that includes the great stories of those who have formed the nation; the great poets—Whitman, Dickinson, Thoreau—the wondrous people who are America." (No doubt she is inspired by National Public Radio's Story Corps project, which collects memorable stories from both ordinary and extraordinary Americans, airs them weekly, and archives them for posterity.) "The more I read about American history, the more I am awestruck as to how we even came to be; I'm amazed by the extraordinary birth of this nation."

Myss is a whirlwind of activity these days: she's on a personal campaign to inspire Americans to reconnect with the vision of our founders. Really, she wants us to "fall in love with your country again." Her latest work, *The Sacred Contract of America: Fulfilling the Vision of Our Mystic Founders* (Sounds True) is a CD series recorded in front of a small audience. The choice of media is effective; throughout, the listener feels her passion and intensity. She is near tears after just the first sentence; "I have been formed deeply by the influence of being the daughter of a marine. There's a great dignity that goes with that history; I grew up with a great deal of patriotism—the kind born of ideas and ideals, not the 'let's get them' kind you see today. I think my father would be choking if he saw America today. He really taught us what the nation stood for, and that freedom and the respect of the world was everything." Known for her no-nonsense, forthright (some would say blunt) style rippled with humor, Myss cuts to the chase with this work. Her sincerity is palpable, and her riveting delivery of a powerful encapsulation of America's beginnings, psychic makeup and current state of affairs summons an urgent call-to-action impossible to ignore.

Citing the last decade's plethora of books about America's founding fathers and mothers ("make no mistake; those women fought that revolution"), she notes *The Return of the Revolutionaries* by Walter Semkiw, M.D., which identifies modern Americans he thinks are reincarnated founders. (Semkiw's designations are based on information gleaned from psychic Kevin Reyerson, famous for his work with Shirley MacLaine.) "I got an email from this man saying that I had been Deborah Franklin," Myss says. I fired back; "Oh my God, no; I'm sure I was Abigail Adams. Supposedly, all of us are back and there is a meeting once a year—I haven't attended yet; I don't have the outfit."

On a more serious note, Myss explains that a contract is a collective of opportunities and challenges, a configuration of systems and patterns of power represented by mythologies that characterize and form the magnetic field of all living things. And, though every nation has one, she considers ours extraordinary. "America's isn't better or less, but if I were a physician, I'd ask: 'Are each of the organs equal?' You can live without your gallbladder (I know, I do). You can live without your appendix, but I wouldn't take out your heart. We just play a pivotal role." Contracts contain archetypes, which are repeated patterns and overarching themes woven into the DNA of its carrier. Whether personal or national, each contract contains twelve major archetypes, four of which are common to all: the Child, the Victim, the Prostitute, and the Saboteur. This quartet interacts to ensure survival and invite us on a journey toward managing power. We are intended to transcend the lower aspects of these archetypes to find self-esteem.

According to Myss, America's "Child" is an orphan. Though a first thought might be one of sorrow or pity, she emphasizes the freeing nature of a child without parents. The orphan represents the freedom to begin a life without past baggage, to neither belong to nor be beholden to anyone, or to belong to anyone or anything you want to. The Statue of Liberty stands as a symbol of the adopting Mother that is without parallel anywhere on the planet.

America's "Victim" represents our collective response to those in need, as well as our refusal to see ourselves as victimizers. Myss says it's important to understand that all cosmic laws contain opposites—the victim contains the victimizer. "Our phenomenal passion to reach out to victims with great generosity comes from having a history of victimizing others [she believes the taking of land from Native Americans is America's 'original sin']. . . . We're on a thin line right now," she thinks, "part of our contract was that America would not be an invader nation." Myss believes 9-11 brought out the victim consciousness in Americans. She says the cry for vengeance following the event "is not typical of us. We have a history of being a kind, loving nation. We have mutated since 9-11; we've become

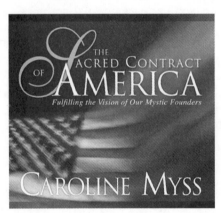

frightened, timid, easily herded and controlled—cowardly. We are anything but Americans." With this, she dives into what she calls the "Saboteur" archetype, explaining he conviction that Vietnam changed everything. "For the first time, the trust between the corps of the military and its government was broken. Like the rebels of the founding days, many soldiers questioned the war and said, "the principle of fighting here doesn't thrive with my soul." "A whole generation disconnected from our government and the fundamental vision of our country," she states. Though she considers such soldiers heroes, Myss finds it unfortunate that people were unable to distinguish between the government in office and the principles of the Republic. "Patriotism meant war," she notes, adding her view that "our current government has shifted the loyalty of the people to itself rather than to the founding principles—very clever—and very dangerous." She also argues that the "New Age" and the narcissism that followed Vietnam completed the work of the saboteur.

Our "Prostitute" isn't one of Miss Kitty's girls from *Gunsmoke*, but represents what we will sell in order to get what we need and ensure our safety in life. It isn't much of a stretch to see that the combination of commercialism/materialism creates our prostitute, bowing to the God of Money. "How much is enough?" asks Myss. "What are these SUVs, these Hummers, these huge Broncos—what does a human being on earth need a creature like that for on the streets of this nation?" When indignant, as she is when considering this, her voice rises in pitch. It stays there as she moves on to describe what she calls "a psychic reptile," the sense of entitlement. "This is the key to America's prostitution," she claims. "It's in the archetypal fiber here, it's part of the American mythology and it has caused us to become emotionally fragile and culturally weak. Even illegal immigrants are tapping into this sense of entitlement!" Myss feels this "reptile" is a large part of America's "shadow." "I don't know how Americans are going to shake free of this." Mentioning that being so litigious a society has reduced our freedoms ("you can't do anything anymore without fear of arrest or a lawsuit"), Myss becomes deeply emotional and states slowly, "What you are entitled to in this land is the rights of the soul, not the right to abuse, to sue, to make someone your economic slave, to hold someone hostage because you've been disappointed. You have the right to free yourself from prostitution!" She's even more concerned about the national debt. "We're owned by foreign nations; we don't even own our highways anymore! A prostitute is someone owned by someone else."

Though she hasn't yet discussed America's unique archetypes, the heart of Myss' message bursts forth: "The responsibility for being a light in this nation falls on your shoulders. Work as a sacred activist within your community. Ask yourself: How much freedom have we negotiated and what can I do in my own way to return the rights of free speech and action?"

Among America's unique archetypes are the self-explanatory pioneer, the visionary, embodied in people like Henry Ford, Howard Hughes and William Randolph Hearst, and the expression "the sky's the limit"; and the mystic, exemplified by many of the founders ("there is some similarity between the two, but the visionary is not associated with a higher power"). Many of the founders were Freemasons ("not like a bunch of Harry Potters, but they had a code of ethics; their word was good. Today, if the contract isn't signed, your word means nothing"). The founders weren't necessarily religious, but they were inspired by the thought that a place could exist where humans could thrive on freedom of spirit. They were high on ideals, high on the potential of what humanity could become if the soul was allowed to thrive in its fullness. "These people scripted the first document ever on this earth that bestowed the rights of free thought, that put the rights of the soul before the body . . . these people were saturated with Light." Though she claims to be "passionately in love with the founders," Myss isn't blind to what she considers their faults (Franklin allowed his only child, a bastard son, to rot in prison during the Revolutionary War because "he chose the wrong side"). Each held to the principles, even when they couldn't stand each other, during all rivalries.

The revolutionaries who put everything on the line for independence were America's first Rebel-Warrior archetypes. This force champions worthy causes when truth has been violated. "Where is our Rebel now," wonders Myss. "It's as if it has been banned, silenced, anesthetized."

From her perspective, the Bill of Rights is the seed of global self-esteem, and America embodies the individuation of the Self. "America came to be against great odds, as if humanity had to be given a chance to create the possibility of equal self-esteem—think of what an amazing thing it was to set this up, when most people can't follow a diet, can't be trusted in their own kitchens! Our contract is to lead the world to a new way." With that mission, Myss feels we couldn't avoid being in the middle of global chaos. "I knew 9-11 was the great turning point for our nation; as significant a turning point as Oppenheimer opening the nuclear age. America was destined to step into the global arena; some event had to trigger that; it might have had to be a hostile act because no one wants to become one planet. We may like the idea in theory, but we don't like it in fact; in terms of mergers of boundaries and power and having people at the table as equals."

The Entrepreneur archetype needs almost no explanation—say the phrase "American ingenuity" and you have the essence of this energy. Though the "can do" spirit is threaded through our DNA, Myss is concerned for America's financial future (because of our debt to other nations, we may find ourselves asking for aid, rather than giving it, she warns).

The Slave-master archetype needs a bit more explanation, and Myss provides an understanding with carefully weighed words. The bottom line? Slavery has always been a part of the human experience; with regard to some of the founders owning slaves (notably, Thomas Jefferson), she says the practice was in place and the work accomplished with the Declaration of Independence. The Constitution and The Bill of Rights set in motion the wheels of its eradication. Today, many Americans are slaves to their jobs (and proud to say so, she says). But the point of her analysis is that this combination is the highest archetype when viewed in its ultimate form as surrender to God or Spirit. "When you turn over your will to the will of God, you are in essence a slave and in that sense, ultimately free."

No discussion of America's archetypes would be complete without the mother. Besides our adoptive Mother Liberty, the apple-pie, do-it-all and do-it-perfectly mother that nourished a revolution, pioneered, and birthed a nation has morphed into an anorexic shadow of herself, anxiously following the dictates of a media mockup. Here Myss is merciless. "The American woman needs to look at what she's literally and symbolically bought into and step into real liberation by being more than cotton candy and the image pushed by cheap magazines."

The last archetype addressed in The *Sacred Contract of America* is that of the Judge, represented by our Supreme Court and the "law of the land." With the recent upheaval regarding the Attorney General [Eric Holder] and seemingly unending political shake-ups and scandals, Myss agrees things seem bleak. Yet, she says, whenever societies move into cycles of chaos, there is a corresponding release of Light to counteract it. "There is a mystical renaissance going on," she notes. "This nation was founded by political mystics and it has to stay alive by the same channel." As for the outcome, "I'm not an Armageddon theologian but I will tell you, we're at a collision of the sky gods. I believe the founding fathers are back in an energy field, just as I believe my beloved Teresa of Avila is back. The nation's vision is on a respirator; the people have dropped the ball. Freedom needs management. We are as unconscious as it gets, and in our narcissism we've been taken over from within—and that is quite extraordinary."

Myss hopes her current work will contribute to refocusing America's out-of-control shadow toward the Light. "I'm not blind to my country's darkness, but I refuse to not see its greatness," she says. "We are very much at the crossroads of a new spiritual paradigm and most certainly America is once again at the forefront of a revolution. This time it's global. The stakes are higher, the consequences far more lethal, but the power of America's vision remains intact if we as a nation reconnect with that vision."

PART THREE

SECRET SOCIETIES, LOST RELIGIONS

9

THE TEMPLAR ENGRAVINGS
AT DOMME

What Can the Mysterious Graffiti in an Obscure French Village Reveal About This Once Powerful Secret Order?

BY WILLIAM HENRY

After a long night enjoying amazing French wine and a bizarre argument over whether Pamela Anderson or Dolly Parton best exemplified the Divine Feminine in our time, our gang of classic American templar and wine enthusiasts left Chartres cathedral way too early that morning.

Before we rolled, our bus' GPS pinged a satellite. We locked on like a guided missile to Domme, a "lost" village in the Dordogne valley no one on the bus had ever heard of but me. Even the satellite appeared to struggle to locate it. "You wanna go where?" it seemed to say.

I was inspired to visit Domme by Ean and Deike Begg. In their book *In Search of the Holy Grail and the Precious Blood*, they describe the bizarre graffiti found in the chateau at Domme, where Knights Templar were imprisoned during the surprise attack by the Catholic church in 1307. Here is found a depiction of Jesus' execution that is slightly twisted from the official Church version. On Jesus' left is a pregnant woman holding a wand or a rod.

Unfortunately, the Begg's book didn't include a photograph of this graffiti. I had been dying to see it for years.

I've written about the perplexing images of a shorthaired, beardless Jesus using a magic rod or wand to perform miracles in several of my books, including *Cloak of the Illuminati*. For example, I present a 5th century portrayal of Jesus turning water into wine with a magic wand at the wedding at Cana. A woman, possibly Mary Magdalene, stands beside him. It was Hebrew custom in Jesus' time that the groom provided the wine at wedding feasts. Many believe this was Jesus' wedding to Mary Magdalene. Early Christian art suggests he produced the wine by magical means.

If this woman at Domme is Mary Magdalene, as I presumed, the wand likely belonged to Jesus. It would suggest that Mary Magdalene brought his technology to France with her after her husband's demise.

On a hot day in July 2005 I had an opportunity to hunt for it.

OVERHEATING

Rolling through the hilly French countryside, I daydreamed about Jesus' wand while looking at fields burned an early shade of brown from the hot summer sun. I hoped I wasn't wasting the time of the 18 revelers who accompanied me to France. The stop at Domme that morning was a surprise to the group. So, too, was the fact that our bus suddenly overheated, forcing us to pull off the road to give it a rest. What do you do when there's nothing to do in France? Whine? No! Find wine!

Back on the road a few anxious hours later, we exited the auto route at Domme. My wilting excitement blossomed. A few fellow travelers commented how I lit up every time we caught the light of certain sites. I thought of my cat, Boo, who loves to chase the red beam of my laser pointer dancing across a wall. I think he knows he'll never catch that light, but its fun flying after it, and good exercise, too.

Creeping along the narrow road toward Domme, our big white bus was an unwanted obstacle to the train of tiny cars behind us. Most were packed to the gills with vacationing Europeans fleeing to the Dordogne valley's famed rivers and hiking trails. The valley is a favorite holiday spot whose postcard-perfect scenery is dotted by romantic medieval chateaus and Harry Potter-esque stone villages.

Suddenly, we entered a forest. The sun disappeared behind the trees. The road turned into a long black serpent making frequent switchbacks. Our land yacht lurched and lunged, surfing the turns that took us from left to right and back again in less then 30 seconds. Side-to-side. Speeding up. Slowing down. Passengers sloshing in the rear of the bus began to complain of nausea and motion sickness. Of course, it was my fault.

When I pointed the laser pointer at Domme on the map on the wall and said, "We're going," I had no idea that it would take so much effort or time to get there. This was turning into a guilt trip.

The towers of Domme's massive eastern gate, the Porte des Tours, were used as a prison for 70 local Templars arrested in the swoop of October 13, 1307. Graffiti scratched on the walls inside the larger, left-hand tower provide poignant evidence of the anguish suffered by the prisoners, who still did not know whether they were incarcerated in what were to be their death cells. (The last of them was not released until 1318.) Equally clear is that they were innocent of the trumped-up charges brought against members of the order. Scratched carvings include crucifixes of different sizes, two seated Virgins with Child, and an object which is almost certainly supposed to represent the Grail. There are also imprecations against Pope Clement V and Philippe le Bel ("the Fair"), France's King Philippe IV—the two "abominables" who had destroyed their order.(Researched by W. Bro. Michael Jacobson LGR)

Nearby is the Templar and Cathar stronghold at Carcassonne

Replica of the Templar graffitti engraved on stone at Domme, France (on display in the Templar Museum at Domme. © William Henry).

Just then the bus swung into a parking area. Our seasick crew spilled out on dry land with shaky legs.

"Oh look," I said, pointing to the last three-quarter mile of steep slope atop which sits Domme. "Remember how good the long walk leading to the Great Pyramid felt? It won't be that bad." They looked at me like I had two heads.

Fortunately, a local entrepreneur was waiting with his miniature railway train. Paying two euros each for the ride, we climbed aboard the tiny train and chugged up the mountain like happy dwarfs with our knees in our chests.

DOMME

The conductor deposited us in the town square, a surprisingly lovely and colorful tourist trap with an astounding panoramic view of the heavenly Dordogne valley.

My fellow travelers scattered into the shops in search of refreshment. I bolted for the tiny Templar museum sandwiched in between two handsome gift shops to inquire about the Templar graffiti.

Inside I was sorely disappointed. The Templar prison was closed! What?!

Seeing my smile melt into disappointment the sophisticated young French woman behind the counter flipped a look to the wall behind me. There sat a stone replica of the Templar graffiti. "That's as close as you'll get, Simon Templar," her look seemed to say as I smiled back at her in appreciation.

I fired off a few shots with my digital camera. Then I settled in for a long gaze.

It was nothing like I had imagined. The drawing was crude. But what should we expect from prisoners drawing on rock?

Sure enough, there was a crudely drawn figure of a person (is it a he or she?) holding a rod that looked like a downward pointing arrow (or the Spear of Longinus?) to me.

Beside the figure is a spread eagle Jesus on a cross.

This surprised me in its similarity to early 5th century Christian depictions that show a muscular, almost superhuman, Jesus spread out against the cross so different from the giant crosses with a small (or often no) Jesus Christians display in America today.

Why, I wondered, would Templars carve crucifixes on the wall of their prison at all? Denial of the crucifixion, or a Savior who hangs on a wooden cross, was the requirement of initiation into their order. To get in they spit on the cross. The reason for this remains a closely guarded secret.

The Templar denial of the crucifixion is similar to that of the Cathars (who were first terrorized then systematically slaughtered by the Church only 60 years before) and their rejection of the cross as a symbol because it was an instrument of torture, a false idol of terrorists. The only source that Christ ("anointed") means "crucified," claimed the Templars, is the belief and the doctrine of the Church. The Templars rejected this belief.

Was this drawing some form of allusion to the secret Rule of the Order, a reminder of their oath? Did they ritualistically spit on it while imprisoned, perhaps to gain resolve? Remember, Jesus used spit on some healings. Did the Templars know his "healing spit" secret?

A fish with a Tree of Life (left) whose branches resemble grape stems (above). The resemblance of the Templar tree to a grape stem makes me think of the Gnostic use of the grape vine and bunch of grapes to symbolize Christ.

Dogon Nommo image. © Robert Temple.

Dogon drawing of the landing of Nommo's craft (left); Templar engraving at Domme (right).

Left: A figure holds a rod or wand. The crucifixion. Right: 2nd century portrayal of Jesus raising Lazarus with a wand. (The Vatican Museum)

Additional out of place details in the Templar graffiti included seven pierced pyramids topped by tall crosses.

Another non-Templar symbol is a fish and a Tree of Life, and another larger creature or object topped by a cross, which we'll discuss momentarily.

THE MYSTICAL TREE

When French king Philip the Fair ordered the arrest of the Knights Templar in 1307, the Order of the Templars was one of the most powerful forces in the world. The Order was supposedly formed to protect pilgrims from the "infidels," although most agree that, during their travels throughout the Middle East during the early 12th century, the Knights Templar were clandestinely in pursuit of ancient knowledge. It's claimed these militaristic monks reclaimed the secrets hidden beneath Solomon's Temple atop Jerusalem's Mount Moriah and subsequently acquired enormous wealth and knowledge ... perhaps beyond earthly riches.

What could be more valuable than gold or other treasure? Whatever it was, it posed a challenge to the temporal power of the king of France and to his supporter, the Roman Catholic Church.

For a clue to this metaphysical treasure we return to the image of the fish and the tree beside the cross at Domme. They are easily comparable to the sephirotic Tree of Life. The sephirot are the ten qualities of the Mystical Tree, set forth as a major doctrine of the Kabbalistic *Book of Splendor* (The

Zohar), which was first published about AD 1280, although its legend claimed a much earlier date.

Mastery of the principles of this enormously powerful spiritual tool allows the manifestation of the Divine into the world and the means by which Divine Union may be achieved. The Zohar compares itself to the Ark that gives shelter.

If we understand their graffiti correctly, its symbolism suggests the Templars imprisoned at Domme had acquired esoteric knowledge. The only way to reconcile the appearance of the crucifix and the Kabbalistic Tree at Domme is to recognize that far from denying Jesus, like the Cathars, the Templars worshiped him as an angel of light who had entered human affairs to deliver a spiritual technology for escaping earth life and to cross into the kingdom of light via the Tree of Life.

The Gnostics frequently called Jesus the "Tree of Life" and a "branch." At Domme, we have a figure holding what may be Jesus' wand. Is it a branch from the Tree of Life?

As noted, the Templars did not confuse Jesus, the man of light, with Christ: that is, the timeless quantum cosmic essence that exists everywhere and nowhere. Instead, they accumulated technology (a cluster of principles including alchemy, sacred geometry, and astronomy) that once belonged to this enlightened person and his apostles and enabled the manifestation of Christ. This "Christ technology" could "feed" us, transmute an individual into a higher being, and even create an advanced social order, a new kingdom of heaven on earth. Philip the Fair and the Church of Rome wanted this technology for their own purposes. Helter skelter. They planned to crush it out of the Templars like a bunch of grapes.

THE MERKABAH

Kabbalists call all ten sephirot collectively the Merkabah or "chariot" of God, whereby the Divine could descend from heaven into men's souls.

Beside the fish and Tree of Life at Domme is another larger "fish creature"(?). Obviously any one can read anything they want into this symbolism. To me, this fish creature bears an amazing resemblance to a drawing presented by Robert Temple in *The Sirius Mystery* of the descent of Nommo. Nommo is the amphibious savior the Dogon tribe of Mali, believed to have

MISSING CONNECTIONS

been sent from Sirius to watch and educate humankind. Is Nommo's craft the Merkabah chariot?

Nommo divided his body to feed humankind. His name is thought to mean "make one drink." Nommo was known as master of waters.

Interestingly, the Merovingians, the alleged "offspring" of Jesus and Mary Magdalene who ruled this part of France, claimed descent from a fish creature that came out of the ocean. This fish-being is widely traced to Oannes in Babylonia and Enki in Sumeria. Both are equated with Nommo . . . and Jesus.

Enki is portrayed in the Babylonian seal shown at right. He hovers in a winged ring or craft (an ark?) above a utensil operated by priests wearing fish suits. It appears to portray Enki descending in a Merkaba chariot. This is a purification ceremony.

The early Christian symbol of the anchor with a cross with a pierced circle and a fish grasping a line of hope or salvation is plainly kin to, if not a copy of, the Sumerian seal portraying the fish-priests beside a radiant tree or pillar above which hovers Enki.

Both are identical in meaning to fish grasping the Tree of Life in the Templar engraving.

The match between these emblems—all three portray fish attached to a tree (or tower?) topped by a symbol for the Lord—leads to a profound question. Were the early Christians devotees of Enki/Nommo? Were the Templars, as well?

FOUNTAIN OF LIVING WATER

The fish at Domme may be the key that unlocks this engraving. In ancient Christian symbolism the fish stands for the concept of the living water referenced in so many traditions. This living water is different from ordinary water. It's cosmic. It has a quickening effect.

John's gospel provides insight into these mysterious waters. Jesus said, "the water that I give him shall become in him a fountain of water, springing up into life everlasting." (John 4: 10-14)

As Ezekiel 47:8-10 tells us, its source is the Temple of Solomon in Jerusalem. The "fountain of living waters" is mentioned in the Old Testament's Song of Solomon (4:15): The living waters flow from the Temple.

What is it about Solomon's Temple that produces the living water? And what does it have to do with the Templar excavations there and the graffiti portraying a Tree of Life/fount of living water? I'm not certain, but this living waters connection is made even more relevant when we acknowledge that in French literary tradition introduced in the 12th to 13th century Mary Magdalene is remembered as *la Dompna del Aquae*: Mistress of the Waters. Is it she holding a branch of the Tree of Life at Domme? Or, could it be a beaker holding living water?

Like the Medieval kabbalists, the Templars who engraved these drawings crammed a tremendous amount of information into a very small space. Whatever it means, this astonishing conglomeration of religious and philosophical symbolism, which taps into the root and runs into the branches of religious beliefs of the ancient Middle East, certainly suggests the Templar prisoners at Domme were aware of mystic traditions.

10

THE FALL OF THE ROYAL SOCIETY

*or How Isaac Newton Settled His Score
with Robert Hooke*

BY PETER BROS

Orthodox history tells us that Robert Hooke was a minor character with no accomplishments to speak of, certainly none to equal those of the majestic Isaac Newton. Instead we learn that he was a jack-of-all-trades who started many projects and finished few, and we discover that he was a colorless, misshapen recluse who attempted, but failed, to claim credit for discovering that Kepler's inverse square law could be mathematically connected to Galileo's inverse square measurement of gravity, the underlying idea that led to Newton's Theory of Universal Gravitation. When Newton's theory was published in the *Principia*—the three-volume work containing Newton's explanations for his laws of motion and universal gravitation—he obliquely credited Hooke, but not with priority, for the basic idea. When Hooke objected, Newton retaliated by having his name excised from the *Principia*—crossed out on existing copies. History sided with Newton, condemning Hooke as an upstart who had attempted to claim what was not his.

From this point on, there is little mention of Hooke in the history of science other than a cryptic reference to the timing of Newton's takeover in 1703 of The Royal Society—that learned society for science founded in 1660, still in operation, which claims to be the oldest such society in existence. Though voluntary, The Royal Society serves in the United Kingdom as the virtual academy of sciences. While Newton could have taken charge any time after 1695, he left his mentor, Sir Charles Montagu, to run it through 1698, and then Montagu's proxy, the Lord Somers, until 1703. The year 1703 is also the year Hooke died. Hooke had actually been running the Society during the last decade of his life.

Based on the frontispiece to *Sprat's History of the Royal Society.* The president of the Royal Society and Francis Bacon are on either side of a bust of Charles II.

The implication from even a casual reading of history is that Newton, for some reason, feared Hooke and thus avoided seizing the Society's reigns during Hooke's lifetime. While history does not ascribe Newton's hesitancy to fear, it does ascribe it to a strong and justifiable dislike for Hooke. However, it is strange that, with Montagu, one of the most powerful men in England, as a mentor, Newton would let a dislike for Hooke get in the way of his desire to seize the reins of English science and thus to direct the scientific worldview in his favor.

HOOKE'S BUSY LIFE

Hooke's claim to the idea underlying the *Principia* was not an idle one. He, along with Edmund Halley of comet fame and Sir Christopher Wren, the man who rebuilt London after the Great Fire of 1666, had been sitting around a café table in London discussing Kepler when Hooke proposed the analogy of Kepler to Galileo. When Halley and Wren suggested Hooke show the relationship mathematically, Hooke begged off. He was the direc-

tor of scientific experiments for The
Royal Society, and others were using
up his time in conducting experiments. The outcome of the informal
meeting was a modest offer by The
Royal Society of an award for anyone who could put the analogy into
mathematical terms.

Robert Hooke   Isaac Newton

Some months later, Halley was
visiting Cambridge where Newton was Lucasian Professor of Mathematics.
When he told Newton about the problem, Newton claimed to have already
solved it. Although he was not forthcoming with the proof, the problem
eventually led to the *Principia*.

Newton, isolated at Cambridge, had only two contacts with The Royal
Society prior to the publication of the *Principia*. He first presented his
reflecting telescope, which was received by the Society with the enthusi-
asm it deserved. This emboldened him to submit his *Theory of Colors*, and
here is where he first crossed swords with Hooke. The Royal Society had
been established with the motto "*nullus in verba*," nothing in word, and
Newton's *Theory of Colors* was basically nothing but words. As the director
of experiments, Hooke lived by the motto, which was based on Francis
Bacon's outline for scientific experimentation. The Society was established
to experiment on practical problems that could lead to technological
improvement. Bacon taught that concepts could not be taken as fact, that
what we thought always had to be updated by what we found out. Newton, running counter to Bacon, thought that theories could be proved, that
ideas could be demonstrated to be fact, an anti-Society position. Hooke
objected to Newton's presentation, and Newton never recovered from the
shock. (His first act as President of The Royal Society three decades later
was, after having the portraits of Hooke destroyed, having the Society publish his *Theory of Colors*!)

To Hooke, objecting to Newton's theory-as-fact approach was simply
another task in his busy life. One of the many tasks he had been assigned
by The Royal Society was to measure the parallax of a star (parallax is the
change of angular position of two stationary points relative to each other
as seen by an observer, caused by the motion of an observer). Although,
on the continent, the Ptolemaic solar system still ruled, England's conver-

sion to Anglicism had removed Catholic authority over scientific observation and most enlightened thinkers in England accepted the Copernican solar system. However, since proof for Copernicus remained to be demonstrated, The Royal Society set out to demonstrate parallax, a measurement that could only be made from opposite sides of the Earth's orbit. It's reasoning went that if parallax could be shown, it would prove the Earth orbited the Sun and therefore validate Copernicus.

The notes of The Royal Society show that, although constantly called on the carpet for not finishing this task during the 1670s, Hooke kept piling excuse on top of excuse for why it hadn't been done, leading to further evidence that he was just a jack-of-all-trades and incapable of handling the highly specialized parallax project.

HOOKE'S FRIENDSHIP

It took over 300 years to uncover the reason for Hooke's foot dragging. Uncovering what Hooke was up to during the 1670s was one of those serendipitous accidents that pop up from time to time. In the 1990s, Lisa Jardine was writing a book about Wren (*On a Grander Scale*, 2002). She was contacted by Channel Four in Britain, which was doing a documentary on the Great Fire of London. As Christopher Wren had rebuilt London after the fire and therefore played a central role in the story, Channel Four invited Jardine to participate in a shoot at the 202-foot tower Wren designed as a monument to the Great Fire.

Jardine arrived early. As cameras were set up around her, she sought shelter from the cold by the ticket booth. After several hours, the attendant, whom she had gotten to know, asked if she had seen the tower's basement. When she said no, the attendant rolled back a carpet revealing a trapdoor. Below, Jardine found a beautifully carved set of curving stone steps leading into a massive chamber below the monument.

Having already published Hooke's definitive biography, *The Curious Life of Robert Hooke: The Man Who Measured London*, Jardine knew exactly what she was seeing. Wren, along with his lifelong friend Hooke, had turned the monument into a massive 202-foot zenith telescope to fix the star he was using to measure parallax.

Hooke finally reported to the society that he had measured parallax. However, the subject became lost in other matters and the honors of discovery went to James Bradley in 1728. While Bradley claimed that his measurement differed significantly from Hooke's, it is understandable since the margin of error in the measurement is 6°S, and the most accurate to date is less than half a degree. Moreover, Bradley went on to state that he had accepted Hooke's measurement (acknowledging Hooke's priority in the process) because of the length of the telescope Hooke used. Bradley, at least, must have been aware of the London Fire Monument telescope that Wren and Hooke had conspired to build.

WREN'S FAMILY AND FRIENDS

Wren's connections superseded The Royal Society, as did Hooke's. Wren's family and friends had held the ultimate positions of power in England.

In 1603, James I took over the throne from the Tudors in what was, at first, a shaky change of royal houses. Subsequently, however, the Stuarts cited The Order of the Garter Knights to claim kinship with the Plantagenet line of kings stretching back into the 12th century, thereby solidifying their hold on the crown.

When Charles I took over from his father, he received the ultimate symbols of Stuart legitimacy: the Order's "George" (in reference to St. George, Patron Saint England), which was a large pendant, and the Garter cloak. Windsor Castle, the home of the king, held the Order's chapel in its northwest corner next to the dean's house, the house where the monarch accommodated visiting dignitaries. The Register of the Order was also, at all times, the dean, and therefore among the most influential members of the monarch's entourage, having both constant access to the ruler and the ability to deny access.

The first dean and register that served under Charles I was Matthew Wren, who was succeeded by his brother, Christopher. Titles reflected sources of income and the Wrens, being very close to the king, carried many and were among the wealthiest men in England.

The "George" pendant

Sir Christopher Wren

Christopher's son Christopher Jr. was the same age as the son of Charles I, the future Charles II. Christopher Jr., who became Hooke's great friend, grew up with the future king and they both shared an interest in mechanical things, an area in which Christopher was highly skilled, both as a draftsman and builder of equipment.

With the start of the Civil War, the king and his son were separated from Christopher, with young Charles staying with his father and his fighting forces, while Christopher (the Wren's assets confiscated by the Cromwell parliament) landed in the hands of royalists who still had assets. Charles II fought beside his father, but eventually was persuaded to take refuge in France as his father's losing cause led him toward Cromwell's ax. When executed in 1649, Charles II was allowed only the presence of his confessor, whom he entrusted with the "George," telling him to "remember." This direction was an instruction to ensure that the "George" found its way into his son's hands, thus legitimizing his future kingship.

While the Wren family was brought low monetarily, it still maintained its social status. Young Christopher was included in the future king Charles's party in its escape to the continent. His father, however, remained in England, spending every waking hour preserving the artifacts of the Order as well as meticulously reconstructing its history and rituals so that, when Charles II succeeded his father, his legitimacy would be secure.

THE ROOTS OF THE ROYAL SOCIETY

After Charles I was beheaded, Cromwell's Commonwealth had turned Oxford into a barracks. Charles I had always supported excellence at Oxford, and under Cromwell, this purpose was carried on by parliament. Thus, John Wilkins, a protégé of the former king, was allowed to remain as warden of Oxford's Wadham College. Wilkins, the future founder of The Royal Society, had very specific interests in developing skilled minds that could handle technological problems and provide answers to them. He did not balk at taking in the talented children of royalists, and indeed began developing a group of these at Wadham College. One of those esteemed very highly was young Christopher, who was taken in despite the fact that his uncle was in the Tower of London and his father was hiding out in the hinterlands.

At this time, Parliament decided to survey Ireland. The man hired to do the survey, William Petty, was not nobility, but was extremely talented both in pushing technology and administration. The survey took at least a thousand people to complete, and when it was done, Petty, an astute businessman who had engaged in land speculation during the survey, returned to England a rich man. While in Ireland, he had met Robert Boyle and had struck up a close friendship with this foremost scientist of the day. Boyle had laboratories in both Ireland and England. His laboratory in England was run by Robert Hooke whose father had been a royalist, but had died before the capture of the king. Like Christopher, Hooke was thrown onto his own skills to make his way in life. His ability in the laboratory to produce any type of equipment that Boyle needed was becoming known throughout the scientific circles of the day.

While Wilkins was establishing his Oxford group to engage in practical experiments, Petty, upon his return, was casting around for ways to improve technology, coming up with idea after idea. He approached Boyle, telling him he was good with ideas, but not so good with perfecting their implementation. While the logical person to do the perfecting for Petty was Boyle's assistant, Hooke, Boyle didn't want to give up any of Hooke's valuable time and therefore referred Petty to the Wilkins group. The only person in Wilkins' group capable of perfecting Petty's designs was Christopher Wren. Petty's contact with the Wilkins' group, ironically, brought Boyle into close association with the group, and with Boyle, Hooke.

The Wilkins group therefore ended up financed with Petty's money, and the group grew form and substance as it worked on practical projects designed to solve real technological problems. Its process is what today we consider the scientific method, although the method today is used, or claimed to be used, to solve problems that, in reality, cannot be technologically tested, such as how the universe began.

THE ESTABLISHMENT OF THE ROYAL SOCIETY

The group continued experimenting on advancing technology with Commonwealth approval right up until the restoration of the monarchy with Charles II. The first thing Charles II did was put on his father's "George" and don the Garter cloak. He, of course, was well acquainted with Wilkins and Petty's activities, as well as with Christopher's. The king was quick to reward old loyalists and he bestowed many honors and commissions on Christopher Wren. Looking for the most competent help, Christopher began including Hooke in these projects because Hooke's interests and his own coincided.

Meanwhile, Charles II wasted no time putting his stamp of approval on the doings of the Oxford group, moving it instead to London and incorporating it as The Royal Society, its purpose still the advancement of practical technological applications. Thus, Christopher Wren, the king, and Robert Hooke were all intimately involved in the Society's creation by Wilkins to do the practical experimentation that could lead to technological advancements. This concern for practicality is the reason the Society quickly embraced Newton's reflective telescope and why it did not embrace his theoretical musings on light, which were not directed at producing practical applications of anything. Although Newton disguised his contempt for Hooke as dislike, it is clear that Newton feared Hooke's powerful ally, Wren, with his long-standing connections to royalty. To Hooke, Newton's theories were just that—theories, not fact. Newton, believing his mathematics to have proved them, was convinced his theories were fact.

Newton didn't dare to use his own lesser connection to take over The Royal Society during Hooke's lifetime. Unfortunately, Hooke was born a sickly person, without a healthy stamina, and succumbed at a relatively young age, several decades before Christopher Wren, leaving Newton free to take over the Society.

Once in full charge, Newton proceeded to pervert the Society's scientific method from one of testing ideas against reality, a procedure that advances technology, to one of proving fantasies about reality, doing the exact reverse of the Society's founding motto, "nothing in word," modifying it to "words are sufficient," crippling technology and destroying the possibility of a scientifically accurate picture of reality to this day.

11

THE OTHER SUN OF GOD

Before There Was Christianity There Was Mithraism

BY STEVEN SORA

When I asked the concierge of my hotel in Rome for directions to the Church of San Clemente, he said no one had ever asked him for these directions before. It was on few tourists' top-ten lists of places of interest. After answering my question, he posed one in return, "Do you know what lies under that church?" I nodded that I did. The church was built over an ancient temple to the god Mithra. This god was significant in Rome before the birth of Christ and was actually the basis of the state religion. His "cult," as it would be referred to much later, had been populated strictly by men and mostly by soldiers.

Mithra was the Persian savior god who predated Jesus by centuries. He was born in a cave on the same day of the year that Jesus was, December 25. His mother was a virgin, his father, the Sun. Magi and shepherds attended his birth, and his life is full of miraculous deeds including the healing of the sick, restoring sight to the blind, and the casting out of devils. Before his ascension to heaven he celebrated a last meal with twelve disciples. His ascension was celebrated at the Christian Easter. His image was then buried in a rock tomb in hopes that someday he would return.

Pleased that I was aware of Rome's ancient god Mithra and this unusual church, the concierge reached over the desk to shake my hand. He then explained that the handshake was started by adherents to the Mithra religion. The handshake was never a Greek or Roman custom, nor was it a greeting in Babylon or Israel. It signified a transfer of power from God to his representatives on earth, his priests, or as a greeting between initiates. It spread as it became custom within areas of Roman military influence.

With that I headed to the Coliseum and continued past it by barely one hundred yards. There, on the quiet side street of Via San Giovanni, the Church of San Clemente stands. There is little of significance on the outside and one might walk by without recognizing it as a church. Inside is another story.

Mithraeum of the Baths of Mithras, Ostia Antica, Italy

The church was built in the 12th century and has a beautiful mosaic from that period as well as some large frescoes of the Crucifixion, the Annunciation, and scenes from the lives of several important saints (including even St. Christopher, who was later deemed to be most likely mythical). It also holds vestiges of an even earlier church that it was built over, including marble choir screens that had been salvaged.

This earlier church is believed to have been built in AD 392 and can be reached by a stairway from the right aisle. It was dedicated to the saint that is believed to be the third Pope of the Catholic Church, Clement. This church was destroyed during the Norman invasions around the time of the crusades. The church is mostly intact as it remained well preserved until being unearthed in 1857 by Irish monks. The discovery may have been a surprise, but a greater mystery was also to be unearthed. Under this 4th century church was still another level. It contains a temple called the Mithraeum, and it is one of the few shrines dedicated to the god Mithra that has survived outside of Asia.

Visitors who venture here, two floors beneath the Church of San Clemente, are greeted by an eerie series of chambers connected to tunnels.

MISSING CONNECTIONS

Many of these rooms simply lead only to another room, and visitors can be forgiven for worrying that they might become lost. The complex holds one large section that once served as a warehouse, another section believed to have once been part of a palace, and a tunnel that was actually a road. In one of the most remote rooms, there can be heard the somewhat disturbing sounds of running water although no water is visible. Behind the stone is an underground stream that flushes out Rome's principle sewer system, the Cloaca Maxima.

Despite the darkness of this underground temple, Mithra was called the God of Light. His religion had been born circa 1000 BC, when Zoroaster preached the concept of one universal god and the eternal war between good and evil. This prophet foreshadowed the tenets of Christianity, as well as Judaism and Islam. In Persia the dualism took form as Ahura-Mazda, the sun god born as the twin of Ahriman, the dark god. The twins had been born of the Creatress, who was later forgotten. The "good" twin later became known as Mithra. One of his titles is the Invincible Sun. His worshippers believed that at the end of the world there would be a great battle fought by the sons of Light and the sons of Darkness. Mithra's followers were the good guys.

A Mithraic prayer says that in the beginning the two spirits came together. They created Life and Non-Life. In the end, the prayer cautions, the followers of evil will suffer the worst existence, while the best existence shall be for those who follow the right. The message is not unlike the Christian message of ever-lasting life.

In practice, however, it was not a message of the meek inheriting the earth. It was the strong. For a soldier to be accepted into the faith was an honor. He would be blessed by the god who on Earth was represented by the bull. He would draw on the powers of the bull god that exhibited both strength and fertility. As the bull was the source of such power, the soldier utilized such strength for the benefit of his nation. The worship of the bull itself was not new—from Egypt and the Levant to the British Isles, the bull was held in high regard and coupled with worship of the sun. Poseidon was regarded as a bull god as was Shiva in India. Italy itself was named for the Vitalia, the Sons of the Bull. The Mithra faith may have simply served as a variation of the practices of Sun and Bull worship.

Constantine was the emperor of Rome until AD 337. He claimed that he, himself, was the incarnation of Mithra. He was also the driving force in the drive to make Christianity "Catholic" or universal. It served his purpose to unite pagans (the Mithraic faith included the soldiers) and early Christians within Rome, as this unity would make his empire stronger as it fought it enemies outside its borders. Constantine had lived his own life in the religion of his father, a follower of the Invincible Sun. During this time, the religion of Mithra had been the established religion of Rome despite the fact that it excluded women.

While many of Constantine's conquering deeds would not today be called "Christian," he did promote tolerance, which allowed pagans and

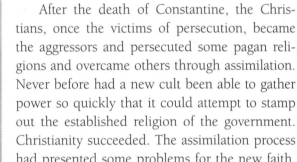

Christians to enjoy freedom from persecution. On his deathbed he converted to Christianity.

After the death of Constantine, the Christians, once the victims of persecution, became the aggressors and persecuted some pagan religions and overcame others through assimilation. Never before had a new cult been able to gather power so quickly that it could attempt to stamp out the established religion of the government. Christianity succeeded. The assimilation process had presented some problems for the new faith. The Mithra religion may have been particularly embarrassing to Christianity because of the obvious similarities that had been adopted by the newer religion. There were so many shared char-

Bust of Constantine (Capitol Museum, Rome)

acteristics that St. Augustine questioned whether both faiths were actually worshipping the same God. Many of these similarities were a result of the influence of Constantine himself. What once enabled Constantine and the Christian Council of Nicaea to ease the transition from Mithra to Jesus, would become difficult to explain away.

Even the holiest day of worship to early Christians and Jews, the Sabbath, always observed on Saturday, was changed by Constantine to Sun-Day. Jesus himself would have observed the Jewish Sabbath. The birth of Jesus, once celebrated on January 6 (and still celebrated on that day by the Eastern Orthodox Church) was moved to December 25 to accommodate Mithra.

New Testament stories were not the only ones to show evidence of being grounded through Persian influence. The Old Testament, attributed to prophets of Judaism (and God himself) carried a version of the Mithraic story of Ahura-Mazda, a dualistic creation. This god was given credit for planting the haoma tree. The fruit of this tree would bring immortal life to those who ate it. The Garden of Eden was, in Persia, a walled garden, a Pairi-daeza in that language.

The church would later alter the myth of Constantine at the Battle of the Milvian Bridge. The famous line of Constantine's, "By this sign I will conquer" refers to the *labarum*, a symbol which today is accepted to be the Christian monogram of Chi and Rho; but the original sign of the labarum was most likely a combination of the symbols of the all-powerful sun and bull—not the Christian cross. The Church nevertheless would declare it was the cross that Constantine had in mind.

Before the worship of Mithra was stamped out by Christianity, along came the Persian prophet Mani. He was born near Baghdad. As a young man he was initiated into a mystical cult by his father. They wore the white robes of the Essenes and practiced baptism. Just as Christianity had apostles spreading the Word, Mithraism had the apostle Mani, and the form of Mithraism that endured through his preaching became known as Manichaeism. Rome for centuries had already accepted belief in Mithra, so it was easy to accept the concept of dualism which was incorporated in Mithraism. Mani preached this doctrine, carrying it from Persia to Europe. Dualism teaches the balance between good and evil, the light and the dark, already present in Mithraic teaching. While Christianity shared the concept in part, it didn't believe the creation of the material world was evil, a concept shared by pre-Christian Essenes, and surviving among later Cathars and Albigensians into and beyond the 14th century. Mani put many of the concepts in writing in his Fundamental Epistle that started: "May the peace of the Invisible God and the Knowledge of truth be with our holy and dearest brothers."

The word "brothers" again reasserts the "male only" orientation of Mithraism, and its probable influence on other secretive, often male-only organizations. It is one of the clues that Mithraic traditions found their way into organizations including the Knights Templar and the Freemasons. Tracing a direct line from the ancient sources to the Knights Templar and modern Freemasonry is difficult, but some the characteristics of the shared influences are glaring evidence:

Mani referred to Jesus as the "Son of the Widow" and to himself as the same. He claimed to have fasted in solitude for a long period and to have "met" Jesus during this time. The Templars would later have a motto for never turning away a "son of the Widow." Another link between the Templar legend and Manichaeanism is that Templars were accused of worshipping a severed head. If this is true, and not another invention used to prove the Templars to be heretics, it can be related to the story of John the Baptist who had preceded Jesus. John the Baptist was beheaded while in prison, and many believe he was part of the Essene sect since they were famous for the Baptism rite. The same rite was found among the sacraments of Mithra and the Christian sacraments as well. Mani, like John the Baptist, was, in AD 276, decapitated. Could a Templar tradition have been rooted in worship of John the Baptist, reverence for the prophet Mani, or both?

Mithraic practice was shared by both Templars and Freemasons and survived in Christianity.

Like Freemasons there were various degrees of initiation. In Freemasonry, arriving at the Third Degree was important, and there are thirty-three levels. In Mithraism there are four initiatory stages and three higher stages. In the four levels of entrance, one would start with the degree of Corax (Raven), which was a symbol of the Moon. The second was Cryphias (the Hidden One), a sign of the planet Mercury. This was followed

A Persian ruler (center) receives his crown from Ahura Mazda (right). Mithra (left) is wearing a crown of sun-rays. (Iranian relief)

MISSING CONNECTIONS

by the Warrior (actually Venus) and the Lion (the Sun). From this stage, one was a full member. The higher degrees included the Persian (Mars), the Sun-Runner (Jupiter) and the Father (Saturn). This highest degree of Father was called in Roman the *Pater Patrum*, similar to the Pope's title.

These seven stages can be compared to Christianity's Baptism (the Moon), Penance (Mercury), Marriage (Venus), Communion (Sun), Confirmation (Mars), Holy Orders (Jupiter), and the Last Rites (Saturn). The number seven is prominent in both faiths, as well as in the Kabbalah where the seven flames of the Menorah represent the seven planets (which in Kabbalistic tradition include the Sun and Moon).

Manichaeanism was a variation of a religion blending Gnostic Christianity and Mithraic traditions. This form of religion had little dogma that would be at odds with Christianity since both faiths were pervaded by the eternal conflict of darkness and light, of good and evil. The commonality between the Roman Catholic Church and the teachings of Mani would separate when it came down to the idea of direct relationship with God. The Church would then accuse Manichaeans, Cathars, Albigensians, and others of heresy, since there was no recognition of a central authority on Earth. Such "heretical" beliefs became the cause of a propaganda war against the pagan cult of Mithra that still pervades modern thought. One 20th century writer claims "there is no evidence that the Mithraists ever preached a morality of love," yet a minor title of Mithra was "mehr," a Persian word literally meaning "love."

The religion of the Invincible Sun was at odds with most of the non-militaristic faiths. In the Mithraic temple two stories beneath the modern Church of San Clemente, one of those eerie places in the complex of tunnels and connecting rooms was the *taurobolium*. It was said to be where the initiates were baptized to enter the first level of the Mithraic religion. The rite was similar to baptism as practiced by the Essenes and Christians, but it is believed that the blood of a sacrificed bull was used in place of water. Bull cults were nearly universal when Christianity began to take root and a bull was annually publicly sacrificed on the Vatican hill, near the location of St. Peter's Cathedral. After three centuries of Christianity in Rome, the practice was stopped. The anointing in the blood of the bull had been practiced elsewhere including Eleusis, in Greece, and as far away as England where Roman soldiers carried the faith. In becoming a more gentle faith, Christianity outlawed the sacrifice of the bull and declared that Jesus was the lamb whose sacrifice took away the sins of the world.

12

FROM SAINT TO SUN GOD

The Many Faces of John the Baptist

BY STEVEN SORA

The party was well underway when the host introduced his daughter to the guests. He asked her to show off her greatest ability, to dance for his guests, but she demurred. He asked again and again, yet his daughter, Salome, denied him. Finally he promised her anything up to half of his kingdom, and at that she consulted with her mother. Yes, she would dance, but her request was surprising, She asked for the head of a man that her father held in his prison.

Her request granted: John the Baptist was executed, and his head brought to Salome on a platter.

The story of Herod and his daughter Salome is accepted as a historical reality. John was an influential religious leader who openly spoke out against Herod's marriage to his second wife Herodias. While Herod feared an uprising, Herodias was further inflamed by the insult of having her marriage deemed illegitimate. Herod had broken both custom and religious law by marrying her while his first wife was still alive. Worse still, this new wife had been married to his brother. Salome was the daughter of Herodias and Philip, therefore now both niece and step-daughter to Herod. It was such a serious breach that the itinerant preacher John continued to harp on it. So irked was Herodias that she wanted him put to death, whereas Herod figured his death would be even more likely to ignite rebellion than his preaching.

Legend continues where the Bible story leaves off. Herod's decision incited neighboring King Aretas to attack his small tetrarchy. He and his wife were exiled to Gaul, and then later Spain, where they were killed in an earthquake. Salome is said to have perished while crossing an ice covered river. She slipped through the ice, which then closed around her neck. She was beheaded while her legs frantically danced under the ice.

The death of John the Baptist brought life to the ministry of Jesus. Jesus had few followers, while John may have been the most important preacher of the day. He attracted thousands to the Jordan River where he baptized all into a new form of gnosis. When Jesus came to him, according to the Gospels, a dove appeared above his head when he received the sacrament from John. The dove, already a symbol of Isis, represented a higher

Salome II (Caravaggio, c. 1609)

form of knowledge: a direct knowledge of God. This initiation brought Jesus into the greater circle that evolved around John, but he was not yet the leader he would become. Even after being baptized Jesus would question the apostles, "Whom do men say the Son of God is?" The answer in Matthew 13:14 was, "Some say John the Baptist." Salome's request would effectively end John's ministry and begin the ministry of Jesus.

John is regarded as the precursor both in an earthly sense and in an astrological sense. John announced the coming of the Son, as the morning star announces the coming of the Sun. As such he is held in high esteem by Christianity and Islam, and in the highest esteem by sects that survived the fall of Jerusalem. Christianity celebrates only one other birth date besides the December 25 birth date of Jesus: the June 24 birth date of John.

Pre-Christian and agricultural-based religions have some interesting similarities with the John-Jesus dates. The summer solstice is generally June 21 or 22, and in Europe regarded as midsummer. The sun at this time is at its greatest strength; from the solstice its power diminishes. Then six months later the winter solstice announces a new sun, or a new king, when the old king is dead.

THE SECRET THE TEMPLARS UNCOVERED

The Christian church held a monopoly over knowledge when the Crusades began in AD 1099. The Bible had not yet been printed, and the stories of the Gospels were filtered through the Church and the priests. Doctrine was rigidly enforced under threat of torture and death. Stories from Adam to Noah, Jonah to John, were repeated in the pulpits across Europe. They were accepted as true.

The Templars arrived in Jerusalem shortly after the city fell to the Fatimid Caliphate in the 11th century. The wars known as the crusades would last over a century, although bitter battles were often separated by years of peace. During the down-time the crusaders in general and the Templars specifically were introduced to a completely different handful of religious concepts. From Persia came the worship of Zoroaster, the Ram of God, who forgave the sins of man. He was born in a cave on December 25. From Egypt came the tale of Isis who resurrected her husband Osiris as her son Horus. Horus was baptized by Anub in the same river where John was said to have baptized Jesus. From the Far East came the Buddha whose birth was announced by Bodhisat, to a virgin mother Maia. Even Hercules was born of a virgin, Alcmene. His father was god, that is, Zeus.

The floodgate of knowledge was opened, and it was a shock the religious sensibilities of Europe. The Templar Knights would be accused of worshipping a bearded head. By itself this was strange although in a different context it linked the Green George head seen throughout Celtic lands, and the head of John the Baptist revered in Asia.

One sect that the Templars encountered was the Mandaeans. They had survived the Roman massacre of Jerusalem in the AD 70 revolt, and had headed into Syria and further west to escape Roman domination. In the 17th century they were still alive and well. Catholic missionaries who encountered the group called them "St. John Christians." This was in modern Iraq.

Despite being surrounded by Islam, this sect survives into modern times. To them, John is the "king of light." Their sacred texts refer to John as Yohanna in their Aramaic-derived language. Other texts written in Arabic refer to John as Yahya, his name in the Koran. The name "Mandaean" comes from "manda" or gnosis, which is given to mean a self-knowledge of God. They had lived in the Jordan River area where John's ministry was started.

Their religion is a mixture of the many religions that have existed between Jerusalem and the Fertile Crescent of Mesopotamia over thousands of years. They have gods and goddesses. Their goddess Libat is an Ishtar-like goddess whose prominence ranged throughout Europe and Asia under various names. Their gods are more like Sumero-Babylonian gods than anything found in the Judeo-Christian world. At the same time they share Adam and Eve, John the Baptist and Jesus. Jesus, however, is regarded as a false prophet whose militancy contributed to their forced emigration. While Christianity uses the symbol of the fish to represent Jesus, the Mandaeans connect the fish-man Oannes with John the Baptist.

John the Baptist of the Christian gospels has been also identified by early Christian syncretists in Egypt with Oannes. He was a bringer of knowledge and light with a widespread cult in the pre-Christian Middle East. Oannes is said to have been born of the sea, and as a result half man, half fish. Further east, the Hindu god Vishnu had his first avatar as a half-fish, half-man. Fast forward to the Bible and we see a similar story of a man surviving being swallowed by a sea creature, a whale. From the belly of this sea

Oannes

creature he reaches land where he preaches (bringing the light of wisdom). Is it coincidence that Jonah and Oannes have some oddly similar stories as well as a phonetically close name.

THE SUN GOD

Somewhere between the ancient knowledge-bringer Oannes, and the Son (Sun) of God, Jesus, there was a Syro-Phoenician god by the name of Hadad. His followers worshipped in a huge temple built to him about 900 years before the ministry of John and Jesus. In the temple were ancient carvings of another era. A basalt bas-relief shows a winged sphinx, possibly an influence of both Mesopotamian and Egyptian religions. It also depicts the head of a bearded man that is remarkably similar to John the Baptist. The act of baptism allows in many faiths a cleansing that is preparation for rebirth and eternal life. Water is also the most important ingredient for the fertilization of the planet.

The Romans brought their own very similar god, Jupiter, and rededicated the temple that had been dedicated to Hadad. After Rome converted to Christianity, a church was built here and dedicated to John the Baptist. Since John looked like the bearded Jupiter and the bearded Hadad, all could worship here. It was reported that the head of John the Baptist was buried here after his execution.

Later Islam grew to become the dominant religion in southwest Asia. Temples to pagan gods and Christian churches alike were converted to Islamic sites of worship. It was decided to change the Christian site of John into a mosque. And not just any mosque. Under a tolerant Islamic leadership the magnificent Umayyad Mosque (the Great Mosque of Damascus) was built. Consent was given by the city's Christians who in exchange were allowed to build a grand St. John church of their own. It took ten years to build the mosque and it became a centerpiece to the modern city of Damascus. It contains an expansive courtyard decorated with sacred mosaics. The courtyard contains a huge fountain of ablutions and several domes. The builders allowed a prominent spot for the skull of John who was important to the Muslim faith as well, as he was a very important prophet. This mosque is very important today as an Arabic pilgrimage site. In size it is grand and one of the few with three minarets. One of those minarets is dedicated to Jesus.

Pope John Paul II was the first leader of the Roman Catholic Church to enter a mosque and visit the shrine of John the Baptist (and Prophet). It was a goodwill visit to promote tolerance between Syria's Christians and Muslims.

In a curious display of just how religion adopts and accepts the unorthodox, Muslim women still come to pray at the shrine to St. John if they cannot get pregnant. Fertility was not one of the aspects of the Baptist however. Are they praying to John, or Hadad, or an ancient god further unknown to Christianity?

John has devotees from other corners of the world. In Portugal the festivities annually dedicated to John are more reminiscent of a popular Phoenician solar deity than a Christian saint. As Baal, he is the sun and his consort goddess is the moon, under the name Astarte (Phoenician) Ishtar (Babylon) Anat (Syria) or the Christianized St. Lucy. In the north where the rooster is the symbol of the sun, the Christian *mass do Galo* (of the Rooster) is an ancient reminder of the odd connection. Twice each year the solar calendar starts a twelve-day celebration. In winter it begins on December 13, also known as St. Lucy's Day, the day of the light, and culminates on December 25, the birth of Jesus. In summer the celebrations begin on June 13, and the highlight is Midsummer's eve, June 24.

Along the Atlantic coast of Europe, long before Christianity, bonfires were lit and dedicated to celebrate the calendar feast day of Hercules (represented under several names) throughout Europe. This was Midsummer's Day Eve. After the spread of Christianity bonfires were lit on Midsummer Day to St. John, whose birth feast is the same date as the Celtic feast. The name had changed although the feast remained the same. In Norway, fires lit to Balder, the Norse god, were now to St. Hans (John). In Ireland, Germany, Austria, and Russia pagan bonfires preceded those of John. He could grant good luck, cure cattle, and protect towns.

The ancient Celts and possibly the Druids before them had a tree calendar. The month that started on June 10 of our calendar and lasted until July 7 was dedicated to the oak. In accord with the tree calendar, the gods Jupiter, Zeus, Hercules, Thor, and Celtic Dagda were celebrated. Midway in the oak month was also Midsummer, on which was celebrated St. John's day. The oak king was killed on this day, preparing for another king.

In Wales, the hero who would become St. David was actually once Dewi. Dewi the Waterman was a god of the sea who dragged men to the infamous locker, as Davy Jones. The Christian Church invented a St. David but almost nothing was known about him except he was meant to replace the pagan god Dewi. The symbol of this David-Dewi became the national symbol of Wales, the Red Dragon.

It may have been animosity toward Wales that led Britain to take the Celtic Green George, the disembodied head similar to John the Baptist, and to make him St. George the Dragon Slayer. Green George survives well into the modern century from his depictions in Rosslyn Chapel to mundane garden decorations. His celebration, a very

St. George (Raphael)

obvious fertility ritual, is notably at the spring equinox, the Christian Easter. The spring goddess predates Christianity and is named Eostre.

SECRET MESSAGE BEHIND THE TALES OF GOD

The furthest corners of Europe preserved their fertility festivals the longest. At the harvest time, often the last of a harvested crop would be made into personified representations of the living food a fertilizing sun, rain, and earth provided. Corn shaped into the form of dolls were burned, honey cakes were cooked and eaten, and barley, used for spirits, was similarly deemed important enough for its own ritual.

The ritual is remembered in the John Barleycorn song that recalls Sir John being both killed in a ritual and consumed. Many consider it to be the same rite of transubstantiation that occurred at the Last Supper. Jesus had his followers promise to remember him by the eating of his flesh and the drinking of his blood. The death-rebirth theme is at least as old as the tale of Osiris, which is a tale of the seasons, and the old crops being harvested to await the young crop.

The basic needs of humanity have not changed in the thousands of years since civilization began. Food, safety, love, and children are desired and heroes, gods, and saints are asked to provide.

In a sense, however, tales of heroes and gods alike are often contrived to pass along a much more complicated message. Understanding the stars and the heavens, predicting seasons and weather, and very specifically having the ability to predict an eclipse, were the province of the learned. Such magicians (like the magi) held power and awe by this talent. To pass these along to the next generation of adepts and priests was done through tales that the majority understood on one level while the initiated understood on a much deeper level. As Jesus said, "Let those with ears, hear," he meant, let those initiated understand.

Were the twelve labors of Hercules a lesson on the zodiac? Were the twelve adventures of Ulysses built on the Hercules "lesson?" Were the twelve apostles or knights of King Arthur an echo of these more ancient tales? We may never know with certainty if the trappings of our modern religious feasts and festivals preserve the knowledge of the gods known to the ancients.

13

TEMPLARS IN MEXICO

*Were the Spanish Conquistadors the First Europeans to
Meet the Aztecs or Not?*

BY STEVEN SORA

The order of the Knights Templar would survive for less than two centuries. In the period between AD 1108 and 1307, the order would have a spectacular rise and a devastating fall. The order's history is based equally on legend and fact, in part because the order wanted it that way. Many of its secrets remain as secrets even today. Written records remain concealed, others have been destroyed, and still others remain in plain sight for those who understand enough to recognize what they actually mean.

One of these secrets left in plain sight is the depiction of maize and aloe carved in stone in Rosslyn Chapel. The journey of Sir Henry Sinclair to the New World in 1398 can account for the depiction of maize, a corn variety known to Native American peoples in New England [See chapter 7, "Return to Oak Island," page 52]. Aloe, however, is a plant grown much further south. While aloe itself could come from Africa's tropics, the aloe cactus is distinctly American and originates far south of New England where Sir Henry left his mark.

Could the Templars have reached Mexico? There is much evidence from the Spanish explorer Hernando Cortés that the Aztecs and the Templars had some common history. The Aztec civilization, like that of the Templars, also had only a brief history. Compared to the other ancient peoples of Mexico and Peru, the Aztecs were modern. Despite the historical portrayal that compares them to the Maya and Incas, like the Templars, their power lasted for only for two centuries. The Aztecs then encountered the Spanish who ended their control. Coincidentally, the rise of the Aztecs occurred at the same time as the demise of the Templar order in Europe. Was it mere coincidence?

Our knowledge of the Aztecs was substantially reduced by the Spanish Catholic bishops who destroyed as much of the Aztec literature as could be found. Bishop Diego de Landa (c. 1562) recorded that the Spanish found a large number of books. Since the bishops could not read them they decided it was all superstition—the work of the devil—and burned them.

All of Mexico shared bound books of bark and skins, and possibly three or four survived. The so-called Madrid codex is decorated and inscribed on both sides of all 56 pages, which gave instructions for raising crops, rainmaking, beekeeping, weaving, and hunting.

All of Mexico shared a calendar as well. That calendar was much more accurate than Europe's Gregorian. The natives were adept at mathematics and possessed the use of the zero, a mathematical concept that Europeans had somehow missed. The Aztec were watchers of the sky and revered Venus as much as the Egyptians had. The Templar Knights also had kept their secrets hidden, not from the illiterate populace, but from the Church.

Hernando Cortés (Mexico Templar art)

Mexico had first been populated mostly by the Maya who peaceably farmed the southern regions of that country and other areas in Central America. Around 1200 BC they met up with the culture historians label "Olmec," whose origin has never been explained. The Olmec may have been the first civilizing force to elevate an agriculturally based culture to that of a highly skilled urban civilization. The visible evidence is in their immense wave of pyramid and temple building as well as in their advanced urban layout.

Further west were other Mexican peoples, including the Otami who ruled over a large region. The head of this people, Tlahtoani Tezozomoc, employed Mexica mercenaries who would later become the Aztecs.

The Aztecs, like many cultures including the Greeks and the Romans, adopted their gods from those of older populations. For the Aztecs it was the

Mexica gods, and they seemed to place importance on a multitude of deities, often warlike or destructive in nature. Oddly enough, Mexican religion depicted the cross, had a flood story, and remarkably the Aztecs even had the sacrament of confession. It was less like the Catholic confession and more like the Cathar confession, usually performed at one's deathbed.

Similarly, the Aztecs placed a great emphasis on martial arts. At some point in their history two elite orders emerged from the basic military, the Knights of the Jaguar and the Eagle Knights. The most illustrious were admitted to these orders. They fought for the sake of glory, for their own wealth, and were regularly singled out for special honors. The Jaguar Warriors, like the Knights Templar, were an organization that was part military and part religious. The Jaguar Knights had their own symbol in an animal that embodied courage and power. They were devoted to the god Tezcatlipoca, whose name translates to "Smoking Mirror" the term given to obsidian used in shamanic practice. He was the great sorcerer, the god of the night sky, associated with enmity, discord, strife, and war. Tezcatlipoca, like a Christian saint, was patron to calendar days and his was any day with Acatl (meaning reed).

The other pivotal order was that of the Eagle Knights. Like the Jaguar Knights, they were mostly men of noble birth, although others were allowed in for bravery, and success in capturing the enemies needed for their devotion to human sacrifice. The eagle was fearless. An Eagle Knight had the duty to fight to the death even if his fellow soldiers were all being killed—there was no retreat, no surrender. A depiction of one Eagle knight shows him to be helmeted. The Eagle Warrior survives on Aero Mexico's logo.

The helmet of the Eagle Knight was not unlike a medieval knight's helmet except it protruded further over and under the face of the warrior. It offered both protection and the ability to induce fear.

Aero Mexico Logo

Both orders had their own temples. They also held privileges granted only to the elite, including that of being allowed to keep concubines and of being welcome to dine in the Royal Palace. At the Eagle Knight temple a large carved basalt eagle served as both a totem and a religious representation of the Sun.

The temple included an entrance hall connected to a courtyard by a long corridor. Inner chambers featured carved reliefs of serpents and warriors and two mysterious skeletons whose meaning today is lost. This motif is used today in some Masonic temples in America. The Eagle Temple also holds life-size images of the Eagle Knights decked out in their beak-like helmets and feathered dress. Remarkably, when they weren't in battle, they wore cloaks of red or white with a red fringe. Did this Templar-like imagery have any roots in encounters with that European order? The timing is certainly interesting with the Aztec orders gaining in power and ability just as the Templar order was leaving Europe to flee the French king, but there is more to the story.

At some point in Aztec history, a white-bearded, fair-skinned figure came among them. His name was Quetzalcoatl, and he brought culture and attempted to show the value of peace over constant warfare. It is hard to understand just how significant this figure was in a cultural sense. In one sense, Quetzalcoatl was like the Micmac Glooscap who influenced the population of Nova Scotia. He arrived by boat, lived for a time in a tent called "winter," traveled widely, and left promising to return again. Through the research of historian Frederick Pohl (and others), we believe that Henry Sinclair, of the Templar family that became the hereditary guardians of Freemasonry, was the basis for Glooscap's legend.

The Glooscap hero is similar to the Norse Loki, a god and a trickster at the same time. It may be that Henry Sinclair became Glooscap through the eyes of the Micmac people. Quetzalcoatl, like Glooscap, was based on an individual with some divine proportions. Like Loki and Glooscap, he represented both dark and light, a dualistic concept shared by several religious groups including the Cathars.

Was Quetzalcoatl a Templar Knight?

Within both the Jaguar and Eagle orders were rankings that compare to the rankings within a Templar Lodge. The native Mexica peoples share the legends of Quetzalcoatl and of his arrival by ship with his white soldiers. According to the Vatican codex, one of the few documents preserved from the massive destruction of Mexican writings, the natives called the newcomers Tecpantlaques, which can be interpreted to mean, "Men of the Temple." Since the extent of the Aztec ruled area bordered on the realm of the Maya, it is no surprise to see that they also commemorated exposure to white, bearded, and mustachioed men who came in ships. The Maya left such depictions on the walls of Yucatan's temples.

A Mayan ruler, long before contact with Europe, was Pacal Votan. One of his titles was "Navigator." This same title was said to be a title of the grand-masters of the Priory of Sion. It also served as the title of the leader of that resurrected Templar order, the Knights of Christ. Specifically, Henry the Navigator of Portugal, not a sailor himself, sent his order's brave ship captains west into the Atlantic.

Historian Jean de la Var-ende was a Norman royalist and an ardent Catholic who wrote about Europe's aristocrats. In his book *Les Gentilhommes*, he stated that the Templars had sailed back and forth across the Atlantic to mine silver. At least three Spanish historians agree

Quetzalcoatl

with each other that the white-bearded Quetzalcoatl and his men were none other than Templars fleeing the 1307 assault on their order. One is Juan de Torquemada who arrived in the New World as a child (not to be confused with the Dominican Inquisitioner of the same name). Torque-mada was the chronologist for the more peaceful Franciscan order and later the provincial superior for the order in Mexico until 1617. He wrote a lengthy text on the rituals and the government of the native Mexican population. Francisco Lopez de Gomara and Toribio de Motolima also wrote on the appearance of white skinned foreigners in pre-colonial times. Modern writers, including Alejandre Vignati (in his 1975 book *El Enigma de los Templarios,* published in Spain), agree with the story of pre-colonial Europeans.

Quetzalcoatl's influence on the warlike Mexica unfortunately did not leave them with a more peaceful attitude. Instead he may have aided them in the art of war. It is possible the warlike Aztecs only understood the glory of battle and victory. If a Templar influence attempted to introduce a peaceful Son of God, the Aztecs did not listen. In fact, in a sad parody of Christianity, the Aztecs treated their captives well until they killed them. The brave captive would live in comfort until the day he would enter the arena with his captor. The capturing Aztec knight would address the captive as if he was his son. The "son" would address his captor as his father. The better armed "father" would then defeat the inadequately armed "son" in a battle that culminated in death.

Quetzalcoatl left Mexico in a ship from the island of Cozumel, promising to return on 1 Reed, the feast day of Tezcatlipoca. Years later, on 1 Reed 1519 (April 22), Hernando Cortés showed up.

If we estimate that Templars had arrived shortly after the 1307 attack on their Paris headquarters and that the Quetzalcoatl-led group left Cozumel, as the legend states, in 1311, it was four Toltec, or Aztec, cycles, of time that the white men had been gone. On the date predicted, they returned, after stopping on the same island of Cozumel. Montezuma II can be forgiven for not believing in coincidence. Whether it was because of the legend, or simply because the Aztec leader was afraid, several hundred Spanish defeated a city of two hundred thousand. When the Spanish arrived at Tenochtitlan they were met with a city so astonishing that Bernal Diaz del Castillo recorded that many soldiers believed it had to be a dream. Twice the size of Rome or London, and three times the size of any city in Spain, Tenochtitlan was built on an island in a blue water lake, surrounded by a ring of mountains. To reach the island one would cross one of three causeways that were 25-feet wide. The city had avenues so wide that ten horses could ride abreast. It held palaces, forums, and large homes. It contained fifty pyramids, the largest taller than anything in Seville. It had an extensive canal system through which most of the commercial traffic moved. The Spanish arriving at the most important Mexican city were not Templars, but again there is irony in the date: it was St. John's Day 1520, sacred, of course, to the Templars, but not to the armies of the Spanish Inquisition.

Cortés proved quickly not to be the peaceful Quetzalcoatl but more like the opposite. He was the dark side of the divine who came to destroy and slaughter. His tiny force was aided by the Totonacs, a client state living near Vera Cruz. He would soon topple Montezuma and wipe out the population. They had a handful of weapons and would hire the Totonac mercenaries to assist them, but that does not explain how hundreds defeated hundreds of thousands. The secret weapon was disease. .

The victors then destroyed everything the culture possessed. Buildings were demolished; books were burned. Centuries later Mexico City would be built over the ruins. While such an immense city cannot be excavated, the Aztec are resurrected every time a subway is built or new electric cable is laid.

At this point the evidence is not conclusive, but in the last quarter century there has been a staggering increase in discoveries. Road building and tourism serve to uncover pyramids on a regular basis, and one historian commented that there could be as many as a hundred thousand pyramids within Mexico and Central America.

It would serve our modern civilization well to find a cache of texts that the Spanish missed.

14

MYSTERY OF THE BLACK MADONNA

What Is the Secret of Her Enduring Appeal Despite Rejection by Orthodoxy?

BY MARK AMARU PINKHAM

Throughout the ages the image of the black madonna has elicited profound veneration, but also intense trepidation and even abhorrence from its observers. While Catholics have sought to denigrate and even to shun the numerous Black Madonnas scattered throughout their own European churches—the followers of the older, nature-centered, and alternative faiths have traditionally praised its beauty and uplifting power. In 1952, during a convention of the American Association for the Advancement of Science, representatives of the church made their feelings clear when a paper on the Black Madonna was presented. Abruptly the attendant priests and nuns rose and walked out in protest. The shocking disdain for the Black Madonna left reporters scrambling for clues to this "skeleton in the (church) closet," which the mere mention of the Black Madonna had invoked. It has since been speculated that paganistic origins for the Black Madonna could have sparked such surprising behavior, and more recently, with the controversy stirred up by *The Da Vinci Code*, it has been conjectured that it was somehow connected to the forbidden secrets of Mary Magdalene.

Members of the modern Knights Templar organization are free to speak and research both the Black Madonna and Mary Magdalene, who is venerated as one of the organization's patrons. Wisdom regarding both forms of the goddess or female principle has been passed down among Templars for centuries. According to the archives of the International Order of Gnostic Templars (*www.GnosticTemplars.org*), a division of the Scottish Knights Templar, Templar history related to Mary and the Black Madonna began with Templar origins, when the founder of the Rule, St. Bernard of Clairvaux, composed literally hundreds of songs and sermons in honor of Mary Magdalene, and even mobilized the second crusade from Mary's

Poland's Black Madonna of Czestochowska

headquarters at Vezelay. But beside Mary Magdalene, St. Bernard has also been acknowledged to be a worshipper of the Goddess in her other forms, including that of the Gnostic Sophia.

When Templars arrived in the Middle East, their "goddess" education was furthered by the Goddess-worshipping Sufis, Islamic adepts who originally created Mecca as a goddess shrine and later inspired the Muslim "goddess" flag, with its goddess-related symbology of eight- or five-pointed stars and crescent moons. These adepts were the guardians of a tradition that had been faithfully preserved for thousands of years in the Middle East. From them, Templars learned that beginning as far back as 4000 BC in ancient Anatolia and Sumeria, the goddess had been worshipped as Cybele, Inanna, Ishtar, Astarte, and Artemis—to name but a few of her manifold personifications. But although Sufi indoctrination opened new vistas for Templars, this wisdom was not entirely foreign to them. Templars had already become familiar with some of the goddess's Middle Eastern manifestations back in France. The image of Cybele had returned from Asia many years previously with the Roman legions and she had been enthusiastically adopted by the ancestors of Lyons as a patroness. Artemis had similarly found a home as patroness of Marseilles, and the Egyptian Isis had been crowned Queen of Paris. But even though her black visage had been part of French culture for many years, it was not until the Templars arrival in the Middle East that they truly began to understand the essence of the goddess.

The Sufis taught that the goddess was actually the third "person" of the Catholic trinity, the Holy Spirit, which was the power that descended upon the apostles on the day of Pentecost. Templars also learned that as the Holy Spirit, the goddess could not only bless us, but could also manifest all our desires. She was the universal energy that emanated from God and possessed the ability to create, preserve, or destroy whenever she was called upon. Her three powers were personified by her diverse images, some of which reflected her role as the beneficent Mother Nature, while others, especially in her more grotesque forms, revealed her power to destroy. The Black Madonna was a reflection of the goddess's destructive power, but the Sufi practitioners of yoga and alchemy also informed the Templars that this power was benevolent since it could alchemically transform a seeker of wisdom into an enlightened adept. This transformation was accomplished by destroying all the distorted concepts and egotistical predispositions that keep a person from knowing the intuitive secrets of the universe that exist within his or her own heart. Such intuitive wisdom, it was learned, is known as gnosis.

The Sufis revealed that the worship of the destructive/transformative power embodied within the black image of the goddess had, over thousands of years, become common-place in the Middle East. And icons of the Black Madonna had been specifically made by craftsmen to amplify this force. The venerated Black Madonnas of the East had been made of a dark or black conductive and amplifying material—such as a hard wood, stone, or meteorite—in order to better transmit her power to their worshippers. A huge black meteorite had been the original image of Cybele, just as it had been for Aphrodite or Venus. Meteorites found along the coast of Asia Minor had been traditionally gathered up as manifestations of Venus and installed in small temples dedicated to the goddess. Goddess mystery school traditions eventually grew up around these black images since it was found that they exerted a magical effect on the human energy system. With current scientific knowledge we have learned that their "magic" created currents of energy which pulsed within the human electro-magnetic field, an effect caused by their high density and concentration of iron and nickel. Ultimately, their effect would have elevated a person to ecstasy while also initiating him or her into spiritual life by activating the normally dormant evolutionary force at the base of the spine. This power, known in the East as Baraka and Kundalini, can lead one, it is believed, to immortality, which is why in ancient times meteorites were recognized as both Holy Grails and Philosophers' Stones.

The Sufi love of the goddess and their unparalleled understanding of her alchemical power personified as the Black Madonna completely resonated with the Templars. Thus, when they returned from their respective tours of duty in the Middle East they made a point of bringing back many statuettes of the Black Madonna for local Templar preceptories and the Gothic cathedrals they were in the process of building. In fact, it was principally because of Templar influence that, by the time of their demise in 1307, it is estimated that there were upwards of 190 prized images of the Black Madonna venerated throughout France.

Templars installed some of their most prized Black Madonnas in chapels in the Languedoc region of France. The Languedoc was a hot bed for all things heretical, and it eventually became famous for harboring perhaps the most hated of Catholic heresies, the Cathar Gnostic faith. Interspersed among the Cathars were many practitioners of alchemy, learned from the Sufis—reputed to be the greatest alchemists of the time. Alchemy, it is believed, leads to the awakening of the inner centers of intuitive wisdom or gnosis. And the pursuit of gnosis leads to inner, alchemical transformation.

Such heretics were safe in the Languedoc to practice the alchemy acquired from the Sufis. Alongside the alchemical experiments were observed the rites of Johannite Christianity, an ancient Gnostic tradition inherited in the Holy Land. The elders of this alternate branch of Christianity taught that Jesus had established not one but two lineages of Christians, the Catholic Christians of St. Peter and the Gnostic/alchemical or Johannite Christian lineage of John the Apostle and Mary Magdalene.

Jesus had, according to their tradition, himself become a Gnostic through his training with John the Baptist, who was regarded by the Johannites as co-Messiah with Jesus. After Jesus transmitted Gnostic Christianity to John the Divine, the alternate Christian lineage had passed down a long line of Grand Masters named "John" until the First Crusade. At that time the lineage was inherited by the Templars and their first Grand Master, Hughes de Payen, became the titular John of the lineage. From that time onward, Templars were married to the Gnostic path.

In recognition of the Johannite Christian heritage, Templars dedicated their churches in the Languedoc to John the Baptist and Mary Magdalene and placed alchemical images of the Black Madonna within them or in close proximity. Templars also built a series of Gothic cathedrals in northern Europe dedicated to John or Mary and installed Black Madonnas upon their main altars. The dimensions of these cathedrals, which were based upon sacred geometry taught by the Sufis, were designed to generate the alchemical power of the Black Madonna and elicit states of gnostic awareness. Seven of these cathedrals were anciently built over the seven chakra points of Europe. An ancient pilgrimage route of the seven sites founded by the early Johannite Templars was designed to activate the seven human chakra points—which are considered to be centers of gnostic awareness. Beginning at Santiago de Compostella in Spain, and then moving up the European spine to the French cities of Toulouse, Orleans, Chartres, Paris, Amiens, and then finally culminating at Rosslyn Chapel in Scotland, these seven cathedrals are marked abundantly with Johannite, alchemical and goddess symbolism. Black Madonnas were once prolific in these cathedrals, and many of them once had labyrinths covering their floors. Even the original floor of Rosslyn Chapel was originally covered with a labyrinth. The Templars understood that the labyrinth, a geometrical form body of the goddess, is one of the best tools for alchemy and gnosis in existence. The idea is that, as one walks the back and forth maze of a labyrinth, the two hemispheres of the brain begin to act in unison and intellect unites with intuition to produce gnosis. Alchemy is also stimulated internally as the body's intrinsic polarity harmonizes and unites to activate the latent alchemical fire.

Some of the sites of Europe's towering cathedrals, such as at Chartres, had since the time of the Celtic Druids been places of goddess worship and divination. Legend has it that there was a Madonna at Chartres hun-

The Black Madonna of Chartres Cathedral

dreds or even thousands of years before the birth of Christ, so obviously the image could not possibly have represented the Virgin Mary holding baby Jesus. It was, no doubt, related to the pre-Christian nature religion that once permeated Europe, and was, therefore, an image of the Goddess holding her Son, the Green Man or Lord of Nature. The time-worn legend of this nature cult held that the goddess was the barren earth who gave birth each spring to a Son manifesting as all the fledgling buds and sprouts of the season. The Son grew very quickly—reflected by the rapidly growing vegetation— and then died each year in the fall with the falling leaves. During his short life he also became the lover of his mother, who then became extremely distraught at his passing in the fall. This popular nature legend spread throughout Europe, the Middle East, and Egypt, and precipitated the creation of many nature festivals, including Easter. Within the Mesopotamian nature cult the early Madonnas represented the goddess Inanna or Ishtar, whose Son/lover was the nature god Dammuzi or Tammuz; in Anatolia they denoted Cybele and her Son/lover Attis; and in Syria they symbolized Astarte or Aphrodite and her beloved was Adonis, a nature god who, like the waxing and waning life force of the growing season, was forced to spend part of the year underground. Even in Egypt, the original Black Madonna and Son—Isis and Horus—represented the Goddess and Green Man. When the Egyptian Green Man, Osiris, died each fall it was said that Isis would revive him long enough to mate with him and conceive Horus. According to one perspective, Horus was thus Green Man Osiris reborn.

When the Catholic Church was formed it borrowed many of the rites, holidays, and images of the early nature cult, including the Black Madonna and her Son. They also co-opted many elements of the legend of the Lord of Nature and wove them into the life story of their savior Son, Jesus. This was possible because the legend of the Lord of Nature had, by that time, acquired both a mundane and spiritual interpretation; to some he represented the forms of nature, and to others he was the savior and archetypal initiate. In Egypt, for example, the mundane understanding of the Green Man, Osiris, maintained that he was the personification of nature that died and is then reborn each year, but the spiritual interpretation of the legend taught within the mystery schools recognized Osiris to be the archetypal initiate whose death in the fall and resurrection in the spring denoted the egoic death and spiritual rebirth of an Egyptian adept.

Thus, the archived Templar histories have revealed that Templars must have known the Black Madonna and her Son as not only the Goddess and Green Man, but also as the transformative goddess who gives "birth" to the archetypal initiate and coddles him to spiritual maturity—or gnosis. Since the Church was no doubt aware of these early "pagan" associations, its current disdain for the Black Madonna is understandable. The Church has always sought to distance itself from the earlier pagan traditions it so abundantly borrowed from, and it has consistently opposed all alchemical paths that lead to gnosis. As some mystics have demonstrated, such a path can invariably lead to the inner revelation of "I am Infinite," or simply "I am God," a proclamation that goes decidedly against the grain of Catholic doctrine.

Finally, the Church's abhorrence of the Black Madonna may also stem from the fact that in some circles she is associated with Mary Magdalene. In fact, there are those who believe it is she who is embodied and immortalized as the dark image. If this is indeed true, the Catholic church is more likely than ever to be virulently opposed to any veneration of the image of the Black Madonna, especially now that the Nag Hammadi gospels have been found to portray Mary as the favorite disciple, wife, and even true successor of Jesus.

15

F. L. WRIGHT VS. G. I. GURDJIEFF

A New Book Uncovers the Strange Story
of the Taliesin Fellowship

BY HERBERT BANGS, ARCHITECT

Roger Friedland, a cultural sociologist, and Harold Zellman, an architect, have written a very good book about a strange and little-known subject, the Taliesin Fellowship of Frank Lloyd Wright (*The Fellowship*, HarperCollins, NY, 2006). Wright, himself, is certainly well known, through his buildings, his writings on architecture, his autobiography, a number of other biographies, and a popular novel, *The Fountainhead*, which became a successful motion picture. Oddly enough, however, until Friedland and Zellman published *The Fellowship*, little was known of the school that Wright set up during the depth of the great depression, ostensibly to train the cream of American youth to be "organic" architects.

In 1932 Frank Lloyd Wright was broke. The notoriety that had followed when he left his first wife and children for an open liaison with Mamah Cheney, her murder, his disastrous second marriage to Miriam Noel, and finally the affair with Olgivanna Hinzenberg, had wrecked his career. And as if all the adverse publicity was not enough, new building construction had come to an abrupt stop all over America as the world sank into the great economic depression of the 1930s. In 1932 there was no architectural work to be had anywhere by anyone, and to Wright, with his extravagant ways and his problem of not enough money—never enough money—the depression was an unmitigated disaster.

But Wright had an answer, an answer perhaps born of desperation and unlikely coincidence, but a brilliant solution for all of that. Wright had toyed for several years with the idea of opening an architectural school at Taliesin, his estate in Wisconsin. After all, his spinster aunts had made a living from the old Hillside Home School on the Taliesin property. As it turned out, however, his school, the "Fellowship," would not be an ordinary school, not even an architectural apprenticeship under his direction,

Frank Lloyd Wright   George I. Gurdjieff   Olgivanna Wright

as Wright had at first thought. It was to be indirectly but inextricably linked to the ideas of another extraordinary man, G. I. Gurdjieff.

Gurdjieff seems to have been an incomprehensible mixture of self-appointed messiah, visionary genius, and mystical seer. Acquainted from an early age with the magical beliefs and powers of the peasants among whom he was raised, he was absorbed in all aspects of the occult. There is little doubt that he possessed remarkable magical powers, which were carefully cultivated throughout his life. He was, in fact, a magus, or magician in the old sense of the word, and he had a messianic message, simple in essence. We are all asleep, he taught, lost in the mechanical repetition of response patterns of behavior. Freedom is to be found in awakening, in becoming aware of who we are, and what we are. This may be achieved through "the Work," a system of constant mental and physical challenges whereby a student may be shaken into a state of higher awareness. An essential part of the Work was the performance of sacred dances that were designed to align the dancer with the mathematical laws of the cosmos. One of the students and dancers that had followed him on his long journey from Tiflis to Paris was Olgivanna Hinzenberg, who eventually became the third wife of Frank Lloyd Wright.

Friedland and Zellman have demonstrated that, unknown to Wright, his involvement with Olgivanna was "set up" in New York by key members of Gurdjieff's "Institute for the Harmonious Development of Man," then located in "le Prieure" a run-down former seminary near Paris. Wright had recently announced, in a spurious attempt to appease his creditors, that he intended to leave Taliesin and make his home in Chicago. Taliesin would presumably be vacant, and Gurdjieff was looking for just such an estate in America to which he could move the Institute. It is not likely that Olgivanna would have been thrown in Frank's way without the concurrence of the "master." Moreover, she, herself, felt she had been commissioned by Gurdjieff to obtain a suitable property in the United States. In any event, the meeting arranged between Wright and Olgivanna was entirely successful. Wright was infatuated with this slender, beautiful dancer, over thirty years his junior, and reveled in his conquest. He soon brought her to Taliesin and embarked upon yet another out-of-wedlock affair.

The Gurdjieff group in New York must have been pleased. Two days after Olgivanna moved in with Wright, according to Friedland and Zellman, they were holding multiple meetings to discuss the situation. Wright, they understood, was not hostile to the idea of some sort of Gurdjieffian use of Taliesin. Friedland and Zellman point out that Wright and Gurdjieff had much in common, and there were "uncanny correspondences in their thinking." Both, for instance, used the term "organic:" Gurdjieff to refer to a harmony with cosmic forces and Wright to his architecture. Both were also inspired by forms found in nature, and both were devoted to the beauty of Gothic art. Moreover, Wright was already aware of Gurdjieff and his ideas through Zona Gale, a Gurdjieff follower whom he had unsuccessfully courted. The group had every reason to be optimistic.

But the whole effort went for naught when Taliesin once again caught fire and burned to the ground. The estate was useless to Gurdjieff and in any case, for the next few years, Wright was absorbed in rebuilding, and absorbed in the further scandal of Olgivanna's pregnancy and the birth of his illegitimate child, in his divorce from the unstable Miriam Noel, and finally in his marriage to Olgivanna. At the same time he was struggling to keep his architectural practice alive, and retain his ownership of Taliesin while the banks threatened to foreclose on the mortgages. Then, just as it seemed he might finally become free of his debts, building stopped all across the country as a result of the economic depression and Wright completely lost his architectural income.

Wright was desperate for money—a lot of money—to pay his debts, to hold on to Taliesin, and to continue to enjoy his lavish life-style. The brilliant stroke he achieved was to capitalize on the beauty of his estate, and his fame and reputation as an architect, by offering "apprenticeships" to those who would pay, and pay handsomely, for the privilege of living at Taliesin and working under his direction. The students came and paid, and the scheme proved highly profitable. The school, however, now called

Taliesin (Photo by Jeff Dean)

the Fellowship, was not what many of them had been led to expect. For one thing, an apprenticeship implies the presence of a master with whom one works and learns, but Wright, at that time, had no work. Olgivanna, however, was eager to incorporate the ideas of Gurdjieff into the structure of the school. What resulted was a curious amalgam whereby the total re-education of the students along lines established at the Priory somehow became the primary goal.

There were, inevitably, complaints from those who had expected that they would learn to become architects in the manner of Frank Lloyd Wright, and found that they would instead learn to cook, hoe corn, labor on the construction of the buildings in which they were to be housed, wait on the table, and act as personal servants to the Wrights. Many left, but they were quickly replaced by others who found the Taliesin communal life deeply rewarding. Those who stayed did the work assigned to them and made the Fellowship function. They listened to lectures by Mr. and Mrs. Wright, as they were formally called, studied and performed the Gurdjieff dance "movements" taught by Olgivanna, and participated in the outings, theatrics, and music that were an important part of life at Taliesin. Later, as the country began to emerge from the depression and architectural commissions began to come in, more time was allotted to architecture, but the emphasis always remained upon the spiritual transformation of the individual apprentice.

The great strength of the book lies in the way Friedland and Zellman build up a picture of life as it was lived in the ivory tower that the Fellowship became for both the Wrights and the apprentices. Through the stories of the apprentices as they reacted to Taliesin and interacted with the Wrights, and through a careful description of the succession of events, both within the Fellowship and in the outside world, that shaped and influenced life within the walls, we begin to sense what a strange place the Fellowship must have been. Most of the apprentices were young men—"my boys" Mr. Wright called them—and it seems that the women applicants were largely "put down" and discouraged. The result was a pervasive male homosexuality that could have been damaging if publicly revealed. Gay men, however, with artistic abilities and devoted to Wright, were essential to the Fellowship. The Wrights privately encouraged them while denouncing homosexuality in general. Wright was similarly an outspoken anti-Semite who depended upon Jewish clients and Jewish apprentices. These deny, despite his rhetoric, that they ever experienced discrimination at Taliesin. His politics, however, which were absorbed by the apprentices, were naïve, to say the least. He admired Germany and Japan, became friends with Lindbergh and with Phillip Johnson, a founder of the Museum of Modern Art, who had tried in the 30s to start an American Nazi party. Even after the attack on Pearl Harbor he had urged "my boys" to resist the draft. Most of them did, for loyalty to "Mr. Wright" and an unquestioning acceptance of whatever he said or was even believed to think became an absolute requirement for those who wished to remain at Taliesin.

And yet Wright certainly had feet of clay, clearly visible to those who were willing to look. The apprentices must have been aware of his obsessive jealousy, overweening conceit, the night-time quarrels with Olgivanna, and the occasional day-time scenes as well. They must have known of his arrogance and cruelty, his gross selfishness, his failure to pay his legitimate debts, and the rage with which he greeted attempts to collect them. They nevertheless put their trust in this supreme egotist, accepted their own exploitation, and remained fanatically loyal. As an F.B.I. agent reported to J. Edgar Hoover, Wright "was regarded by members of the Fellowship as somewhat of an idol, a tin god, or a master who could do no wrong."

Friedland and Zellman are carefully noncommittal regarding their opinion of this unusual micro-society. Only in their prologue do they use the word "bizarre" and conclude that Frank and Olgivanna "brought a passion, indeed a madness, to the place."

And mad it may well have been. In the early 1950s, when I was an architectural student at the University of Pennsylvania, I made a short visit to Taliesin and had a direct experience of the Fellowship as it was in its heyday. I can, therefore, confirm the accuracy of the description given in the book. If anything, the atmosphere of the place is understated. The slavish adulation of Wright, the aggressive insistence that he be recognized even by a casual visitor as "the world's greatest architect," and the abject fear and reverence that he seemed to inspire, at least in David Dodge, the apprentice who took me on a tour and introduced me to "Mr. Wright," were puzzling and troubling. This odd looking, little man, wearing a cape, and curiously androgynous with his long, white hair, rosy cheeks, and bright blue eyes, was certainly not a god, but was, nevertheless, obviously regarded as one. In some way I felt then, and feel now, that the Fellowship, as it came to be under the megalomaniac direction of Frank Lloyd Wright, was an affront to our common humanity.

Despite the "madness," the Fellowship persisted. It always seemed to be on the edge of failure and dissolution but Frank and Olgivanna somehow surmounted the successive crises, and perhaps through sheer force of will managed to keep it going. In its financial and emotional shelter Wright's career revived, and in his later years he came to be considered the accepted major icon of American architecture. The Fellowship has even persisted after Wright's death in 1959. It persists now, long after the backlog of building designs that he left has been exhausted, and the world has moved on to newer and more fashionable architectural styles.

But what of Georgi Gurdjieff, who through Olgivanna and the example of his own institute may be responsible in some way for what the Fellowship became? The first visit of Gurdjieff to Taliesin took place in 1934.

He had lost the Priory and was desperately searching for money, supporters, and an American home. Olgivanna, who despite her marriage to Wright always considered Gurdjieff her "master," would have led him to think that he would find all of these things at Taliesin. He must have decided to use his considerable psychic powers and remarkable strength of character to seize control at the outset. According to Svetlana, Wright's stepdaughter, he behaved as if Wright were one of his followers. He ordered him about. He dominated Wright in his own home, and with Olgivanna's support, humiliated him in front of the apprentices. But not even Gurdjieff could subdue Wright's enormous ego for long. A violent, screaming quarrel between Wright and Olgivanna in their apartments after the public humiliation was audible to the apprentices across the compound. It led to Gurdjieff's departure, and soon afterward Wright made it clear that there would be no Gurdjieff center at Taliesin.

Gurdjieff died in October, 1949. He nevertheless continued to be a force in the Fellowship through Olgivanna and her daughter Iovanna, born to Frank before their marriage. As Frank declined in his last few years, Olgivanna moved to take more and more control of the Fellowship. Immediately after her husband's death, she seized control of the Frank Lloyd Wright Foundation, under which the Fellowship was organized. The Foundation, under Olgivanna, continued the architectural practice, but her chief interest was, as always, in forwarding the ideas of her master, G. I. Gurdjieff. The death of her husband gave her the free hand that she always wanted to teach Gurdjieff's principles as she understood them, and the authority to shape the lives of those within the Fellowship as one who had received the light directly from the master. Friedland and Zellman show us that the result of her meddling in the lives of others was an increase of unhappiness and misery.

Friedland and Zellman seem to believe that the Fellowship, with all its faults and problems, and Wright, with the enormous ego that the Fellowship fed, were justified by the buildings designed and constructed in the last decades of his astonishing career. They cite Fallingwater, the Johnson Wax Administration Building, and the Guggenheim Museum as great architectural icons that could not have come into being without the emotional and financial support of the Fellowship and the Gurdjieffian philosophy that came to the architect through Olgivanna. Very likely this is so, but the vital question then becomes, are they really great buildings? Granted they are famous, admired by both the critics and the public, and are enormously influential—but are they great buildings? In my opinion, they are not. They are all three fatally flawed by the very conditions cited by the authors as responsible for their creation. They demonstrate the presence of a remarkable talent, a great courage, and a willingness to dare and achieve, but they are all three fatally tainted by the unbridled arrogance of their creator. In pursuit of his goal to be "the world's greatest architect" Wright was willing, if not eager, to ignore the needs of his clients, to indulge in grandiose fancies, to sacrifice the integrity of his buildings to one dramatic view or photograph, to design for one or two spectacular effects at the expense of the harmony and cohesion of the whole. These buildings, like the man, are irresponsible. They are showy rather than dramatic. They are fundamentally flawed and yet they reveal, even in their flaws, the tragedy of what might have been.

The day of Wright's death I was in Philadelphia, and that evening I returned to the university to hear a lecture by Lewis Mumford. Above the entrance to the School of Fine Arts a huge black flag was flapping in the wind. Mumford, who had been one of Wright's earliest supporters, elected to discard his notes and speak extemporaneously on the life and work of Frank Lloyd Wright. It was, in a sense, a funeral oration, and I think that Mumford saw it as such. I shall never forget it. The theme was tragedy, the tragedy of what might have been. What might have been, had he kept faith with Louis Sullivan, with his first wife and children, with all those he cheated, betrayed, with those like Mumford, whom he had excoriated at a breath of honest critical appraisal, and finally with himself in his refusal to see the contradictions and evasions that were characteristic of his behavior. As Louis Sullivan had written of the Marshall Field Warehouse in Chicago, when we look at a building we see a man. When we look at Wright's buildings we see a man possessed of an enormous talent and an enormous ambition who was terribly flawed.

And what was the role of the Fellowship, of Olgivanna and Gurdjieff in the working out of this tragedy? I think that they all three aided and abetted the destruction of Wright's artistic integrity. The unquestioning adulation of the apprentices, the need to secure the love and admiration of his young and beautiful wife, who apparently never wavered in her devotion to the other man, and the powerful personality of that other man, whom Wright seems to have at once admired and resented, all reinforced his megalomaniac drive for success in architecture at whatever cost. Without the Fellowship Wright would probably be remembered as a footnote for the value of his early work. With the Fellowship he is a household word, and known for the famous buildings of his later years. But the fame was purchased at a terrible cost both to the architect, and to the society that he served.

PART FOUR

THE UNKNOWN JESUS

The Baptism of Jesus, Leonardo da Vinci

16

THE MYTHICAL JESUS

*Is Christianity Based on Historical Facts or
Ancient Mystery Traditions?*

BY ROBERT M. SCHOCH, PH.D.

D id Christianity spring onto the scene two millennia ago as a divine
revelation that came directly from the one true God, as to this day
some of its more fundamentalist adherents contend? Was there
a real individual, a historical person, a genuine Jesus Christ—a teacher
and, according to his followers, a theurgist and wonder-worker—who was
crucified in Jerusalem? Was such a man the Messiah for whom many Jews
longed?

I would venture to guess that most people who call themselves Christians (today there are estimated to be over two billion throughout the world,
making it the single largest religion, although divided among thousands of
sects), as well as those of many of other faiths, do not doubt that a historical Jesus walked the earth. Of course many might doubt his reputed birth
from a virgin, question his working of miracles (such as turning water
into wine or raising the dead), and deny his resurrection after supposedly being dead for several days, but they still accept that there was a real
Jesus. Indeed, there is a small industry that revolves around presumably
identifying and tracking the historical Jesus. There are those who contend
he survived being nailed to the cross. Another idea popular in some circles
is that Jesus sired a bloodline by his wife (usually considered to be Mary
Magdalene), which some claim can be traced historically through various
Dark Age and Medieval lineages, such as through the Merovingian royal
family in Europe (ruling in parts of modern France and Germany). Others
would trace Jesus and his bloodline in the opposite geographic direction,
such as to Kashmir, Tibet, or India. Still others attempt to identify Jesus
and members of his immediate family based on the physical evidence of
tombs and ossuaries (bone boxes) from 1st century Jerusalem. No matter

which approach is taken, the point here is that it is assumed there is a historical man behind the myth of Christ.

On the other extreme are people like D. M. Murdock (also known as Acharya S., the pseudonym she used for her earlier works) who deny completely that there is any historical basis for the Jesus of Christianity. Murdock in such books as *The Christ Conspiracy* (1999) and *Suns of God* (2004), builds on the research of scholars such as Gerald Massey (1828-1907) and Egyptologist E. A. Wallis Budge (1857-1934) who point out the many similarities between the ancient Egyptian religion and Christianity (which is not to say these earlier scholars held Murdock's extreme views). Murdock argues that the Jesus of the gospels, ostensibly the founder and linchpin of Christianity, never actually existed. He was a creation of those who "invented" the cult that was to become Christianity. Forget about arguing whether Jesus was the result of a god's (presumably the one true God) miraculously inseminating a virgin (though Mary was betrothed to Joseph at the time), or if he performed miracles and preached the truth, much less ponder the concept that he was killed and resurrected on the third day. This is all nonsense—or is it?

Ironically, it may seem to some, regardless of whether Jesus ever existed as a real person, the story of his life is rich in meaning and fits into a bigger and deeper picture than many professed Christians dare imagine. Whatever the reality or non-reality of a historical Jesus—total fabrication or obscure rabble-rouser and anti-Roman independence fighter upon whose personage many myths were grafted—Christianity as such, interpreted in hindsight, arose in the broader context of the Roman Empire from a syncretism of near-Eastern beliefs, incorporating especially Hellenistic, Egyptian, and Judaic elements, during the period of the Flavian, adoptive, and Antonine emperors of the late 1st and 2nd centuries AD. Furthermore, it is slowly becoming more widely recognized that the whole concept of a messiah, and even the specifics of such a messiah's death and resurrection three days later, was an element of Jewish thought and tradition in the decades before the supposed historical Jesus was presumed to have lived and carried out his ministry and passion (see Ethan Bronner, "Ancient Tablet Ignites Debate on Messiah and Resurrection." *New York Times*, 6 July 2008). In this sense, there was nothing new about Jesus.

The Christian concept of Jesus as the Messiah fits into a broad historical, cosmological, and astrological context. The life of Jesus reflects many elements found in religious traditions current in the 1st and 2nd centuries, as

Osiris, Horus, and Isis

well as much earlier. In particular, the Jesus myth mimics important aspects of the well-known and widely popular mythology of the Osiris-Isis Cycle, and the later Greco-Roman Serapis and Isis cult derived from it. Indeed, with Osiris, Isis, Horus, and Set we see so many familiar "Christian" themes, I find it personally incomprehensible that this evidence of a connection between Egypt and Christianity can be so easily brushed aside by certain people who find such concepts inconvenient or even threatening to their religious beliefs. Listed below are a few examples discussed by Murdock, Massey, and Budge in their various works. Murdock elaborates on these further as well as recounts more, and I recommend her books to interested readers. (Note that there are many versions of the Egyptian myths, and the versions highlighted here are those that best parallel Christian beliefs.)

Osiris/Horus (father and son, to a certain extent interchangeable, just as in Christianity) died and was resurrected on the third day, just as was Jesus. The rebirth or resurrection, as one might expect, for both Jesus and the Egyptian deities traditionally coincides roughly with the Spring Equinox when the Sun moves north from below the celestial equator to above it.

Like Jesus, Horus was born of a Virgin (Isis), and descended from a royal lineage.

The birth of both Jesus and Horus, and indeed many other ancient deities as well, occurred on December 25 (correlated with the Winter Solstice when the Sun has reached its furthest point south in the sky and just begun to move north again), and both were born in a manger. In both birth accounts there is a star in the east and three wise men or kings visit the child.

Anup/Anubis is the equivalent of the Christian John the Baptist, and he baptizes and initiates Horus, just as John baptized Jesus; pivotal ages for both Horus and Jesus are 12 and 30.

Osiris/Horus, like Jesus, is a teacher and miracle worker; both he and Jesus had twelve companions or followers.

Set/Seth (Sut, Sata), more or less the equivalent of the Judeo-Christian Satan, "tempts" and does battle with Horus/Osiris; likewise Satan tempted Jesus.

Horus is said to have been anointed and beloved, the son of the god and solar deity, and acts as the light, the truth, the way, the messiah, the son of man, the lamb, and the shepherd; he was even referred to as the holy child, the anointed one, and has the epithet of Iusa ("ever-becoming of the father")—all very similar to how Jesus is regarded.

We must also consider the cosmological meaning and significance of the Jesus Christ myth, and concomitantly the earlier myths and beliefs that were its predecessors. Thus the birth and resurrection certainly reflect both the daily cycle of the Sun (rising or birth, high noon or zenith, setting or death, the midnight nadir, and rising or rebirth the next day) as well as the annual cycle of the Sun (Winter Solstice, Spring/Vernal Equinox, Summer Solstice, Autumnal/Fall Equinox, and Winter Solstice once again). The crown of thorns, placed on the head of Jesus when he was crucified, is an obvious solar motif representing the rays of the Sun. The twelve disciples or followers find correspondence in both the twelve months and the twelve constellations of the zodiac. The significance of the numbers 12 and 30 (Jesus was questioning and learning in the temple when 12 years old and began his ministry at around the age of 30 years) reflects astrological phenomena. Twelve is high noon. The twelve months are, in the classic Egyptian calendar, each composed of 30 days (for a total of 360 days, plus 5 days added to the end of the year). The twelve zodiacal signs in the heavens each span, ideally at least, 30 degrees (for a total of 360 degrees completing the full circle). The star in the east (possibly Sirius) and the three kings (possibly the three belt stars of Orion) are clearly stellar.

When discussing these issues, there is something we should not underestimate: The importance and influence of astrology during the early centuries of the Common Era. *Logos* can be translated as reason, and thus astrology can be viewed as the reason or logic of the stars, or applying logic and reason to the understanding of celestial phenomena. Though natal ("sunsign") astrology (that which is most familiar colloquially today) played a role in the Roman Empire (for a discussion of astrology in Greco-Roman Egypt, see James Evans, "The Astrologer's Apparatus: A Picture of Professional Practice in Greco-Roman Egypt," *Journal for the History of Astronomy*,

Jesus at the center of the zodiac

vol. 35, part 1, no. 118, 2004, pp. 1–44.), arguably it was the deeper meanings and broader implications of astrology that were of primary importance. This astrological understanding is found throughout the Judeo-Christian Bible, and indeed it has been argued that this collection of ancient writings is primarily a reflection of astrological knowledge (Ron Watson, *The Greatest Story Never Told*, 2005).

Interestingly and tellingly, a series of coins was produced at Alexandria, Egypt, during the reign of the emperor Antoninus Pius (reigned AD 138 to 161; most or all of the coins in this series were minted circa AD 144/145) bearing zodiacal themes. Individual coins were struck for each of the twelve zodiac signs, and each such coin included the sign's ruling planet (in ancient times the "planets" in this context were the Sun, the Moon, Mercury, Venus, Mars, Jupiter, and Saturn). Additionally, various coins were struck depicting the entire zodiac, including a famous coin depicting on its reverse a double zodiac surrounding the conjoined heads of Serapis (essentially the equivalent of the older Osiris in this context) and Isis (Figure 1; the obverse of the coin bears the portrait of Antoninus Pius). An early Christian, or Gnostic/Christian, would (I believe) feel comfortable with such iconography, perhaps interpreting the central figures as simply variations on the themes, or different incarnations, of Jesus Christ and/or the Father of Christ with his mother or wife the Virgin Mary. They are surrounded by the twelve apostles (the zodiacal signs of the inner zodiacal circle), which encompass Earth and the terrestrial realm, and in turn are part of the larger cosmos and the progression of the aeons (the outer zodiacal circle). Here, on a "pagan" coin of 2nd century Alexandrian Egypt we have, when understood in context, powerful Gnostic and proto-Christian motifs.

Figure 1

Other meanings have been attributed to this coin in particular, but they are not mutually exclusive with the understanding expressed above. Indeed, part of the richness of such symbology is the multiple layers of meaning seen in the same depictions. Thus, the double zodiac coins have been interpreted as a model or illustration of a contemporary astrologer's board used for casting horoscopes of two persons simultaneously (for instance, husband and wife). These same coins have been interpreted as commemorating the alignment of the Sothic (Sothaic) and Civil calendars, and the beginning of a new Sothic Cycle (also known as a Canicular Period), which happens only once every 1460/1461 years and occurred during the reign of Antoninus Pius. The Egyptian calendar year of 365 days was slightly short of a full year, and thus lost a slight amount of time each year. After 1,461 Egyptian years (1,460 Julian/ Roman years of 365.25 days each) the start of the year had come full cycle again, to correspond with the heliacal rising (visibly rising at dawn with or just before the Sun) of the star Sirius (Sothis to the ancient Greeks, Sopdet to the ancient Egyptians), which in turn correlated with the annual flooding of the Nile. On a grander scale, these coins may also symbolize the precessional cycle and the changing of the world ages, with the inner ring representing the yearly zodiac cycle and the outer ring representing the so-called Great Year, or progression of astrological ages. Approximately 2,000 years ago at the birth of Christianity, the Sun had just entered the late degrees of the sign of Pisces, marking the beginning of the Age of Pisces; not coincidentally, an early symbol of Christianity was the fish, the sign of Pisces. Shortly (within the next century or two, depending on one's analysis) we will enter a new age, the Age of Aquarius.

The first and second centuries were a time of change, the beginning of a new age, a new world order—a concept taken very seriously by a large proportion of the populace at the time. The Roman Empire had conquered, subdued, and consolidated much of the known world. But there were continued rebellions and uprisings in many quarters. Directly applicable to the birth of the new Egyptian-Jewish-Greek-Roman cult that we now label Christianity were the uprisings, followed by brutal suppressions and dispersals, of the Jews from the Holy Land. These occurred in AD 66–73 and AD 132–135. This was a time when many looked for the Messiah, the Savior, and apparently the myth of the Savior was reified and enhanced during the formation of the religion that would eventually become known as Christianity. Some argue that this occurred in 2nd century Alexandrian Egypt, in at least part founded upon or influenced by the writings of Philo. Alexandria at that time was a center of a large Jewish population, and Philo Judaeus (circa 20 BC to circa AD 50) was a prominent Jewish philosopher. Consciously a new syncretic universal religion was being created, one that by the early 4th century would be adopted as the official religion of the Roman Empire.

Any religion tends to have its sacred sites, relics, and other objects of veneration. These help consolidate and reinforce the beliefs among the masses. Christianity is certainly not lacking for such holy spots and artifacts. In ancient Egypt sacred sites and relics of Osiris, Isis, and Horus (and of course other gods, saints, prophets, and deities at different times and in different places) were popular and venerated, and also confirmed for the faithful that their gods and holy personages were "real." This concept was simply transferred to Christianity, and to this day relics of early Christendom are venerated by the faithful. Among the most sacred and sought after relics associated with Christianity are the Holy Grail and the True Cross.

Many people interested in such matters cannot even agree on what the Holy Grail is. Is it the cup Jesus reputedly drank from at the Last Supper? This is the traditional view. Or is it the cup in which the blood of Jesus was collected from the wound in his side as he was dying on the cross? Or is the Holy Grail actually the womb of Mary Magdalene who sired the offspring of Jesus, and thus it represents his bloodline? Could the Holy Grail be a set of records or documents related to Jesus and his family and bloodline? It appears that there has never been unanimous agreement on exactly what constitutes the Holy Grail, much less definitive identification of its physical remains. The matter of the True Cross seems a bit more straightforward. The True Cross was the wooden cross that was reputedly used in the crucifixion of Jesus. According to legend, toward the end of her life, the Empress Helena (circa AD 250 to circa AD 330), the Christian mother of the Roman Emperor Constantine the Great, traveled to Jerusalem and miraculously discovered the True Cross.

The True Cross, or at least the cross reputedly found by Helena, was venerated during the 4th century, as described in writings of the time. In AD 614 Jerusalem was captured by the Sassanian Emperor Khusro (Khosrau) II and the True Cross was carted off as a spoil of war. In AD 628–630

Figure 2

(different dates are given by various authorities) the Byzantine Emperor Heraclius regained the True Cross, first taking it to Constantinople, and subsequently returning it to Jerusalem in AD 630. While being transported back to Jerusalem, a piece of the True Cross broke off or was removed. This fragment was burnt, the ashes mixed with clay, and from the clay small tokens, sometimes referred to as a type of pilgrimage tokens, were made commemorating the return of this most sacred relic to Jerusalem (Figure 2; on the obverse is pictured the True Cross with two indistinct figures beneath, variously interpreted as Saints Peter and Paul or the Emperor Constantine and his mother, the Empress Helena; the reverse bears what are apparently the marks of a piece of wood used to press the clay into the mold). Indeed, each token so produced became a miniature reliquary and sacred relic since it contains within its matrix a miniscule bit of the True Cross. These tokens continue to be highly prized and venerated by some Christians to this day, as do larger reputed pieces of the True Cross. Even if these tokens do not actually contain the ashes of the True Cross, they apparently do contain the ashes of the cross "discovered" by Helena in the early 4th century and venerated ever since.

So, are the veneration of relics, the belief in a savior god, the concept of holy places, and a general sense of the sacred and the divine, all nonsense and simply a primitive throwback to the Dark Ages? I would contend not, as relics and associated beliefs can serve a positive function, although any particular religion (Christianity included), if taken too literally, may be based on apparent historical and hagiographic falsehoods. The truth and significance of a viable religion lies deep in a nexus of historical, psychological, and social concepts that must be brought to the surface and explored in order to gain a full appreciation of the rich cultural heritage of humanity.

17

DID JESUS VISIT INDIA?

New Research Tracks His Missing Years to the Far East

BY LEN KASTEN

It appears to be a subject that no Christian wishes to discuss. Priests, bishops, ministers, and laymen alike avoid it like the plague. Why? Because they have no answers. And yet, it is a simple and important question—where was Jesus between the ages of 13 and 30? Are we to understand that he spent those years laboring as a carpenter in his father's shop? Would this have been an appropriate endeavor for a young man whose birth was heralded by angels and who was debating brilliantly with rabbis at the age of 12? Clearly, the man who showed up in Jerusalem at the age of 30 to undertake what he knew to be a very dangerous mission that would probably end in his death was well-prepared, and one might even say "trained" for that mission, and fully confident of his ability to carry it to completion. It seems highly unlikely that he achieved that preparation and confidence in his father's carpentry shop. The failure of the Gospels to address this subject is suspicious. Logic would dictate that his followers would want to know the history of such a "miracle-man" and self-proclaimed Son of God. It suggests that somehow, sometime, this information may have been excised from the Gospels, perhaps at the Council of Nicaea in AD 323. It is possible that some in the early Church knew this history and found it incompatible with the new religion proclaimed by Constantine, built around the divinity of Jesus. A belief in this possibility is encouraged by the fact that the story of the so-called "lost years of Jesus" was well-known at the time—in India!

WAS JESUS "A YOGI?"

In the modern era, there have been numerous references to the travels of Jesus in India and Tibet, and they are all remarkably consistent. Perhaps the most noteworthy is *The Second Coming of the Christ* by Paramahansa Yogananda (1893–1951), originally written in the 1940s, but re-published in a slip-case edition in 2004. Yogananda, who founded Self-Realization Fellowship in Los Angeles in 1920, is best known for his classic best-seller *Autobiography of a Yogi*. In *The Second Coming* he recasts the teachings of Jesus in the light of Eastern religious philosophy, taking the position that Jesus was influenced by Hinduism and Buddhism, and higher esoteric Eastern wisdom, believed to be the province of the Himalayan masters. This influence, he claims, was the result of the youthful Jesus having lived and studied with monks and teachers in India and Tibet. Such sayings as "the kingdom of heaven is within you" and "know ye not that ye are gods?" can easily be discerned as deriving from Eastern religious thought. Jesus also made indirect references to karma and reincarnation, and much of what he taught about love and compassion seems clearly influenced by the teachings of the Buddha. One reviewer of *The Second Coming* says, "...a deeper esoteric study of what Christ was saying ... this interpretation is laced with eastern mysticism and Christ is seen as a self-realized Yogi come to awaken mankind to their own cosmic consciousness."

Art by Ron O. Cook

Yogananda's view of Jesus as a "self-realized yogi" becomes more acceptable when one takes a closer look at the "miracles" that Jesus performed. All of them, it is said, have been duplicated by generations of yogis in the Himalayan foothills. These powers are the so-called "siddhis" developed by years of rigorous adherence to spiritual development through yoga and meditation with the help of a guru, especially the arts of Raja Yoga. According to Shri Prakash Ji, "A yogi is one whose soul has linked to the Universal Soul, one who has reached God ... Yogi is within God and God is in Him. God and Yogi are Oneness." And once this union has been achieved, the spiritual powers or "siddhis" manifest. The ability to walk on water, or to levitate, is known as "vayu-siddhi" and is considered one of the minor siddhis. Jesus was even able to teach his disciples the technique. The power to raise the dead is known as "ishitvam" and is one of the eight major siddhis. Kabir, Tulsidas, Akalkot Swami, and others had the power of bringing back life to the dead. Raja yogins routinely appear and disappear, heal the sick, calm the elements, and manifest solid objects out of thin air. Could the evidence that Jesus had these powers mean that he studied Raja Yoga with high yogis in India and Tibet until he became "self-realized?"

SHANGRI-LA

The most recent book on the subject is *The King of Travelers* (1999) by Edward T. Martin. Martin traveled to India in 1974, while stationed in Kabul, Afghanistan, with the Peace Corps. In what is clearly a case of synchronicity, Martin, who had already read extensively on the subject of Jesus in India, came across the book *Christ in Kashmir* by Aziz Kashmiri in a small bookstore in Srinigar, and was able to immediately meet the author through the bookstore owner. In his book, Martin describes that fateful meeting, "...over steaming cups of tea, we had a far-ranging discussion about the subject of Jesus in India. To my surprise, I found out that in India itself there is a very long-standing tradition and folklore that Jesus did indeed live in India." That meeting with Kashmiri started Martin off on a life-long research odyssey that culminated in his book twenty-five years later. We interviewed him to discuss the book, and his recent trip back to India with Hollywood producer Paul Davids, in which they traveled 4,000 miles across the continent filming a new documentary on the subject; the movie was released in 2008 as *Jesus in India.*

In our interview with Martin, he focused on the so-called "chain of evidence," that is, all the reliable sources of information on the subject. In his book, he mentions Edgar Cayce, who made frequent references to the travels of Jesus, and to *The Aquarian Gospel of Jesus the Christ* by Levi Dowling (1907). Martin's opinion is that the most thorough coverage of this subject is to be found in *The Lost Years of Jesus* by Elizabeth Clare Prophet (1984). The evidence seems to revolve almost entirely around the secluded and mysterious Buddhist monastery of Himis in Leh in the province of Ladakh in northern Kashmir. Himis is a "gompa" or "solitary place of refuge from the world of temptation" prized by Buddhist monks. Prophet says that Himis is "tucked away in a hidden valley in the Himalayas 11,000 feet above sea level. Some who have visited it say it brings to mind visions of Shangri-La." It was to Himis that 29-year-old Russian journalist Nicolas Notovitch traveled in late 1887 because a lama had told him that he might find a manuscript there about the life of the prophet Issa who had traveled there as a young man. Issa is the Indian name for Jesus. In the course of a conversation, the chief lama at Himis mentioned that there were scrolls there in which "are to be found the life and acts of the Buddha Issa who preached the holy doctrine in India and among the children of Israel." These scrolls in Tibetan, the lama explained, were copied from the original version kept in Lhasa and written in ancient language of Pali.

During an extended stay at Himis convalescing from a broken leg, Notovitch persuaded the lama to show him the scrolls, "two large bound volumes with leaves yellowed by time," and to allow him to translate and record the verses. This ultimately became the book, *The Life of St. Issa: Best of the Sons of Men*, published by Notovitch in 1894. It consisted of 244 of the scattered, translated verses organized by Notovitch into 14 chapters. The complete story by Notovitch with the verses incorporated was titled *The Unknown Life of Jesus Christ*. That book, originally in French, was an instant success, going through eighteen editions in France, three in the U.S. and one in England, and was translated into German, Spanish, Swedish, and Italian. It is still in print today.

ISSA PREACHES TO THE LOWER CASTES

The Life of St. Issa could really be considered the earliest gospel, even though related by merchants rather than disciples, since it was supposedly written in the 1st or 2nd century AD. It begins with the story of the

The Ancient Meenakshi Temple, Madurai, India

Jewish enslavement in Egypt and ends with the Crucifixion. Regarding the departure of Jesus to India, it says that at the age of 13, he was expected to take a wife, and the modest house of Joseph and Mary became crowded with "the rich and noble" seeking to make the illustrious, brilliant youth a son-in-law. "It was then that Issa clandestinely left his father's house, went out of Jerusalem, and, in company with some merchants, traveled toward Sindh (India), that he might perfect himself in the divine word and study the laws of the great Buddhas." Almost certainly, the merchants' camel caravan traveled over the Silk Road, the main East-West trade route.

Issa crossed the Indus River and moved on across the continent to the Temple of Jagganath in the province of Orissa in Southeast India. There, he was enthusiastically welcomed by the white Brahmin priests, and spent six years studying the Vedas, and learning how to teach, heal the sick, and perform exorcisms, in Jagganath, Rajagriha, Benares and other holy cities. Then, in an early display of his characteristic anti-establishment trouble-making, the 21-year-old Issa defiantly preached the holy Hindu scriptures to the lower castes—the farmers, merchants, and laborers, thus enraging the Brahmins and Kshatriyas (priests and warriors), who promptly put out a contract on his life. According to the verses, "He strongly denounced the men who robbed their fellow-beings of their rights as men, saying 'God the Father establishes no difference between his children, who are all equally dear to him.'" Warned by his friends, Issa fled to the Himalayan foothills in Nepal, the birthplace of Gautama Buddha with whom he evidently felt a strong connection. Having learned the Pali tongue, Issa spent the next six years studying the ancient scrolls in the Buddhist monasteries of Nepal and Tibet, including Himis where he remained for about two months, until he "whom the Buddha had chosen to spread his holy word, could perfectly explain the sacred rolls." And then he turned his face westward, and began the fateful journey back to Palestine, to live out his hard destiny.

While popular, *The Unknown Life* got some rough treatment from critics, notably Max Muller, a well-known Orientalist and professor of Philology at Oxford University, who declared the book to be fraudulent in an article in *The Nineteenth Century*, a scholarly review. And so, the authenticity of St. Issa remained in question for many years. Then in 1922, Swami Abhedananda traveled to the Himis Monastery to determine once and for all whether or not Notovitch had told the truth. Abhedananda, who was 56 at that time, had lived a life of unquestioned spiritual integrity and authority, having walked the length and breadth of India himself barefoot and without money at the age of 20. In 1929, in his book *Kashmir and Tibet*, Abhedananda stated that while he was skeptical at first, he was able to verify that everything Notovitch had said was absolutely true. Ironically, Max Muller, then deceased, had been one of the Swami's closest friends! This confirmation of the Issa legend by Abhedananda might have been enough to silence the critics. But then came an even grander endorsement from an unexpected, and very impressive source.

Nicolas Notovitch

"THESE BOOKS SAY YOUR JESUS WAS HERE"

Nicholas Roerich was truly a Renaissance Man in every sense of the word. Born in St. Petersburg, Russia, in 1874 to an upper-middle class family, and educated as both a lawyer and artist, Roerich was an accomplished painter, professor, and art impresario during his early life, but he sought to bring all the arts together. Prophet says, "Typically described in biographical notes as 'a Russian-born painter, poet, archaeologist, philosopher, and mystic,' Roerich was also a diplomat, writer, critic, educator, set and costume designer, and explorer." But underneath it all, the mystic prevailed, and he had a strong urge to travel to India and Tibet. In 1924, at the age of 50, his worldly success behind him, Roerich, his wife Helena, his two sons, and Tibetan lama Lobzang Mingyur Dorje, mounted an expedition

Nicholas Roerich

to Central Asia consisting of "nine Europeans, thirty-six natives, and 102 camels, yaks, horses and mules." The eldest son, George Roerich, was a noted archaeologist and Orientalist who had studied at Harvard as well as the School of Oriental Languages in Paris. He was conversant in Persian, Sanskrit, Chinese, and all of the many Tibetan dialects. One of the several goals of the journey was the study of ancient monuments and the conditions and origins of contemporary religions.

Unexpectedly, wherever they traveled, they heard legends about Jesus. In his book *Altai-Himalaya* published in 1929, which was more of a travel diary, he says, "In Srinigar we first encountered the curious legend about Christ's visit to this place. Afterward, we saw how widely spread in India, in Ladak and in Central Asia, was the legend of the visit of Christ to these parts..." He said further that he heard several versions of the legend, but that they all agreed on one point, "that during the time of His absence, Christ was in India and Asia." Then Roerich started hearing about the manuscript of the life of St. Issa. In his second book, *Himalaya*, he writes about Himis. "Regarding the manuscripts of Christ—first there was a complete denial... Then slowly, little by little, are creeping fragmentary reticent details, difficult to obtain. Finally, it appears—that about the manuscripts, the old people in Ladak have heard and know." Roerich knew about Notovitch's book. He says, "Many remember the lines from the book of Notovitch, but it is still more wonderful to discover, on this site, in several variants, the same version of the legend of Issa."

There were others after Roerich. In the summer of 1939, Madame Elisabeth G. Caspari, a Swiss musician, and her husband were on a pilgrimage to Mt. Kailas in Tibet, and stopped at Himis on the way. While seated on the roof of the convent, she was approached by the librarian of the monastery, and two monks. They carried three manuscripts with elegant coverings. As he carefully unwrapped the parchment leaves, the librarian said to her, "These books say your Jesus was here."

All of these reports basically take the position that Jesus was a conscious disciple of Gautama Buddha, and that's why the monks at Himis treated the manuscript so reverently. Some believe that he was actually a reincarnation of the Buddha. They claim that he understood that his mission was to spread the Buddhist doctrine in the West, and that Christianity is simply a Westernized version of Buddhism. There have been several books on this subject, giving impressive lists of parallels between Buddhism and Christianity. This idea argues for a long and hoary history of continued and connected revelations by successive "standard bearers" coming at precise intervals, and all dedicated to elevating the spiritual consciousness of the human race. From this perspective, it certainly makes sense that the young Jesus, conscious of the role he was to play, would travel to the only place on the planet where he knew he could be prepared for that role.

18

JESUS & ARTHUR

Were These Two Enigmatic Figures the Same Person?

BY RALPH ELLIS

C ould the biblical Jesus really be the historical character upon which all of Arthurian mythology was founded? This might sound like a speculation too far—far too far—but bear with me a while, for there is much more to this theory than initial thoughts might suggest. And perhaps I should state, before I start on this radical reassessment of the New Testament, that this is a scholarly, in-depth investigation using the original documents of this early era, including the Tanakh, Talmud, Josephus, Origen, Eusebius, Irenaeus, Herodian, Suetonius, Tacitus, Clement, and many others besides.

It is of no dispute that the authors of the *Vulgate Cycle*, the great Middle Ages epic that records the life and deeds of King Arthur, based their story on biblical events. The Vulgate begins, for instance, with the story of Joseph of Arimathea traveling to Britain and bringing with him the Holy Grail, in the form of a cup that held Jesus' blood. It then relates that Arthur's Round Table was a direct copy of the Last Supper table, which is why King Arthur's table was surrounded by twelve knights while King Jesus was graced by twelve disciples. There is a degree of equivalence here, and the reason for this is that these are both components of the same story. However, while readers may readily see this New Testament influence on the Grail myths, they may well balk at Jesus being a king or Arthur being a 1st century monarch. How on earth, one might ask, can these particular circles be squared?

The answer lies in a tangential but key factor—the true identity of Saul (St. Paul). It is my belief that Saul, the creator of Christianity, was actually the 1st century historian called Josephus Flavius. This seemingly unrelated discovery actually provides us with the key to unlocking the deliberate New Testament code that has obscured the biblical story for nearly 2,000

Jesus   King Arthur

years—for it is apparent that Josephus records the entire life-story of Jesus, but he just calls him Jesus of Gamala.

Now this is quite a revelation, because it lifts Jesus from the standard portrayal of a populist pauper, and projects him into being a hugely influential aristocrat who lived in the AD 60s and controlled his own private army. This might sound like a pack of nonsense, bearing in mind the barrage of the Church's propaganda we have all endured during our early education, but it is actually what parts of the New Testament really *do* say. Hebrews 11, for instance, says that Jesus became one of the first elected high priests of Jerusalem; and yet we know when this unusual event happened and who was involved—for both the Talmud and Josephus say that this was Jesus of Gamala, who became High Priest in AD 64. Again we see a strong link between the biblical Jesus and Jesus of Gamala.

Jesus the High Priest?—now that is a revelation. Actually, that is only the half of it, for the Talmud further records that this Jesus of Gamala was the husband of Mary of Bethany, the lady who was regularly identified as being Mary Magdalene in Renaissance artistry. Indeed, the Talmud records that this same Mary—Mary Magdalene—was the richest woman in Jerusalem, an observation that rather overturns our common perceptions of biblical history.

But there is more, for Jesus was also a king, and I don't just say this because he was styled as the "king of the Jews" at his crucifixion. No, we know that "pauper Jesus" was actually king Jesus, because that is what his titles mean. "Christ" and "Messiah" are not ethereal spiritual titles, they simply mean "king"—just as kings Saul and David were also Jewish messiahs. So who was this important prince and king called Jesus, and why did a record of his being born in poverty circulate during the 1st century AD?

Well, in my 2006 book, *Cleopatra to Christ*, I identified Jesus as being the great grandson of Queen Cleopatra of Egypt, through a lost daughter of hers known as Queen Thea Muse Ourania. Now Thea Muse became Queen of Persia in the 20s BC, but was thrown out of that country in about AD 4 and was exiled to the borders of Syrio-Judaea. Within this potted history of Queen Thea Muse we have the first elements of the New Testament narrative in a nutshell—a powerful royal prince who was born in temporary accommodation in Judaea at the turn of the 1st century, due to this family's forced travels.

Moving on to my 2008 book, *King Jesus*, I further identify Queen Thea Muse of Persia with Queen Helena of Adiabene, another semi-ethereal exiled queen from Persia who has distinct affiliations with Jerusalem and great similarities with Queen Thea Muse. It may even have been Queen Helena who built the great Syrian desert city of Palmyra. What is known for certain is that it was Queen Helena who built a great palace in Jerusalem and fabricated the great golden menorah for the Jerusalem Temple.

CAESAR

Here is a radically different account of the life of the biblical Jesus than the one we are accustomed to, but one that is fully supported by contemporary and near-contemporary records. But we are no nearer in discovering how this princely Jesus can be equated with the semi-mythical King Arthur, for the life and times of the latter are said to have taken place in a completely different country and era. How, then, might we aspire to transport the Judaean King Jesus to the opposite end of the Roman Empire? The answer lies in the ambitions and objectives of this princely Jesus.

In the guise of Jesus of Gamala—the leader of the Fourth Sect of Judaism and the leader of 600 rebel "fishermen," as Josephus describes him—it is clear that this Jesus was involved in a political struggle against the Jerusalem and Roman regimes. This may initially seem to be at odds with the essence of the biblical Jesus' goals as we generally perceive them, but it is not. Even a cursory glance at verses like Matthew 10:34, Mark 13:12-14, and Luke 22:36 will be sufficient to place an alternative view on the gospel message, for the pauper pacifist was actually an aristocratic revolutionary. In fact, the biblical Jesus was a political revolutionary in exactly the same guise as Jesus of Gamala, and the latter's political power-base was known as the Fourth Sect, a religio-political sect that closely mirrors the principles and goals of Jesus and his disciples. But this was not simply a struggle for the political and religious soul of Judaea, for the Talmud makes it clear that the biblical Jesus was being hailed by his disciples as "Caesar." Jesus also wanted to become Emperor of Rome.

This might seem like a fanciful notion, but readers have to recall that all of these events—as narrated by Josephus, the New Testament, and the Talmud—are from the AD 60s, not the AD 30s, and Bishop Irenaeus of the 2nd century confirms this later era for the life and ministry of King Jesus. In this era, the rule of Emperor Nero was nearing its climactic end, while the most influential prophecy circulating within the Roman Empire was the Star Prophecy, which said that the new Emperor would be a king from the East. In reality this prophecy referred to Jesus, the Egypto-Persian prince who was born under an Eastern star, but it was eventually to be commander Vespasian who rode this prophesy back to Rome to become the new emperor. With the assistance of Saul-Josephus, Emperor Vespasian claimed the prophecy was his, because he was the commander of Rome's eastern forces.

Jewish War

The truth of the matter is that the New Testament story actually relates one of the most bitter political struggles in recorded history. This was not the relative calm of the Judaean AD 30s, this was actually an account of the tumultuous events of the Jewish Civil War of the late AD 60s. Great literary works do not usually emerge from periods of stability and wealth; instead they are incubated and fostered during periods of conflict and strife, and the New Testament is no exception to this rule.

According to Josephus Flavius (Saul) the Jewish revolt was inspired and fomented by the Fourth Sect of Judaism, the sect led by Jesus of Gamala, the biblical King Jesus. The goal was not simply to claim the throne of Judaea, but the throne of Rome. As a direct descendant of Julius Caesar, Queen Cleopatra, and Phraates IV of Persia, King Jesus not only had the royal credentials to aspire to this position, he was also from the esteemed lineage of the greatest of the Caesars and the rightful emperor of Rome.

However, Jesus' grand strategy failed at the first hurdle. The Jewish revolt he engineered quickly morphed into a quagmire of civil war,

Jesus in a Vesica Piscis

and the Romans restored order to the region by destroying Jerusalem and condemning many of its citizens to exile and slavery. It was from this tumultuous event that the modern Jewish Diaspora were created. Furthermore, Josephus Flavius records that Jesus of Gamala (the biblical King Jesus) and two other leaders of the Fourth Sect were crucified in the Kidron Valley, but were reprieved by Josephus himself. In this historical account of the crucifixion we can probably see the first links to the Arthurian legend of the *Vulgate Cycle*, for in being the savior of the crucified Jesus, Josephus Flavius was actually Joseph(us) of Arimathea.

Of the three crucified leaders of the Jewish revolt, only one survived, an account that again tallies with the biblical version of these events, and so the lone survivor just has to be Jesus himself. But this is not the last mention we have of King Jesus within the historical record, for all of the Roman historians record a peculiar audience in Alexandria, between a "King of Egypt" and Emperor Vespasian, before the latter formally accepted the imperial purple. This unknown, ethereal king was said to be lame, blind, and have a dislocated shoulder, a description that tallies well with a derogatory description of the biblical Jesus from the Talmud. This Egyptian king then confers a great oracle upon Vespasian, that enables the latter to confidently accept the throne of Rome.

It is apparent from the details of this meeting that this crippled monarch was King Jesus himself—a King Jesus suffering from post-crucifixion wounds—and he had just conferred the Star Prophesy upon Emperor Vespasian. In exchange, it seems likely that King Jesus negotiated clemency, and he was therefore condemned to exile rather than death. But to where does one exile such a dangerous rebel? The answer, surely, is the opposite end of the empire, and in this early era the diametrically opposite end of the empire was the newly established province of Britannia—England.

Strange as it may seem, in exactly this same era, during the early years of Vespasian's reign, a peculiar fortress was constructed at Dewa, modern Chester. Archaeologists and historians have long been puzzled by this fortress, because it was not only the largest fortress in the empire, it was also hidden away in the remotest of locations behind impenetrable marshlands. Just what was the purpose of hiding a fortress in such a remote location, instead of using it to dominate the empire's northwestern hinterland? What, also, was the purpose of the strange buildings that made this fortress so large, buildings that included a unique "elliptical building"? Archaeologists are mystified by this building, for it was the most prestigious construction in the Dewa fortress and its design is unique in the empire—in other words, this is unlikely to have been a Roman building. But if this prestigious building was not Roman, then what was it doing in a Roman fortress?

Actually, the archaeologists are mistaken, for this is not an elliptical building at all. In fact, it is a very un-Roman Vesica Piscis Temple dedicated to the zodiac and constructed in Egyptian units of measure. But no temple, let alone a distinctly eastern, Vesica Piscis Temple, should have been built in a Roman fortress. Fortresses did not contain temples, as they wasted precious space, so why construct a foreign temple in the Dewa fortress? The answer is twofold. In my many books I have strongly connected both the Fourth Sect and the biblical Jesus with Egypt in general and the zodiac in particular, which is why the disciples were known as fishers of men and why the fish became the symbol of Christianity. In reality, this maritime symbolism was a simple allusion to the precessional zodiac, for the constellation of Pisces had just become the dominant constellation in the early 1st century AD, and King Jesus was the first Egypto-Judaic monarch of this new era of Pisces. This is why Jesus was always associated with Vesica Piscis symbolism, the very same symbolism that we see in the Dewa fortress' Temple of the Zodiac.

SPANDAU

Secondly, the Dewa fortress was designed to accommodate a foreign temple because it was actually a prison—a Spandau prison of the 1st century

AD, designed solely for the purpose of incarcerating a few dangerous rebels whose claim to the leadership of Rome threatened to ignite another civil war.

The end result of all these many new perspectives and arguments is that King Jesus was actually a very famous monarch who had been exiled to England, the very location that spawned the later Arthurian legends. William Blake was right—those feet, in ancient times, did walk upon England's mountains green. But the local population of Chester, inquisitive as to who this very important prisoner was, were simply told that he was some rebel Egyptian king. The common name that the Celtic people used for Egypt in this era, as recorded in the Scottish historical epic called *Scotichronicon*, was actually Aturi. Thus Jesus became known as a powerful monarch called King Aturi, or King Arthur.

However, this was not a story that the later troubadours of the medieval period could freely relate, for it was Catholic heresy. To relate the exile of King Jesus to England in the AD 70s was to proclaim that Jesus did not die on the cross in AD 33, and that kind of story could earn the author a slow roasting by the Vatican's storm-troopers. By necessity, the characters in this important historical tale had to be changed, both in name and era; and the result is a King Arthur of England who lived in the 6th century AD.

19

THE OTHER SHROUD

*Does the Sudarium Cloth in Oviedo, Spain
Prove the Turin Shroud Is Genuine and that the
Resurrection of Jesus Actually Occurred?*

BY PHILIP COPPENS

One of the most controversial relics ever, the Turin Shroud, is said to be the burial cloth of Jesus. For some, it is the ultimate relic, proving the reality of his resurrection. For academics, it remains an enigma, since the image embedded on the cloth has never been fully reproduced. For others, it is nothing more than a medieval fake, for which a 1988 carbon-dating result provides the only evidence. And yet, recent research has indicated that the swatches taken for dating the shroud came from sections which had been rewoven into the original material as part of a medieval repair campaign, implying that the date of the original shroud material remains to be determined.

The Shroud, therefore, acts very much like a mirror: if you believe in Christ and the Resurrection, you are more likely to believe it is genuine. If you are an atheist, you will likely adhere to the official conclusion that it's a medieval fake. As for the official position of the Church: there is none. Individual Christians are left to believe or not. There is, of course, also a scientific position to consider, but, alas, it turns out that the "scientific position" is not very scientific. It relies on the 1988 carbon-dating, which places the shroud's origins between 1260 and 1390, but one very important problem remains: there is no conclusive evidence that the material submitted for carbon-dating originates from the actual shroud. Indeed, mysteriously, for the key part of the sample taking process—in which pieces of the shroud were placed in containers to be sent out for analysis—the Vatican, for unknown reasons, demanded that the video cameras, set up to record the entire process—this key sequence in particular—be turned off.

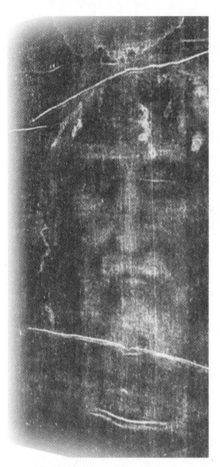

Turin Shroud

If this were a forensic investigation for an actual trial, the carbon-dating results would be inadmissible in court. That would mean we would have to rely on other evidence, most, if not all, of which suggests that the shroud is much older than the 14th century. It is known, for example, that there is pollen present, which shows the Shroud was once in Palestine. We know the weaving technique is contemporary with Jesus. And we know there is genuine blood on the shroud, blood type AB, rare in Europe, but common in the Middle East. Moreover, the position of the hands is consistent with a crucifixion. There are many other examples, and some scientists now argue the carbon-dating—being the odd-one out—should be treated with skepticism. Few, though, dare to point the finger of suspicion directly to the Vatican, instead arguing that other problems with the tests might have occurred.

The story of the Shroud has inspired dozens of books and documentaries, most of which treat it in isolation. What is little known, but completely true, is that the shroud has a little brother: the Oviedo sudarium, which has been residing in Spain for more than a millennium.

The Oviedo Shroud or sudarium is a bloodstained sweat cloth, believed to have been wrapped around the head of Jesus after his death—as mentioned in the Gospel of John. Unlike the Turin Shroud, it does not show an image, merely blood marks and the like. Interest in the Oviedo sudarium came about when Monsignor Ricci visited Oviedo in 1965. He was, in fact, the first to suggest that there was a correspondence between the stains on the cloth of Oviedo and those found on the Shroud's facial area. It would take another two decades before a local organization could

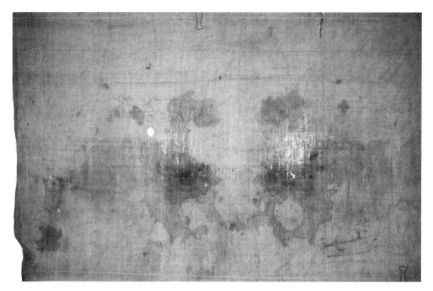

The Oviedo Shroud (Sudarium Cloth)

be formed to begin a series of scientific tests to determine the veracity of the Gospels.

The Oviedo Shroud was meant to be used only for a short period. The linen is composed of taffeta ligaments with the threads twisted in the form of a Z, which is the simplest form of weaving. It is fairly coarse, inexpensive cloth, unlike the Turin Shroud, which would have been intended to remain about the dead person's body for a year or so, after which the bones would have been collected for placement in an ossuary. Unlike the Turin Shroud, the sudarium has no image; it is stained only with blood and bodily fluids. Measuring 85 by 53 centimeters (34 by 21 inches), the sudarium is kept in the Cathedral of San Salvador in Oviedo, where it is put on display three times a year: Good Friday, the Feast of the Triumph of the Cross on September 14, and its octave on September 21, the Feast of St. Matthew.

Part of the problem with the Turin Shroud is that its history is fully documented only from the late 15th century onward, after it came into the hands of Marguerite of Austria, who ordered a special chapel to be built for it in the castle of Chambery. But the history of the sudarium, it turns out, is far better known. Its existence has been known since at least the 11th century, when it was first placed inside the cathedral; and few object to pushing its date back to the 8th, or even 7th century.

Some go as far back as AD 570, when a manuscript by Antoninus of Piacenza mentions that the sudarium was being cared for in a cave near the monastery of Saint Mark. In the vicinity of Jerusalem, it was said, there lived seven nuns in seven cells, who "looked after the sudarium of Christ." Soon afterward, though, the sudarium was moved. In AD 614, Jerusalem was attacked and conquered by the Persian King Chosroes II, but the cloth had been spirited away in anticipation of the invasion. It journeyed first to Alexandria but remained threatened even there. Chosroes conquered that town in AD 616. To protect the relic, it was taken across northern Africa, and it possibly entered Spain at Cartagena. The bishop of Ecija, Fulgentius, it is reported, welcomed the refugees fleeing from the Persians as well as the chest of relics that they brought with them.

Containing the sudarium and other precious artifacts, the chest was known as the "Arca Santa." Fulgentius surrendered it to Leandro, bishop of Seville, where it remained for a number of years. Later, it was taken to Toledo; but when the Muslims invaded Spain in the 8th century, the chest was once again moved, this time to be secured in a cave or well on the mountain known as Monsacro, near Oviedo.

The Arca Santa in Oviedo. Photo © Copyright Catedral de San Salvador de Oviedo

Some of the details of how the Arca Santa reached Oviedo are open for speculation, but there is hard evidence on how this cloth arrived in the Northern Spanish region. A key date and a key man is King Alfonso II of Asturias, who had a special chapel, the Cámara Santa (also known as the Chapel of St. Michael), built for the chest in AD 840, which served as the royal chapel and which was later incorporated into Oviedo Cathedral. Alfonso II is the king who had the bones of Saint James at Santiago de Compostela legitimized by the Pope and Charlemagne. Afterward, he created the Pilgrim's Route to Santiago de Compostela and made sure that Oviedo, his new capital, was on one of the routes.

Even though a chapel had been built for the chest, for a very long time, there was great fear of actually opening it. In fact, the sudarium did not officially enter the annals of history until March 13, 1075, the fourth Friday of Lent, when the chest was officially opened in the presence of King Alfonso VI, his sister Doña Urraca, as well as the Infanta Doña Elvira, several bishops and Rodrigo Díaz de Vivar, better known as El Cid. All had arrived in Oviedo on February 2 and had, by fasting for forty days, prepared themselves to behold the relics. When opened, the chest included, as expected, the sudarium. It has not left the cathedral since. Other relics included were the sole of Peter's sandal, a piece of Mary's garment, some of Mary Magdalene's hair, the hands of St. Stephen (the first martyr), and much more.

After 1075, the chest once again remained closed for centuries, with no opening until 1547–56, when Don Cristóbal de Rojas y Sandoval ordered it opened for him. Then, as now, no one was overtly promoting the sudarium's existence, and then, as now, it was only exhibited three times a year. But even though obscure, it did not escape skirmishes with disaster. Like the Turin Shroud, it survived an almost fatal fire in 1532. The Holy Chamber in which the sudarium was kept was almost destroyed on October 12, 1934, when dynamite that had been placed in the crypt, exploded. The sudarium was unharmed, though severe damage had occurred to the chapel.

As mentioned, the Gospel of John speaks of a sudarium present in the empty tomb (John 20:7): "The handkerchief, which had been on His head, was not lying with the linen cloths, but was rolled up in a place by itself." It was common usage for the Jews to take care of the dead this way. A sudarium was placed over the head of a corpse so that onlookers and the family of the deceased would be spared the horror of seeing the face go into rigor mortis. Jewish culture also had a specific code of conduct for dealing with blood, and all accounts agree that Jesus had been bleeding severely on the cross. Most interestingly, scientific analysis has shown that the stains of the sudarium match those on the head portion of the Shroud, a notion first suggested by Monsignor Ricci in 1965. The clear implication is that both cloths at some point covered the same body. This conclusion is supported by the fact that the same blood type (AB) can be found on both relics, as well as identical pollens (e.g. *Gundelia tournefortii*). In fact, the sudarium contains pollen from Palestine, Africa, and Spain, thus confirming the relic's historical journey. It also contains aloe and myrrh, known to be common ingredients in the preparation of the dead for burial. The scientific analysis of the sudarium has also shown that the person who was laid inside the sudarium and the Shroud was tortured and died on a cross. If this was a fake (that is, not the covering of Jesus Christ), then someone went to a great deal of trouble perfectly simulating the forensics of Jesus' death.

Given that the sudarium has a recorded history from AD 1075 onward, the conclusion has to be that the sudarium and the shroud predate AD 1075—if not the 6th century—thus negating the carbon-dating report.

One of the principal researchers into the Oviedo shroud is Mark Guscin, who in 1999 presented the conclusion of the scientific committee that both the sudarium and the Shroud had covered the same injured head. The analysis also revealed that the man for whom the sudarium had been used had been dead and had suffered wounds before death, while the formation of the stains showed that both arms had been outstretched above his head and that the feet were in such a position as to make breathing very difficult—in short, that he was likely crucified. Finally, Guscin added that the man had a beard, moustache, and long hair tied up at the nape of his neck into a ponytail. This conforms to other research carried out on the Turin Shroud, including the recent work by Ray Downing—creating a three-dimensional reconstruction of the face from the image on the Shroud—which reveals a beard, a moustache, and long hair.

The scientific evidence compiled from the sudarium follows the Bible's timeline: it would have been over the head of Jesus for about 45 minutes, when Joseph of Arimathea went to Pilate to have the body removed from the cross and to allow it to be buried. From the position of the blood and fluid stains, scientists have been able to show that the sudarium covered the head of a dead man who was first in a vertical position and later in a horizontal position—for another hour or so. The cause of death in crucifixion is asphyxiation, after which fluid builds up in the lungs. When the body is put in a horizontal position, this fluid exits through the mouth and nose as seen on the sudarium.

Jewish custom also allows that during the transport to the tomb, a cloth was wrapped around the body, which would have been removed and exchanged for the burial cloth. The gospels argue that a new, clean linen was indeed wrapped around Jesus for transport. This "transport shroud" might have been the cloth given to Charlemagne in circa 797, brought to the Abbey of St. Cornelius in Compiègne a century later—where it became the object of many pilgrimages—and where it was destroyed during the tumult of the French Revolution.

Three shrouds were reported, two of which survived the ages but whose whereabouts, for most of two millennia were unknown and which are, therefore, the subject of great controversy. Though the Gospel of John makes reference to both a sudarium and the Shroud, it seems that after their

The Sudarium (Dürer, 16th century)

discovery in the empty tomb, both objects took different trajectories. Most sources argue that Peter had taken charge of the sudarium and had hidden it, while the burial cloth itself was given to Joseph of Arimathea. Interestingly, Isodad says that Peter used the cloth in a rite known as the imposition of the hands, in which the relic was used to obtain cures (Peter placing the sudarium on his head, like a mitre). Interestingly, the miraculous powers of the sudarium might also be fact, not legend. Janice Bennett, who has had a long interest in the sudarium, wrote how in 1988 she was given an image of the sudarium, which had touched the blood on the sudarium.

She reports how on a number of occasions, when she used it, it was able to heal. Indeed, other relics having to do with the Passion are said to have similar abilities.

Some relics, though, are more interesting than others, and the Turin Shroud could be the most interesting of all. When we read the Gospel of John, it is clear that when "the other disciple"—John—entered the empty tomb, it was from the position in which the Shroud was seen, that he "believed." Maybe he also saw the image on the Shroud, though this is unconfirmed. But from that position alone, John was convinced something out of the ordinary had occurred.

The anomalous image on the Turin Shroud, the creation of which science still cannot explain, is further evidence to substantiate this theory. Indeed, scientists agree that the Shroud and the testimony of John argue that a paranormal event did indeed occur. The methodology of just how the image on the Turin Shroud was created, cannot, at present, be reproduced. The closest that one has come has been outlined by Ray Downing, namely that a state-of-the-art computer scanner is best able to create a similar image; but that fails to account for just how the tiny dots became attached to the actual cloth, since, of course, there were no such scanners at the time the Shroud was created.

PART FIVE

NAZIS AND ETS

Mussolini & Hitler. Illustration by Randy Haragan

20

MUSSOLINI'S ROSWELL?

*What Do Once-Secret Pre-War Documents
Reveal About It?*

BY FRANK JOSEPH

While events surrounding Roswell, New Mexico, in 1947 are world famous, it was not the first time that a crashed alien space-craft was allegedly found and concealed by government officials. In this case, it was the Italian government, and the year was 1933. Yet, the existence of this crashed alien vessel is virtually unknown outside Italy despite an abundance of authenticated contemporary documents confirming reports of a downed UFO before World War II.

To make the long, somewhat complex history of this Close Encounter of the Second Kind accessible for readers, a chronological outline is here presented, pieced together from various accounts which serve to clarify its development over a period lasting over seventy years. Let's begin at the beginning.

June 13, 1933: A circular craft resembling a pair of saucers joined at their outer rims crashes near the town of Maderno, in Lombardy, northern Italy. The object, made of thin, silvery-grey metal, is approximately 50 feet in diameter and less than 7 feet thick. Dorsal twin-booms or antenna-like features face in opposite directions from a delta-shaped configuration enclosed by a transparent blister. Two tubes are coupled where the design slopes upward from a flat underside, itself slung with two more pairs of oblong details. Eleven portholes run in a straight line on either side of the craft's upper half. Another eight appear on its lower portion, again on both sides, but are interrupted in the center of their line on one side by a trio of oval windows in what appears to be a rectangular hatch. An additional six, smaller, ovoid windows or lights are positioned at either end of the craft, which suffers extensive damage in the crash. No occupants of the object are found.

Several witnesses of the crash report it to local officials, who contact their superiors in Milan for instructions. Government authorities in Rome are alerted, and, within hours, "top secret" (*riservatissima*) commands are issued by none other than the nation's head of state. "On the orders of Il Duce Benito Mussolini" are issued three, separate telegrams to the official Fascist Stefani Agency, in Milan, demanding the authorities "recuperate" the downed craft at once, remove it to a secure location away from public view, and enforce strict censorship on anything to do with the crash.

June 14, 1933, Squads of Mussolini's most trusted Black Shirt followers virtually occupy Maderno to, as researcher Alfredo Lissoni writes, follow the protocol of "a Senatorial letter describing in detail the strategy to be followed after the craft had been recovered, i.e., censorship of the newspapers, arrest of the eyewitnesses by the O.U.R.A. (the Fascist secret police), elaboration of a series of conventional explanations for the UFO (i.e., balloons, meteors, etc.) to be fed to the public via the Breda Astronomical Observatory at Milan." Wreckage from the site is transported under strict secrecy to a nearby hanger at the Sesto Calende airfield in the Varese region of Ticino, then under the direct control of General Italo Balbo, head of the Aeronautica Regia, the Italian Air Force.

June 15, 1933: In a secret meeting held with his joint chiefs of staff, Mussolini learns that the object retrieved from outside Maderna is not comparable to anything in their arsenals or even on their drawing boards. He and they presume it is a specimen of superior technology operated by a foreign power, possibly hostile to Italy, which miscarried during an operational test over Lombardy. Eyewitnesses to the incident are unanimous in their recollection that the object was traveling at a speed far in excess of any known aircraft, and in absolute silence, before its collision with the earth.

Il Duce is particularly alarmed, because he has just spent a considerable portion of the national budget on making his Aeronautica Regia, the world's most powerful air force, which appears to have been rendered suddenly obsolete by the Maderno object. With typical decisiveness, he wastes no time, immediately creating a top-secret commission to thoroughly study and investigate the downed craft, and reproduce or "back-engineer" it for Italian military advancement. Christened RS/33 Cabinet ("Research-Espionage/1933"), it is headquartered at Rome's prestigious La Spezia University, where it is headed by one of the great geniuses of modern science,

Guglielmo Marconi, winner of the Nobel Prize and generally credited with invention of the radio.

"Among its members," according to Lissoni, "the Cabinet had many of the most highly respected of Italian academics, members of the Royal Italian Academy of Sciences," including the renowned Turin astronomer, Gino Cecchini. Marconi's political assistant to ensure censorship and promote public disinformation is Tommaso David, code named "De Santi," one of Italy's leading spies, who would go on to engage in important espionage until the end of World War II.

June 20, 1933: Despite RS/33 efforts at an official cover-up, word of the Maderno crash somehow reaches a Varese newspaper, the *Cronaca Prealpina*, which breaks the story, but comes to a conclusion not shared by Mussolini and his military advisors; namely, the object proves that "forms of life on Mars were in contact with men of Earth." David, the suspected "leak," is told in no uncertain terms by his superiors "to keep his mouth shut about the activities of the RS/33 Cabinet." He complies by making sure the Maderno incident is henceforward kept out of all Italian newspapers.

January 1936: After reconstructing the Maderno object to the best of their ability and nearly three years of investigation, the scientifically distinguished members of RS/33 come to a final assessment. They began their examination on the assumption that the "velivoli sconoscuti" or "unknown aircraft" is an example "of secret, new Western weaponry," but eventually conclude that it had not been manufactured by any industrial power on Earth, but was made by a vastly superior civilization from another world. Unfortunately, the technology represented by the object is largely beyond restoration, due to its extremely advanced sophistication and the extent of its wreckage.

Relieved to know that his new air force has not been outclassed by any terrestrial rival, Mussolini frees the imprisoned eyewitnesses, and decides on a policy of gradual disclosure about the spacecraft, thereby acclimating the public to the possibility of visitors from other planets, without risking sudden mass-hysteria. Henceforward, stories about UFO sightings and the strong "possibility" of intelligent life elsewhere throughout the universe appear with greater frequency in the Italian press. Respectable newspapers like the *Gronaca Prealpino*, *Italia*, *L'Italiano*, and even the official publication of the Fascist youth organizations, *Balilla*, begin writing "that there

Mod. 101-/

Indicazioni di urgenza

PRIORITA: SU TUTTE
LE PRIORITA

UFFICIO TELEGRAFICO DI MILANO

TELEGRAMMA

Circuito sul quale si deve fare
==RISERVATISSIMO==

Spedito .... al ...... ore ...... sul circuito N.

All'Ufficio di .... Trasmittente .

Origine	Denominazione	Provenienza	N.	Parole	DATA DELLA PRESENTAZIONE		Via d'instradamento	Mittente ricevuti
					Giorno e mese	Ora e minuti		
							0 Z	

= = D'ORDINE PERSONALE DEL D U C E DISPONESI ASSOLUTO SILENZIO SU PRESUNTO
ATTERRAGGIO SU SUOLO NAZIONALE AT OPERA AEROMOBILE SCONOSCIUTO STOP
CONFERMASI VERSIONE PUBBLICANDA DIFFUSA DISPACCIO STEFANI ODIERNO STOP
IDEM VERSIONE ANCHE AT PERSONALE ET GIORNALISTI STOP PREVISTE MAX PENE PER
TRASGRESSORI FINO AT DEFERIMENTO TRIBUNALE SICUREZZA DELLO STATO STOP
DARE IMMEDIATA CONFERMA RICEVIMENTO STOP - DIR GEN AFFARI SPECIALI = = FINE
STOP = =

N O
C O P I A   R I S

R I S

2412

Mittente: Agenzia Stefani - Milano

Marked "Top Secret," this purported telegram is the first from Mussolini instructing officials in northern Italy to be silent about the crashed UFO

was already telepathic communication with Martians, for such is what the 'aliens' were at that time reputed to be," according to Lissoni. "Nobody made any explicit reference to happenings in Lombardy, but in all of the papers, all at once, was infiltrated the suspicion that extraterrestrial life might exist."

Meanwhile, the RS/33 Cabinet becomes the world's first government-sponsored organization for the study of unidentified flying objects, investigating sightings and collecting data for the next nine years. Marconi himself, although avoiding all mention of the still-classified Maderno incident, publicly proclaims his firm belief in the existence of extraterrestrial civilizations "far more advanced than our own."

August 17, 1936: An RS/33 memorandum reports "the sighting of a flying cigar over the regions of Venice and Mestre." Described as "torpedo-shaped," it is escorted by two flying spheres, one of which "resembled the planet Saturn." An Italian fighter plane dispatched to intercept the objects is easily out-distanced by the intruders, which are graphically depicted in an artist's reconstruction on a two-page insert in the RS/33 memorandum. Shortly after the Venice–Mestre encounter, Mussolini meets with RS/33 members, as documented in the written agenda of the "Camera dei Deputati," or Chamber of Deputies, to discuss public disclosure of the mid-August incident.

Summer 1938: After three years of documenting "velivoli non identificabili," or "unidentifiable aircraft," Milan's Prefettura, the civil governor's office, has nine telegrams reporting "flying disks" and "flying cigars" in the region.

September 22, 1938: During his state visit to Italy, Adolf Hitler is personally informed of the "velivoli non identificabili" by Mussolini in the hope that German scientists can back-engineer the Maderno wreckage, to which they are allowed exclusive access, although, as Italian state property, it remains stored in its hanger at Lombardy's Sesto Calende airfield. Mussolini has RS/33 turn over its files, films, photographs, and illustrations to the Germans, whose flying saucer experiments, said to have achieved exceptional results by the close of World War II, may stem directly from Italian cooperation.

February 22, 1941: Responding to President Franklin Roosevelt's allegation that Italy and Germany had the will and ability to invade North America, Mussolini tells the Federation of Fascist Combatants, "The United States is far more likely to be invaded, not by Axis soldiers, but by the less-well-known, though rather warlike inhabitants of the planet Mars, who will descend from outer space in their unimaginable flying fortresses."

At the time, he is thought to have made a joke referring to Orson Welles' infamous "War of the Worlds" radio broadcast that panicked American listeners just two years before. In view of Il Duce's close involvement with RS/33, however, he may have meant something altogether different.

April 1945: As Allied forces invade northern Italy near the close of World War II, Director Moretti, in charge of the Sesto Calende airfield, incinerates the hanger concealing Maderno's UFO wreckage to prevent it from falling into enemy hands. First, officers of the SD (Sicherheitsdienst, the German SS security service) sift through the hanger's ashes, looking for anything which might have survived the conflagration. They are followed soon after by U.S. Air Force intelligence personnel. It is not known if either the Germans or the Americans find something of value. In the greater fire-storm that consumes the Third Reich, most of the RS/33 materials are destroyed.

March 1996: Bologna's daily *Il Resto del Carlino* receives 34 photo-copied pages of classified government reports documenting UFO sightings over Italy from 1933 to 1940. A Regia Aeronautica description of a close encounter with one of its warplanes has written across it in block letters, "Say nothing to Il Duce!" The newspaper editor trashes the anonymously sent dossier as an obvious hoax. Over the next three years, similar photo-copies arrive at many of Italy's leading newspapers, none of which publish the materials.

1999: Shunned by the mainstream press, the anonymous purveyor of RS/33 documents reluctantly submits them as a last resort to *La Visita Extraterrestre*, Italy's prominent ufology journal. Editor Giorgio Bongiovanni turns over the materials to Naples' ufologist, Umberto Telarico, who suggests they are all probably "fake." But Dr. Roberto Pinotti—a sociologist with a Master's Degree from the University of Florence, a former NATO officer in the Italian III Missile Brigade, and a consultant for the SETI (Search for Extraterrestrial Intelligence) research group—receives a dossier of original RS/33 reports, which he has tested for their provenance. According to Antonio Garavaglia, a Como chemist, the documents' ink and paper are consistent with and dated to official government records of the mid to late 1930s. Encouraged by Garavaglia's findings, Dr. Pinotti searches for additional supporting evidence. He tracks down the elderly Faustino V, who, shortly before his death, testifies that, as a young man in 1936, he was an eyewitness to "the flying cigar" and its spherical escorts that passed over Venice vigorously but hopelessly pursued by Italian inter-ceptors. Dr. Pinotti also confirms the former existence of RS/33, when Marcello Coppetti, a renowned scholar and former friend of the Italian Defense Minister, Legorio, documented the "Cabinet" as far back as 1978, eighteen years before the RS/33 disclosures of 1996.

October 9, 2000: Alfredo Lissoni, editor of *Giornale dei Misteri*, receives a communication from the nameless sender of the RS/33 documents. The unsigned letter explains how the author came into possession of the UFO materials from a family relative who served in the secret Cabinet.

He goes on to suggest that anonymity has been necessitated by his former rank in the Fascist diplomatic corps, where he was a colleague of the Italy's Foreign Minister, Galeazzo Ciano, Mussolini's own son-in-law, during the

Was Hitler's alleged flying saucer technology (represented in this artist's conjecture) based on a crashed UFO from Italy?

unknown writer's tenure as the young Italian Consul in Shanghai just before World War II. Violent anti-Fascist feeling since the aftermath of that conflict would put the anonymous sender at too great a personal risk. He implies that, as an old man with not much longer to live, he wants to bequeath the important RS/33 documents to posterity while there is yet time.

While skeptics dismiss his material as an incredible hoax, it has brought him neither fame nor fortune in the more than ten years he has endeavored to publicize these reports. The ink and paper they comprise have been chemically proved to date to the period and government with which their texts are concerned. RS/33 actually did exist, and at least one of its reported UFO sightings was independently verified by a surviving eyewitness. Investigators with the impressive, academic credentials of Dr. Roberto Pinotti are convinced the documents are authentic. The real mystery here is not their provenance, but where did the strange object that crashed in northern Italy come from, and what brought it down fourteen years before the Roswell incident.

Though apparently unrelated, the events seem to have shared an even more sinister common denominator: both were victims of government censorship and disinformation that persists to this day.

21

HITLER'S NUCLEAR THREAT

*Were America and Her Allies in More Danger
than Anyone Dared to Admit?*

BY JOHN KETTLER

Historians working in Germany have found a 1945 diagram that shows a German nuke. The picture held in a private archive is a rough schematic and doesn't prove the bomb existed, but the document has been used to support the arguments of researcher Dr. Rainer Karlsch.

NAZI NUKE DESIGN?

Karlsch provoked a major controversy by claiming that, toward the end of the war, the Nazis had actually tested a small atomic bomb. Karlsch's book *Hitler's Bomb* (2005) says the Germans planned to combine a mini nuke with a rocket similar to the ones they used to attack England during the blitz.

According to Karlsch, despite the widely publicized failure of a group led by scientist Werner Heisenberg to develop the German bomb, another group headed by physicist Kurt Diebner had a firmer grasp of the technical challenges involved and took their research all the way to a primitive test in Thuringia in Eastern Germany.

Einstein's 1939 letter to President Roosevelt expressing serious concern that the Nazis might develop an atomic bomb caused the U.S. to launch an accelerated program to get there first. The resultant "Manhattan Project" spent over $2 billion ($23 billion in today's dollars) to develop one plutonium implosion test article, code named "the Gadget," and two actually delivered weapons, with more to be delivered in months. The first, "Little Boy," was a uranium weapon utterly unlike the originally tested device. It destroyed Hiroshima. The second, "Fat Man," was a plutonium implosion device and it destroyed Nagasaki. Orthodox—and some would say uninformed—history lists the Hiroshima strike as the world's first atomic attack.

Uninformed? Evidence of ancient nuclear warfare has been repeatedly written about in this *Atlantis Rising* magazine and elsewhere (see "Was There an Ancient Armageddon?" Sylvia Dailey, A.R. #26). But has there been something more recent we should be concerned about? Astonishing, recently uncovered evidence indicates the existence of a threat far more tangible than even Einstein ever realized—evidence that Hitler not only developed but actually tested an atomic weapon that he planned to deliver to the heart of Manhattan.

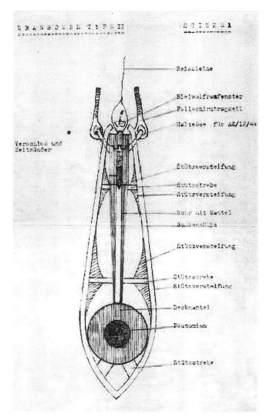

1945 diagram shows a German nuke

THE STANDARD STORY

Here, courtesy of the Nuclear Weapons archive, is the conventional account: The world's first atomic detonation, at the tower test site known as Trinity, using a 20–22 kiloton (KT) device called "the Gadget," took place July 12, 1945. The bomb called "Little Boy" had a yield of 15–16 KT and the one called "Fat Man" had a yield of 21 KT (*http://nuclearweaponarchive.org/Usa/Med/Lbfm.html*). To wrap up the official story, we note that Hiroshima was struck August 6, 1945, while Nagasaki was hit on August 9, 1945, the primary target, Kokura, being weather obscured.

This is what the American government told its people and the world. The war was fought with conventional weapons but finished with two nuclear blasts—American nuclear blasts. From these, other advanced technologies and America's dominant economic position after the war stem its superpower status, which continues to the present day.

But what, then, are we to make of this headline from *The London Daily Mail* (October 11, 1944)? "Berlin Is 'Silent': Still No Phones for 60 Hours."

The official German explanation was "bomb damage," but the evidence suggests that is only partial truth. How about "Bomb damage," as in disruption by EMP (electromagnetic pulse)?

This startling suggestion rests upon multiple witnesses and evidence. Let's start, though, with the sworn affidavit of Hans Zinsser, pilot and rocket expert, interviewed by Allied Intelligence after World War II. Quoting from the online version of Joseph Farrell's (*Giza Death Star*, etc.) astounding *Reich of the Black Sun: Nazi Secret Weapons & The Cold War Allied Legend*, pages 17–18 (http://missilegate.com/rfz/swaz/chapter1.htm):

"His affidavit is contained in a military intelligence report of August 19, 1945, roll number A1007, filmed in 1973 at Maxwell Air Force Base in Alabama. Zinsser's statement is found on the last page of the report (Farrell's excerpts are renumbered to make his points, but the last one was left in the original):

A man named Zinsser, a Flak rocket expert, mentioned what he noticed one day: "In the beginning of October, 1944 I flew from Ludwigslust (south of Lubeck), about 12 to 15 km from an atomic bomb test station, when I noticed a strong, bright illumination of the whole atmosphere, lasting about 2 seconds.

"The clearly visible, pressure wave escaped the approaching and following cloud formed by the explosion. This wave had a diameter of about 1 km when it became visible and the color of the cloud changed frequently. It became dotted after a short period of darkness with all sorts of light spots, which were, in contrast to normal explosions, of a pale blue color.

"After about 10 seconds the sharp outlines of the explosion cloud disappeared, then the cloud began to take on a lighter color against the sky covered with a gray overcast. The diameter of the still visible pressure wave was at least 9000 meters while remaining visible for at least 15 seconds.

"Personal observations of the colors of the explosion cloud found an almost blue-violet shade. During this manifestation reddish-colored rims were to be seen, changing to a dirty-like shade in very rapid succession.

5. The combustion was lightly felt from my observation plane in the form of pulling and pushing.

6. About one hour later, I started with an He 111 from the A/D [probably means "aerodrome," Ed.] at Ludwigslust and flew in an easterly direction. Shortly after the start, I passed through the almost complete overcast (between 3000 and 4000 meter altitude). A cloud shaped like a mushroom with turbulent, billowing sections (at about 7000 meter altitude) stood, without any seeming connections, over the spot where the explosion took place. Strong electrical disturbances and the impossibility to continue radio communication as by lightning, turned up.

53. Because of the P-38s operating in the area Wittenberg-Mersburg I had to turn to the north but observed a better visibility at the bottom of the cloud where the explosion occurred [sic]. Note: It does not seem very clear to me why these experiments took place in such crowded areas."

Farrell comments that the German pilot had observed the test of a weapon having all the signatures of a nuclear bomb: electromagnetic pulse and resulting malfunction of his radio, mushroom cloud, continuing fire and combustion of nuclear material in the cloud and so forth, on territory clearly under German control in October of 1944—eight months before the first American A-bomb test in New Mexico! Note the curious fact that Zinsser maintains that the test took place in a populated area.

Farrell also asks: how did Zinsser know it was a test? He concludes that Zinsser was briefed into the program and knew exactly what he reported seeing.

So, Zinsser reports observing a bomb test, occurring at an "atomic bomb test station" according to his own words, and this test neatly and exactly fits the known atomic bomb phenomenology. In this same time frame, the city of Berlin, possessor of one of the most modern telephone systems in the world, suffers a complete collapse of its phone system lasting over 60 hours.

Additional evidence reported in a contemporary newspaper account and cited by Farrell, says Britain went on secret alert for atomic attack at about the same time as the Zinsser reported test: "Nazis Atom Bomb Plans," (London Daily Telegraph, August 11, 1945), describing the British gearing up for an atomic attack beginning "August, 1944," only to be canceled when the test was an apparent "failure." A single chilling sentence makes the point: "An elaborate scheme was drawn up by the Ministry of Home Security for prompt and adequate measures to cope with the widespread devastation and heavy casualties if the Germans succeeded in launching atomic bombs on this country."

The story continues, "Reports received from our agents on the Continent early last year indicated that German scientists were experimenting with an atomic bomb in Norway. According to these reports, the bomb was launched by catapult and had an explosive radius of more than two miles.

"...the Government gave the reports serious consideration. Thousands of men and women of the police and defence services were held in readiness for several months until reliable agents in Germany reported that the bomb had been tested and proved a failure."

The time discrepancy is easily explained by a late slippage in the German test schedule after the intelligence report had been made and Farrell argues persuasively that the test was only a failure insofar as it had some effects, such as EMP, the Germans hadn't anticipated. Losing communications in your capital in wartime is quite a side effect.

HITLER'S "MANHATTAN" PROJECT

For a low level burst, Norway is too far away to "fry" the Berlin telephone exchange, but it makes a very nice launch platform for heavy bombers flying great circle routes to attack the U.S. This may be why the Germans kept a sorely needed, fully equipped army there and may explain this remarkable story from the *Washington Post*, June 29, 1945.

"R.A.F. officers said today that the Germans had nearly completed preparations for bombing New York from a 'colossal air field' near Oslo when the war ended.

"Forty giant bombers with a 7,000-mile range were found on this base—the largest Luftwaffe field I have ever seen," one officer said. "They were a new-type bomber developed by Heinkel. They now are being dismantled for study. German ground crews said the planes were held in readiness for a mission to New York."

That mission, it turns out, was pre-rehearsed, flown on a nonstop flight by a giant Ju-390 in 1944 from Bordeaux, Occupied France, to within twelve miles of New York City and back. This flight takes on the gravest import when we take a look at an October 1943 Luftwaffe High Command (Oberkommando des Luftwaffe) feasibility study map for a full blown, Hiroshima sized atomic attack on New York City. This is not a beautifully rendered History Channel hypothetical attack using a "dirty" bomb dropped from a Horten flying wing, but the thoroughly analyzed real thing.

Thus, it seems fair to assign the June 6—September 12, 1944 Battle of Northern France a second, vital yet unknown, strategic role. Its capture may have deprived the Germans of not just the known V-1 cruise missile bases and V-2 ballistic missile bases, but of a nuclear strike platform against both the U.K. and the U.S.

Trailblazing research and ground truth studies by British engineer Philip Henshall, as reported in his *Vengeance: Hitler's Nuclear Weapon Fact or Fiction?* (1999) showed there was a reworked, reinforced V-2 (V-4) intended to deliver a ton-class "dirty" bomb (high yield of radioactive debris) from special V-1/V-2 facilities and hardened silos. Such weapons, coupled with dirty-bomb-equipped surface bursting V-1s could have rapidly made London and various port cities uninhabitable. These combined facilities were also designed to accommodate the A9/A10 Super V-2 intended to hit America. The loss of coastal bases such as Bordeaux seems to be the driver behind the fast-track building of the already described Luftwaffe heavy bomber base near Oslo, Norway. Fortunately for the United States, Nazi Germany fell before that airbase became operational. The weapons existed, though, and they were expected to be used.

On April 22, 1945, Mussolini wrote of them: "The well-known mass destruction bombs are nearly ready. In only a few days… Hitler will probably execute this fearful blow, because he will have full confidence…. It

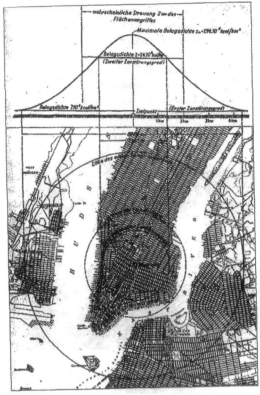

The Luftwaffe's "Feasibility Study" of an Atom Bomb Blast of Hiroshima Size over Manhattan

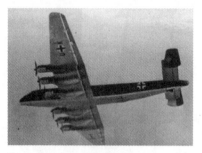

The enormous Ju-390

appears…there are three bombs—and each has an astonishing operation. The construction of each unit is fearfully complex and of a lengthy time of completion."

Mussolini was very much in the loop, for his best scientists and engineers were hard at work on SS black projects, including several types of manned and unmanned saucers.

Hitler himself said, "We have … unbelievably powerful rockets and a bomb…that will astonish the whole world. The enemy knows this… and attempts to destroy us. But we will answer this destruction with a storm and that without unleashing a bacteriological war, for which we are also prepared…. All my words are the purest truth. That you will see!"

By April 30, 1945, however, Hitler was dead and Germany surrendered May 8, 1945.

Italian officer and observer Luigi Romersa was at Rugen Island in the Baltic and reports on the test and aftermath which he witnessed. "There were four of us: my two attendants, a man with worker's clothes and me. 'We will see a test of the disintegration bomb…the most powerful explosive yet…developed. Nothing can withstand it,' said one of them…. He glanced at his watch and waited until noon, the hour for the experiment. Our observation post was a kilometer from the point of the explosion. 'We must wait here,' the man with the worker's clothes ordered, 'until this evening. When it is dark we may leave. The bomb gives off deathly rays, of utmost toxicity. Its effective area is much larger than the most powerful conventional bomb. Around 1.5 kilometers'…."

Romersa doesn't describe the actual blast, but the aftermath is clear.

"Around 4:00 PM, in the twilight, shadows appeared running toward our bunker. They were soldiers and they had on a strange type of 'diving suit.' They entered and quickly shut the door. 'Everything is kaput,' one said, as he removed protective clothing. We also had to put on white, coarse, fibrous cloaks. I cannot say what material this cloak was made of… it could have been asbestos, the headgear had a piece of mica-glass in front of the eyes.

"The houses that I had seen only an hour earlier had disappeared, broken into little pebbles of debris, as we drew nearer ground zero, the more fearsome was the devastation. The grass had the same color as leather, the few trees that still stood upright had no more leaves."

It further appears that the ever pragmatic SS used the Rugen test to get human data, as evidenced by Judge Robert Jackson's remarkable question to Speer at the Nuremberg Tribunal about this intel report:

"A village, a small village was provisionally erected, with temporary structures and in it approximately 20,000 Jews were put. By means of this newly invented weapon of destruction, these 20,000 people were eradicated almost instantaneously and in such a way that there was no trace left of them; the explosive developed temperatures of from 400 degrees to 500 degrees centigrade and destroyed them without leaving any trace at all."

Judge Jackson said "near Auschwitz," but that could have been source protection. Recall the statements of both Hans Zinsser and Luigi Romersa?

A German on the Bomb projects says the German Bomb was ready July 2, 1944, the perhaps not so coincidental date of a coup attempt against Hitler! There may have been another test, with more hapless Jews, in Thuringia at Ohrdruf on May 4, 1945, using a radical lightweight boosted fission device.

Remember the H-Bomb? Its design was patented in Austria before the war and a mature design was patented by Dr. Karl Nowak of Germany in 1943 (German patent 905.847, March 16, 1943). More disturbingly, Nowak's design specifically intended *not* to create the radioactive fallout of atomic and hydrogen bombs. So much for Dr. Edward Teller's inventing the H-Bomb in 1944!

LEFT UNDISCUSSED

Undiscussed in the limited space here are mysteries such as: Oppenheimer's "bombs of German provenance;" the dud first Nagasaki bomb later given by Japan to the Russians (per Russian Marshal Malinovsky's Japanese surrender translator Titarenko); the Nazi uranium and fuses in the U.S. Bomb program; their connection to the Japanese nuclear test on August 12, 1945, at what is now Hungnam, North Korea; German fuel-air explosives and the real exotic weapons of the SS, secret name Schwarze Sonne (Black Sun); transplanted together, it is said, with its weapons to the U.S. (Operation Paperclip), Russia, and elsewhere.

22

THE TRUE CONFESSIONS OF LT. HAUT

A Previously Unheard Account from Beyond the Grave Reinvigorates the Roswell Case

BY JOHN KETTLER

I n June of 2007, the famous dispute over reports of a crashed UFO near Roswell, New Mexico, in 1947 got a new lease on life from a dead man. One important witness to those controversial events, whatever they were, had previously refused to talk, but now he has, from beyond the grave.

Lieutenant Walter Haut was the public relations officer at the Roswell Army Air base in 1947, and was the man who issued the original and subsequent press releases after the crash on the orders of the base commander.

Haut died in 2005, and left a sworn affidavit to be opened only after his death.

In the text released in June 2007, Haut adds several details to the familiar story, including an assertion that the famous claim by the air force that the wreckage was merely a weather balloon was simply a cover story, and that the real object had been recovered by the military and stored in a hangar. Haut described seeing not just the craft, but alien bodies as well.

The affidavit has been the subject of considerable media attention, and researcher John Kettler has looked further into the case. Here is his report. —Editor.

A TALE OF TWO AFFIDAVITS

Haut's supposed "deathbed" affidavit turns out, despite the recent sensational coverage, to not be quite what it seems. In reality, the affidavit was sworn and notarized five years prior to his death, and was held by his attorney with instructions to release it only upon his death.

Why it took two years more (Haut died in December 2005) is unknown, but his original stated goal was to fulfill a promise he had made to then Roswell Base Commander, Colonel William Blanchard, not to reveal certain highly sensitive experiences while Blanchard was still alive.

It would appear that Haut erred on the side of caution and waited until he himself had left the scene to set the record straight and to provide what had carefully been left unstated in his public affidavit. The differences are major and highly significant. Indeed, they add some explosive new angles to the familiar Roswell story. The confirmation of ET bodies at Roswell is hardly new. Haut's swearing he saw them personally, though, is. The real shocker is that Haut explicitly describes the famous press release he wrote, the one which caused a global sensation in July of 1947, as a deliberate diversion and coverup of something much more important than ET craft wreckage strewn on Mac Brazel's ranch.

Crashed Saucer Art

According to Roswell researcher David Rudiak (*http://roswellproof. homestead.com/Haut.html*) here's what really happened. Not only did Haut have an expurgated and unexpurgated version of his affidavit, but he also spilled the beans earlier privately in 1989 to Robert Shirkey, Sr., a good friend and the former Assistant Operations Officer at Roswell (attested by his son, Robert Shirkey, Jr.; audio clip at website) and also gave a lengthy personal oral recounting in 2000 to researchers Wendy Connor and Dennis Balthauser, people he knew well and could absolutely rely upon to keep their promise not to release the interview until he died.

THE 1993 AFFIDAVIT

If we dispense with the boilerplate, Walter Haut basically says five things:

1) While serving as the PIO, Col. Blanchard called him, informed him of the existence of the "flying saucer or parts thereof," origin, a ranch NW of Roswell, and that the Base Intelligence Officer, Major Jesse Marcel "would fly the debris to Fort Worth;"

2) Col. Blanchard ordered him to write a press release and deliver it first to local radio and newspapers;

3) Haut reports reading in the newspaper the following day General Roger Ramey's weather balloon explanation;

4) Haut believes not only that Col. Blanchard saw the original debris, would never have confused the actual crash debris with a weather balloon, and neither would have Jesse Marcel; Haut confirms Jesse Marcel personally told him that what he recovered wasn't what was shown to the press;

5) Haut is convinced "the material recovered is from some craft from outer space."

His first affidavit, while ostensibly confirming many elements of the now well-known Roswell standard story, is hardly inflammatory or world-stopping. What did he swear really happened, though, when he knew he wouldn't be around to deal with the aftermath of his truth telling?

THE 2002 AFFIDAVIT

In the new affidavit, things start out innocuously enough, then head rapidly into high strangeness. Instead of five principal points, we now have fifteen (the website link given earlier has all the details, together with full sourcing for the two affidavits):

1) Haut restates his official job at Roswell, but adds that he spent the 4th of July weekend at home.

2) By mid morning, July 7, he already knew of a downed vehicle report and that Major Jesse Marcel was detailed by Col. Blanchard to investigate.

3) By late that afternoon, he had civilian reports of a second site just north of Roswell (Brazel's ranch was 75 miles NW of the base; the second site was 40 miles N).

4) Tuesday, July 7, 1947 saw a most unusual "usual" staff meeting held, with the long hard-to-identify Capt. Sheridan Cavitt of the Counterintelligence Corps (CIC), Col. James I. Hopkins, the Operations Officer (boss of Robert Shirkey, Sr.), and the Base Supply Officer, Lt. Col. Ulysses S. Nero, to which were added Blanchard's boss, Brigadier General Roger Ramey, his Chief of Staff, Col. Thomas J. Dubose, both from

The infamous Weather Balloon wreckage

Carswell Army Air Field in Fort Worth, Texas (where Marcel and other sources say the crash debris was flown). The main topic was the debrief of Marcel and Cavitt on the Brazel ranch site, with a preliminary report by Col. Blanchard on the second site. What's said is so strange it bears quoting. "Samples of wreckage were passed around the table. It was unlike any material I had or have ever seen in my life. Pieces which resembled metal foil, paper thin yet extremely strong, and pieces with unusual markings along their length were handled from man to man, each voicing their opinion. No one was able to identify the crash debris." All of a sudden, the number of people who handled the crash debris and are identifiable by name goes up from a handful to a roomful. They're describing the same items Jesse Marcel, his son, Jesse Marcel, Jr., and several others have previously reported handling.

5) Here we find ourselves face-to-face with a veritable smoking gun, in the form of discussion regarding the use of a Cover & Deception plan

to hide "the more important site north of town by acknowledging the other location" as part of the larger issue of whether to "go public or not with the discovery."

6) Haut reports that after the meeting (9:30 a.m.) was when Col. Blanchard called him and dictated the soon-to-be-famous and later notorious press release. Distribution was as above.

7) Haut says the press release generated such enormous reaction (calls from around the world) that Col. Blanchard suggested he go home and "hide out."

8) Here, Haut drops a bombshell, stating that Col. Blanchard took him to Building 84 (known to ufologists as Hangar 84, but actually Hangar P-3), where he was shown the object just recovered north of town. "It was approx. 12 to 15 feet in length, not quite as wide, about 6 feet high, and more of an egg shape. Lighting was poor, but its surface did appear metallic. No windows, portholes, wings, tail section, or landing gear were visible." One can see why the government was willing to admit what was already widely known by civilians, in order to protect this stunner. Haut confirms the multiple reports by eyewitnesses of heavy inner and outer guards. The apparent craft recovery's only part of the story.

9) Haut says he saw bodies outlined under a tarp, with "oversized heads protruding." He guesstimated the size as that of a "10 year old child," going on to say that Col. Blanchard, by holding his arm 4 feet above the floor in his office, indicated the height of the beings.

10) Haut confirms that a temporary morgue was set up, which nicely dovetails with the call to Glenn Dennis wanting several child coffins and dry ice for apparent preservation.

11) Fortunately for all concerned, none of the recovered material was radioactive.

12) Right after he got back from Carswell, Major Jesse Marcel personally and irately informed Haut of the switcheroo from real crash debris to the prosaic weather balloon wreckage done by General Ramey while Marcel was briefly out of General Ramey's office. Thereafter, the matter was never discussed again.

13) Haut mentions that he would be permitted to "make at least one visit to one of the recovery sites during the military cleanup." Further, he'd be allowed to collect some of what was recovered and display it in his office. Weirdly, he doesn't say whether he actually did either.

14) The thoroughness of evidence retrieval and site cleanup is evidenced by his statement that two separate teams were used and revisited each site months after the primary cleanup.

15) Where in the 1993 Affidavit Haut mentioned only a craft, here he used an expanded formula, "craft and crew."

Thus, by comparing the two affidavits, it is readily evident that Walter Haut not only knew all along there was a cover-up regarding the craft debris littering Mac Brazel's ranch, but was directly involved in creating and disseminating a cover story that hid the far more significant, maybe even vital information of the recovery of a separate, mostly intact craft at the second site. Further, Haut constitutes another primary eyewitness to many hotly disputed prior aspects of the story, such as the bodies, their size, and characteristics.

From a historical standpoint, Haut has greatly broadened the research possibilities regarding Roswell, for we now have a whole new batch of people and their survivors to interview, documents to pore over.

23

THE ROSWELL MIRACLE METAL

Newly Declassified Memo, the Smoking Gun
for Secret Back Engineering

BY LEN KASTEN

The Battelle Memorial Institute is not well known to the general public. That is fine with the Department of Defense (DOD), since they would prefer that the work that is done there remain "below the radar" as much as possible. And yet, this sprawling complex outside of Columbus, Ohio, adjacent to the Ohio State campus, along with the six, huge, associated national laboratories that it manages, is the center of the most sensitive and important research and development on the planet. Founded in 1929 under the terms of the will of Ohio industrialist Gordon Battelle, it originally focused on research and development in metals to support the burgeoning iron and steel industries in the 1930s. According to its website (*www.battelle.org*), "Battelle now owns more than two million square feet of laboratories in several locations that perform cutting edge research in national security; environment, energy, and transportation; and health and life sciences," and serves "more than 800 federal, state, and local government agencies; some of the largest corporations in the world; and private sector customers and partners through offices in more than 100 national and international locations." Battelle also manages or co-manages the Brookhaven, Idaho, Oak Ridge, Pacific Northwest, and Law-rence Livermore National Laboratories, as well as the National Renewable Energy Laboratory. And as of 2006, Battelle was selected to manage the new National Biodefense Analysis & Countermeasures Center (NBACC). In all, Battelle oversees 20,000 staff members and conducts $3.9 billion in annual research and development. Many of their highly classified research facilities are involved in development projects linked to the military.

Battelle's military connection is no secret and is openly proclaimed on their website. They say, "With more than 50 years' experience in military

Battelle Memorial Institute

chemical, biological, radiological, and nuclear defense programs, Battelle is a leader in using science and technology to detect hazards and protect people and facilities against weapons of mass destruction. Battelle's expertise covers all aspects of anti-terrorism defenses—from threat and vulnerability assessments, to testing of security systems, equipment, vaccines, medical and community response; and training and evaluations." Battelle's close ties to the military began during World War II. Because of the Institute's expertise in metallurgy, it was called upon to study and develop refined uranium for the Manhattan Project, and it was instrumental in the making of the atomic bomb. As a consequence, it became one of the leading nuclear research facilities in the world, which resulted in a leadership position in nuclear propulsion. This led to the development of the first nuclear submarine, the *Nautilus*, in 1948. In the early 1950s, Battelle built the world's first privately-owned nuclear research facility on a 10-acre tract of land near Columbus. It included a reactor, a critical assembly capability, and hot cells. Battelle's innovative history is legendary. They developed xerography, have originated over 2,000 U.S. patents, and have received numerous awards and citations.

The Wright-Patterson Connection

Given their deep expertise in metallics and their wartime military affiliation, it should come as no surprise that when an alien spacecraft crashed in the New Mexico desert near Roswell in 1947, leaving metal-like fragments scattered all over the sheep ranch of Mac Brazel, the Army Air Force would turn to Battelle to analyze the debris— especially since Battelle knew how to keep secrets, as was amply demonstrated by their airtight participation in the Manhattan Project. In fact, it would actually be expected. So, the recent revelation by veteran UFO researcher and writer, Anthony Bragalia, that this is exactly what happened makes perfect sense. Furthermore, it makes even more sense since there is now overwhelming evidence that the recovered parts of the spacecraft were immediately flown to Wright-Patterson Air Force Base in Dayton, Ohio, which is just down the road (about 100 miles) from Columbus. In fact, it seems very likely that the AAF had originally located their Foreign Technology Division at Wright-Patterson entirely because of this proximity to Battelle.

Bragalia writes about a document that was retrieved under the Freedom of Information Act (FOIA) that clearly implicates Battelle in the analysis of the metallic pieces that were found at the Roswell crash site and the subsequent project to duplicate the so-called "memory metal" that astounded everyone who handled it at Roswell. Bragalia's research was recently revealed on his blogsite *Ufoblogspot.com*, titled "The UFO Iconoclast(s)," and is incorporated into the new revised and expanded edition of the book by Thomas R. Carey and Donald J. Schmitt, *Witness to Roswell: Unmasking the Government's Biggest Cover-Up* (2009).

The FOIA request was submitted by Billy Cox, a reporter for the Sarasota, Florida *Herald Tribune*. In August, 2009, after a wait of 10 weeks, the Battelle document finally arrived and was shared with Bragalia. It is titled, "Second Progress Report Covering the Period September 1 to October 21, 1949 on Research and Development on Titanium Alloys Contract No. 33 (038)-3736." The authors are Battelle analysts C. W. Simmons, C. T. Greenidge, C. M. Craighead "and others." The report was produced for Wright-Patterson Air Force Base (by 1949 the AAF had become the Air Force). Bragalia learned that the document had previously been restricted to viewing only by authorized DOD personnel. The FOIA release had to be approved even now, 60 years later, by the Secretary of the Air Force! About 30 percent of the original 119 pages was missing. The receipt of this docu-

Saucer Wreckage art

ment by Cox and Bragalia was the final chapter in a long investigation. They had previously found references to such a report in various footnotes in studies sponsored by the military on "shape-memory" alloys. In searching for this "missing" document, the paper trail led to Battelle. Initially, historians at both Battelle and Wright-Patterson claimed they couldn't find it. But, thanks to the FOIA request, it was ultimately located in the archives of the Defense Technical Information Center at the Department of Defense.

IT FLOATED DOWN LIKE KLEENEX

Many people handled the strange metallic-appearing debris that littered Mac Brazel's ranch after the crash of the spacecraft. They were all astonished at the bizarre qualities of the small samples they managed to get their hands on. Major Jesse Marcel said "[There were] many bits of metallic foil that looked like, but was not, aluminum, for no matter how often one crumpled it, it regained its original shape. Besides that, they were indestructible, even with a sledgehammer." William Brazel Jr. (son of Mac Brazel) said, "The odd thing about this foil was that you could wrinkle it and lay it back down and it immediately resumed its original shape. It was quite pliable, yet you couldn't crease or bend it like ordinary metal. It was almost more like a plastic of some sort except that it was definitely metallic in nature. I don't know what it was, but I do know that Dad once said that the Army had told him that they had definitely established it wasn't anything made by us." Don Burleson (Roswell researcher) said, "Brazel set the object up at the base of a pinyon tree and suggested that they fire at it—which they did—with 30.06 deer rifles from a distance of about

30 feet, an easy target for experienced deer hunters. Mr. Croft (Phillip Croft, hunting companion of Mac Brazel) said that when the foil was hit, it spun a considerable distance up in the air and came floating down "like Kleenex." Upon examining the material, the men found that it showed no effects from having been hit—not even a dent, and certainly no tears or punctures." The Battelle "Second Progress Report" to Wright-Patterson is basically a review of Battelle's effort to develop just such a metal as was reported by the Roswell witnesses. Although there is no direct reference to the Roswell crash in the Report, there are so many personnel links and clues to ongoing UFO research at Battelle that there can be very little doubt that the document was a report on a contract with the AAF to duplicate the metal found at Roswell.

THE BATTELLE UFO CULTURE

Perhaps the major clue was the discovery that one of the authors of the Report, who was included in the "and others," category, was Elroy John Center. Center, a Senior Research Chemist at Battelle from 1939 to 1957, authored the section dealing with the chemical analysis of Titanium-Base Alloys. The Report had already concluded that a "shape-memory" metal must be a titanium alloy of exceptional purity. Center's job was to find ways to detect the oxygen levels in the titanium. It was already known that Center had told a friend in 1960 that while he was a research chemist at Battelle in the late 1940s, he had been given the job of evaluating an unknown material that they told him had been retrieved from a crashed "flying saucer." He also told his friend that the material had "hieroglyphic-like" markings. In his blog, Bragalia tells us that Center's family confirmed that he had an "intense interest" in UFOs and extraterrestrials while working at Battelle.

Center's interest in UFOs was not unusual at Battelle. In fact, it was apparently embedded within the organizational culture. Bragalia reports that the Director of Battelle in the late 1940s was Clyde Williams. Williams was, at the same time, serving on the government's Research and Development Board, which also included in its membership Dr. Eric Walker and Dr. Robert Sarbacher, both of whom later acknowledged that they knew about the Roswell crash. This is certainly a strong indication that the entire government R&D Board was deeply involved in the UFO/ET issue. And this connection would explain why, in 1952, it was Battelle that was chosen to do all the analysis for the infamous Project Blue Book, although, supposedly, it was Air Force Captain Edward J. Ruppelt, the head of Blue Book, who selected Battelle for this job. Given Battelle's influence at such high levels, it is extremely unlikely that it was left to a lowly Air Force captain to make this selection. In any case, Battelle was commissioned to design the questionnaire as well as to computerize and analyze the data for all reported UFO incidents nationally. Ruppelt took his job very seriously and every Air Force base in the country had a Blue Book officer who was required to submit all UFO reports. Starting in March, 1952, Battelle performed a massive statistical analysis of about 3200 cases using the then state-of-the-art IBM punched-card data processing technology. The project was completed in 1954, after Ruppelt's departure, and resulted in the now well-known and contentious, "Special Report No. 14."

THE MYSTERIOUS DR. CROSS

The key intermediary between Wright-Patterson and Battelle after the Roswell crash was undoubtedly Dr. Howard Clinton Cross. It is known that Cross was a senior metallurgical researcher prior to the crash, but after the contract was awarded to Battelle, he apparently emerged as the research director for the memory-metal project. This placed him squarely at the crossroads of interaction with several government agencies; and he became the point man for all matters relating to UFOs at Battelle. Bragalia has done extensive research on Cross, and has unearthed important details about his role in producing the "Second Progress Report," and with regard to Project Blue Book. Battelle learned that the Roswell metal was a combination of extremely pure titanium and another metal combined in a new way, and decided that it could best be duplicated by combining titanium with nickel, to produce the alloy NiTi. The challenge faced by Dr. Cross was how to combine extremely pure titanium and nickel to produce a memory-metal rather than a simple alloy. The "Second Progress Report" summarizes the research and experimentation in that two month period in 1949 attempting to produce a "morphing metal," that is, a metal that is pliable but always returns to its original shape. In a subsection of the report titled, "Investigation of Melting Titanium," Battelle scientist L. W. Eastwood examined ways to optimize the melting of titanium. This had to be done in a certain way to produce NiTi and required the use of an advanced arc furnace. It is known that Eastwood reported to Cross, as did Elroy Center, confirming Cross's role as director of the project. In a section titled "Evaluation of Titanium Base Alloys," the authors discuss ways to create a "recipe" for mixing nickel and titanium to produce NiTi. A nickel-titanium phase diagram is included. The Report also evaluated other possible titanium alloys including titanium-zirconium (TiZr) and included a chart showing the "elongation" and "bendability" of various advanced titanium alloys.

In the early 1950s, Howard Cross emerged as the director of the Project Blue Book research. During that time, Bragalia says, "Cross worked quietly—but very closely—with the heads of various departments of the U.S. Government on various aspects of the UFO phenomena... He held technical knowledge about the craft's construction and was given security clearances that enabled him to become a valuable asset to U.S. military and intelligence in analyzing and investigating especially complex UFO cases... The Battelle metallurgist was of such importance that he was able to deal freely with the heads of the U.S. Office of Naval Research, the CIA, and Air Force Intelligence."

NITINOL

Cross became an expert on titanium and authored a technical summary report titled "Titanium Base Alloys" which was presented to the Office of Naval Intelligence in December, 1948. While it can be shown that "The

Second Progress Report" was the first document to ever discuss the new nickel-titanium alloy (NiTi), the metal wasn't officially "discovered" as a matter of record until 1961 by the U.S. Naval Ordinance Lab (NOL). Bragalia believes this was the result of Cross having originally turned over his data to the Office of Naval Research. The invention of Nitinol is now officially credited to William Buehler and Dr.

Nitinol

Frederick Wang, researchers at the NOL. Apparently, the NiTi data languished in the archives at the NOL for ten years until Buehler came along and started looking for inter-metallic compounds to use for the nose cone of the Navy's Polaris Missile. He quickly focused on NiTi in 1959, and then renamed it Nitinol, combining "NiTi" with "NOL," in 1961 when he discovered its amazing characteristics. Then Dr. Wang joined his group in 1962 and started to find new applications for the unique alloy. Today, Nitinol is used in coupling hydraulic lines on jet aircraft, orthodontics, orthopedic surgery, bone fracture splints, cardiovascular stents, medical catheters, scoliosis spinal correction, and other medical applications. Wang has built Nitinol engines that convert thermal energy to mechanical. It is also being used now in ocean engineering, electrical connector products, robotics, laser beam alignments, tap water valves, sprinkler systems (developed by Battelle), eyeglass frames, automatic window openers, coffee maker valves, and mechanical toys. New uses are being continually identified.

There is really no way to know what life would be like today if that spacecraft from a distant star had not crashed into the New Mexico desert that stormy night in July, 1947. It would certainly be very different. It was truly the opening event of the Space Age, and we are just now beginning to comprehend the magnitude of the change that it brought about.

PART SIX

MYSTIC TRAVEL

Grail Cup

24

QUEST FOR THE GRAIL:
THE SRI LANKA CONNECTION

Did the Legends Originate in the Mystic East?

BY MARK AMARU PINKHAM

The Holy Grail legends written during the Middle Ages in Europe were the first to reveal that the Knights Templar were the true and eternal Guardians of the Holy Grail. This notion was initially popularized by a knight, Wolfram von Eschenbach, who in AD 1200 made it public record in *Parzival*, the most comprehensive and compelling rendition of the grail legend ever written. In addition to this revelation regarding the Templars, Eschenbach also proclaimed in his magnum opus that the Holy Grail could be something other than a chalice or platter (he claimed it was a stone), and that the original legend of the Holy Grail came not from the West but from the East. Eschenbach was explicit on this latter point, stating that the incipient author of the grail legend was Flegetanis, an astrologer from the ancient Middle East, perhaps Babylonia, who "found it in the stars."

Thus, with Knight Eschenbach the world became suddenly well-informed that the Knights Templar were guardians of a Holy Grail, although their grail may or may not have been a chalice. The world also learned that the Templars apparently acquired their Holy Grail during their two hundred years in the East because that is the direction of the incipient Holy Grail mysteries. Eschenbach's insightful revelations proved to be fodder for a host of other grail questions that have emerged since the publication of *Parzival*, including: "Who were the Templars' Holy Grail teachers and benefactors in the Middle East?" Although the answer to this question has always been known in certain occult circles, it was not until very recently that the Sufi master Idries Shah made it public knowledge.

In *The Sufis*, published in the 1960s, Shah disclosed that many of the Templars' early mentors were the Sufis, the enlightened adepts of Islam who had previously accompanied the Muslim juggernaut in its march to eastern Asia and then returned to the Middle East with hundreds of exotic scrolls and mysteries related to alchemy and the Holy Grail mysteries. Apparently, from the moment King Baldwin II gave the Templars the Al Aqsa Mosque on the Temple Mount to reside within and administer, the knights had been in frequent contact with Sufi adepts, including many members of the Al-banna, the Masonic Sufi Order that built the nearby Dome of the Rock. Shah's information has since been found to be supported by credible historical sources, such as signed treaties, that indicate that the knights were indeed allied with many fringe Sufi sects, some of which are known to have taught occult alchemy and the Holy Grail mysteries.

One such "Holy Grail" sect was the Assassins, a mystery order founded by the Sufi Hasan-i-Sabah, a renowned alchemist from Persia. The Persian Assassins, who often allied with the Templars against a common foe, such as Saladin, acquired the Holy Grail mysteries from Cairo's "House of Wisdom," a Sufi mystery academy of which Hasan had been an initiate, as well as from their Persian forebears. For thousands of years, a tradition had existed in Persia regarding ancient alchemists and Narts, or "Knights," who had dedicated their lives to finding the Nartmongue, or Holy Grail, while in the service of certain Persian kings, such as King Key-Khosrow of the 19th century BC. The Templars no doubt learned much from the Assassins and other Sufis, but we also know that there was at least one important non-Sufi "Holy Grail" influence that influenced the Templars.

In the 19th century AD, it became public record through the works of various European Knights and occultists, such as Eliphas Levi, that while in the Middle East the Knights Templar had been initiated into a Johannite or Holy Grail lineage of spiritual adepts that originated in the East and included in its ranks such illustrious spiritual giants as John the Baptist, Jesus, and John the Apostle. When the Templars were formed, the first Templar Grand Master, Hughes de Payen, was initiated into this Holy Grail lineage as its sixty-eighth Grand Master. Then, from that time onward, the ancient Holy Grail lineage became synonymous with the Templars and each Templar Grand Master became the principal patron and Guardian of the Holy Grail. Thus, if the Templars were indeed in the possession of a Holy Grail it was no doubt acquired from this ancient lineage. But what form did their Holy Grail take? Was it a secret, a power, or an object? And from where in the East did it and the Holy Grail mysteries originate?

In order to trace the roots of the Holy Grail mysteries to their source we must begin with John the Baptist, the Western founder of the Holy Grail lineage that the Templars inherited, and then move backward in time. Records show that John the Baptist was part of a lineage of Holy Grail masters known as the Mandean Nasurai that did indeed originate in the East. This lineage began its journey on the paradisaical island of Sri Lanka before traveling west and eventually settling on the banks of the Tigris and Euphrates Rivers in southern Iraq. Thus, for the Mandeans, Sri Lanka was the Garden of Eden, a notion that has also been promoted by certain world religions, such as Islam, which in addition recognizes the island as the home of the Water of Life or Fountain of Youth.

In order to prove their assertion that Sri Lanka was indeed the Garden of Eden and the original land of immortality, both Sufis and Mandeans maintain that Adam's footprint can still be found on the summit of Adam's Peak, the second highest mountain on the island. Here, after a very arduous climb, one can find a small temple enclosing Adam's five-foot-long footprint set in stone, which according to local legend was exactly where God placed him before Adam descended the mountain and walked eastward in the direction of the Water of Life. Adam's journey eventually took him to a place now known as Kataragama, which became his home. Thus, Kataragama can be considered a possibility for being the location of the

Adam's peak

Shrine of Adam's footprint

Eden scenario described in Genesis that involved Adam, Eve, and the wily Serpent on the tree. Such a radical notion is, surprisingly, supported by a growing body of evidence, not the least of which is that Kataragama is today an international holy temple shrine where Muslims, Hindus, and Buddhists all worship a deity whose forms include that of a snake or serpent. Was this deity the original serpent on the tree?

Today, a visitor to Kataragama can find its principal deity addressed by many names, some of which ostensibly identify it as being the serpent on the tree. Such names include the Hindu Skanda, a "snake" epithet that wraps itself around the root word Can or Kan, the universal sound syllable for "serpent." The Hindus also invoke the Kataragama deity as Jnana Pandita, meaning the "Instructor" or "Teacher of Jnana" (Gnostic wisdom). This, of course, was certainly not the function of the serpent on the tree according to the standard Christian or Jewish interpretation of Genesis, but it was definitely an understanding promulgated within the early heretical Gnostic sects that populated the Middle East and Egypt during the first centuries after Christ. These mystics claimed that the Serpent on the Tree had been sent down to Eden by his mother, the beneficent Goddess Sophia, to teach all humans gnosis, that is, the truth of their divine nature. Because of his pivotal service of revealing Gnostic truth to humanity, the

MISSING CONNECTIONS

serpent on the tree was referred to by Gnostics as humankind's original "Instructor" of truth and "Savior." If not for him, the path to enlightenment would not exist for us today.

Were the Gnostics right? Did the serpent on the tree really reveal to Adam and Eve their divine natures? Perhaps another branch of Gnostics, the Gnostic yogis of India, can shed some light on this mystery. They maintain that the serpent on the tree in the Garden of Eden was both an actual human entity of ancient times who taught the secrets of the Holy Grail to humanity, but it was also a metaphorical symbol for the Kundalini serpent that coils upon a human's spine, the "Tree of Life," while bestowing both immortality and gnosis. As it ascends the spine, state the yogis, the Kundalini serpent "teaches" a human gnosis by activating certain psychic centers or chakras that are positioned along it. Once the Kundalini serpent reaches the head it precipitates complete gnosis or intuitive understanding of a person's true, divine nature.

When speaking of him as an ancient human entity, the yogis identify the serpent on the tree as the Kataragama deity himself, whom they venerate as the first teacher of the "Siddha Marga," the path of enlightenment. To them, he was the first Kundalini Master, the first teacher of Yoga, and the first Instructor of Gnosis. In order to perpetuate his work and enable future generations of humans to achieve gnosis and immortality, the yogis contend that the ancient Kataragama deity founded numerous lineages of Kundalini masters, most of which went north into India and continue to exist there today within a multitude of yoga sects. But, as previously mentioned, he also founded an alternate Kundalini lineage that was taken west by the Nasurai Mandeans and gave rise to the Western Holy Grail tradition. According to E. S. Lady Drower, a British woman who lived for years among the Mandeans in their current settlements in southern Iraq during the early decades of the 20th century, after leaving the island of Sri Lanka the sect of Mandeans traveled west and became sequentially assimilated into the Sumerian, Egyptian, and Persian cultures before finally merging with the highly spiritual Jewish Essene tradition. Within this branch of Judaism the Mandeans formed a sect of adepts known as the Nasoreans or Nazarenes, a term which according to the Gnostic Gospels denoted "those of true wisdom." It was within this sect that the Mandean prophet John the Baptist and his cousin Jesus Christ were born. John, the Nasurai Baptist, who preceded Jesus and served as his teacher, went on to become

Hindu shrine in Colombo, Sri Lanka

the official founder of the Gnostic tradition and Holy Grail lineage in the West. His transference of Kundalini, the Holy Grail power of the lineage, to his disciple Jesus occurred during his student's baptism in the River Jordan when the white dove, symbol of the Holy Spirit (a Western term for Kundalini), descended on Jesus with "lightning upon it."

John the Apostle and Mary Magdalene became Jesus' successors in the ancient Holy Grail lineage, and afterward they served as patron and patroness of many fledgling Gnostic sects. John's symbol, a chalice from which emerges a snake or dragon, symbolized his exalted position as a Holy Grail Grand Master. He was the chalice full of serpentine Kundalini power, that is to say, a human Holy Grail. Mary's distinguishing symbol became a human skull, the Gnostic symbol of the death and spiritual rebirth one experiences on the Kundalini or Holy Grail path to immortality.

After John the Divine, the Holy Grail lineage continued for another thousand years until the time of the Templars. When the lineage finally passed to Hughes de Payen, the first Templar Grand Master, the Templar Knights became the eternal Guardians of the Holy Grail. This transformative power, they learned, was the true Holy Grail. It can surround and interpenetrate an object, thus making it a "Holy Grail," but the true Holy Grail is the Kundalini/Holy Spirit power an object or person possesses, not the object itself. In most cases, the Holy Grail power of a recognized Holy Grail object had been infused into it by a human Holy Grail, like Jesus, who had touched it or somehow transferred his or her spiritual power into it.

When the Templars returned to Europe they began authoring numerous renditions of the Holy Grail legend within which they discreetly inserted the Holy Grail mysteries. Their texts proved that any object could be a Holy Grail, and they enumerated a few of its forms, including a stone, a spear, a platter, a book, a cup, etc. They also referred to the founder of the Holy Grail path, the ancient Kataragama deity, as both the first Fisher King and as the primal knight, St. George, the patron of the Templars. The Kundalini power was often identified in the texts as the Holy Spirit dove, but it was also personified as the demonic-looking Kundry, who assisted in the transformation of Percival during his quest to find the Holy Grail.

The Templars' Gnostic practices eventually led to their mass arrest and torture on Friday 13, 1307. But unbeknownst to their persecutors, most Templars escaped from France and continued the observance of their Holy Grail mysteries in other European countries. In Britain, for example, they incorporated many of their Gnostic rites and secrets into fledgling Freemasonry while placing the craft under the patronage of the Holy Grail masters John the Baptist and John the Apostle. In England, the Templar ritual of drinking wine from a human skull while toasting to their patron John the Baptist was incorporated into the rite of the 13th and final degree of the York Rite of Freemasonry, the Knights Templar degree. In Scotland, the Templars' Gnostic and alchemical rites were infused into the 17th and 18th degrees of the Scottish Rite. In the 17th degree, the degree of the Knight of East and West, the initiation ceremony was conducted by a "warden" acting the role of John the Baptist, while entrance into the 18th degree, the Knight of the Rose Croix, involved a rite that mirrored one the Templars themselves had undergone when they anciently became "Knights of the Rose Cross." The fiery red rose, which denoted the fiery kundalini and the alchemical unfoldment that occurs under its inspiration, was the symbol of not only the Templars but many Holy Grail sects of Europe that evolved from or were influenced by the knights, including the Rosicrucians, the Illuminati, the Royal Order of Heredom, the Order of the Garter, and the OTO.

But while much of the Templars' Gnostic wisdom has been either lost or disguised since 1307, many researchers currently believe that their Holy Grail wisdom exists in its purity as an abundance of priceless texts hidden deep within certain Templar chapels and crypts, such as Rosslyn Chapel in Scotland, which they refer to as the Chapel of the Holy Grail. The Sinclair builders of Rosslyn were intimately associated with the Templars from the order's beginning, and they became the preservers of its Gnostic wisdom. Thus, as we decipher the images lining the walls of Rosslyn Chapel and eventually open its crypt, perhaps the true wisdom and power of the Holy Grail mysteries from the East will again emerge.

25

THE PYRAMIDS OF SCOTLAND: REVISITED

How Much Does Egypt Owe to Scotland for Her Ancient Landmarks?

BY JEFF NISBET

The Internet has become the long and investigative arm of Everyman, and in no field of inquiry is this more apparent than in genealogy. The new breed of genealogical cyber-sleuth has shown that ordinary people share an abiding interest in their past, where they came from, and how they got where they are today.

If societies are the sum of their parts, we might then assume that the ancient Egyptians entertained those same motives when they built their pyramid complex at Giza exactly where they did.

But first, let's go back to a more recent time.

On February 11, 2009, several UK newspapers reported that the Israeli "spoon bender" of the 1970s, Uri Geller, had purchased Scotland's tiny Lamb Island, and that my article, "The Pyramids of Scotland" (see *Atlantis Rising* magazine, issue #35, 2002), had inspired the purchase. It was enough to create a huge increase in my website traffic and to waken my article from its seven-year slumber.

Lamb Island, a.k.a. "The Lamb," sits about a mile from the seaside town of North Berwick and is the central island of three that I claimed mirrored the layout of the belt stars of the constellation Orion, which, according to the hotly debated Orion Correlation Theory, were also mirrored in the layout of the "Gizamids."

I had demonstrated how Orion's stars, acting with Sirius, an important star in Egyptian cosmology, dictated the locations of several sacred sites connected to the Knights Templar, the order of warrior monks exterminated in 1307 for reasons that still spark controversy. One of those sites, Rosslyn Chapel, would later capture worldwide attention in Dan Brown's book, *The Da Vinci Code*.

The correlation also showed connections with Tara, legendary seat of the High Kings of Ireland, and with Dunsinane Castle, one-time repository of Scotland's Stone of Destiny, the fabled stone thought to have been brought to Scotland by followers of Egyptian Princess Scota, a legend told by Walter Bower, Abbot of Inchcolm, in his 15th century history, *The Scotichronicon*.

North Berwick Law (Photos courtesy of Jeff Nisbet)

Academics dismiss that legend as a tale fabricated to give Scotland's monarchs an ancient lineage and ignore such discoveries as the UK excavations of Egyptian artifacts, the superabundance of a common strain of mitochondrial DNA in both regions, and a Bradley University report claiming that Egypt imported certain construction techniques from Scotland. Moreover, the *Scotichronicon* is not the legend's only record. Travel writer William Dalrymple claims that a letter to Charlemagne from English scholar Alcuin refers to the Scots as "Pueri Egyptiaci," the Children of Egypt, and author Ralph Ellis traces the story's origin back farther, to Manetho's 300 BC *History of Egypt*.

But I've discovered much more.

Walter Ferrier, in his 1980 *The North Berwick Story*, explains the etymology of the town's name, writing that *bere* is the Old English word for "barley," and *wic* means "village." In *Star Names: Their Lore and Meaning* (1899), Richard Hinckley Allen reports that in the Egyptian "Book of the Dead" Orion was known as Smati-Osiris, the Barley God.

In my article, I drew attention to a mid-17th century map on which The Lamb was named Long Bellenden—curious because it is the shortest of the three islands. I then speculated that the islands may have been "one long island at some point, carved from the mainland by a cataclysm the ancient 'mythmakers' would only hint at, and then cut into three," and that the nearby North Berwick Law, just three feet shorter than Giza's Great

Pyramid, might have been "shaped" into the pyramidal form we now recognize it by. My theories, needless to say, have met with some amusement in certain quarters, and I'm told that one alternate researcher has been known to go for a few cheap laughs at my expense.

Nevertheless, I've since found two local folk tales that suggest a bit of "terraforming" might indeed have occurred.

The Tale of the Saint: Legend has it that there once existed a rock that was a danger to shipping. A monk named Baldred miraculously moved it around the coast and out of harm's way, creating a geological feature since known as St. Baldred's Boat.

The Tale of the Devil: One day the Devil was strolling up the surf and so frightened a local woman that she let out a shriek. Startled, the Devil dropped his walking stick and splashed away. His stick shattered, becoming the three islands in my article. The nearby Bass Rock, upon which can be seen the ruins of Baldred's Chapel, is also known as the Devil's Hoof.

And then there are the lions.

Lying next to The Lamb is the sleeping lion that many see in the shape of Craigleith Island; and 20 miles to the west stands Arthur's Seat, the sphinx-shaped extinct volcano that dominates Edinburgh's skyline. A third lion may be seen in Scotland's Royal Standard, the flag that shows a red rampant lion; and archaeologist Mark Lehner has established that the Great Sphinx was once painted red.

The fourth lion is found in the *Legend of Lyonesse*, the tale of a land that sunk beneath the waves off England's southwest coast. Etymologically, however, the name has been traced as an alteration of the French word Léoneis, which itself developed out of Lodonesia, the Roman name for Lothian. North Berwick lies in East Lothian.

Within a day of Geller's purchase, a conversation began on the Cabinet of Wonders website. One poster duplicated my original graphic and confirmed that Sirius, the alpha star of constellation Canis Major, did indeed fall on Inchcolm Island, where Walter Bower compiled his *Scoticronichon*. Interestingly, the poster discovered that the constellation's beta star, often referred to as "The Herald" because it rises before Sirius, fell within Edinburgh, and wondered if the spot held significance. In fact, it fell on an area I knew well—an area named Starbank Park, which has a star cut out in the slope of its hill, flanked by two crescent moons, with a circular area above, presumably the sun. I have been unable to discover how the park was

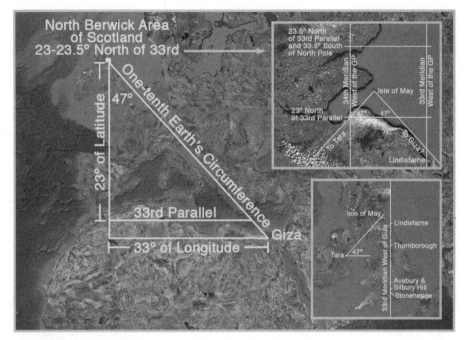

From Scotland to Giza: the Atlantean bridge over time and distance
(Map courtesy of Jeff Nisbet)

named, but it is not unlikely that Edinburgh's Grand Lodge of Freemasons might have had a hand in it.

Inchcolm lies within sight of Starbank Park, and there is a local tradition that names it "Isle of the Druids." Eighteenth-century intellectual Thomas Paine, in his treatise on "The Origin of Freemasonry," claims that the fraternity's roots are found in the solar-centric religion of the Druids, the priestly caste extant in Britain during the Roman occupation, driven underground by the rise of Christianity. Paine attributes the importance of Freemasonic secrecy to fear, observing, "When any new religion overruns a former religion, the professors of the new become the persecutors of the old. We see this in all instances that history brings before us;" and concludes that "this would naturally and necessarily oblige such of them as remained attached to their original religion to meet in secret, and under the strongest injunctions of secrecy. Their safety depended upon it."

By far the most obvious Freemasonic symbology, however, appears to be rooted in Egyptian cosmology, but the fraternity has forgotten why. Also, in Masonic ritual, great emphasis is placed on geometry, exemplified by the enigmatic "G" within the craft's ubiquitous square and compass insignia, and on the cardinal directions of the geographic compass.

Frank C. Higgins' 1919 *Ancient Freemasonry: An Introduction to Masonic Archaeology* states that the 23.5° angle and its 47° double are two of Freemasonry's "Cosmic Angles," and that they "are encoded on coins showing pre-Christian Phoenician temples of Cypress, ancient Greek paintings of Hermes and Ceres, as well as in the Masonic Keystone and Compass of the present day."

To those two numbers we should add a third—33—the highest attainable degree of rank in Scottish Rite Freemasonry, as well as the number of the latitudinal line along which, for reasons unknown, many of the world's sacred sites are located. Using these three numbers, I have discovered an ancient message encoded by the pyramid builders. To understand that message, and its implications, we must first consider the Prime Meridian.

The Prime Meridian is an invisible line that stretches between the North and South Poles, which, due to the rotation of the Earth, passes the Sun every 24 hours. It calibrates the hours of the day around the world, and begins the first of 360 vertical slices of one degree each. Its position is arbitrary, but in 1884 it was agreed that Greenwich, England, should mark the International Prime Meridian, and it has done so ever since.

The Great Pyramid sits 31.08 degrees east of Greenwich, and researchers Scott Creighton and Gary Osborn have recently demonstrated that Freemasonry's cosmic angles of 23.5 and 47 degrees, relating to Earth's axial tilt, have been encoded in its internal geometry. Osborn has found those same angles encoded in countless works of art over many centuries.

I decided that any civilization advanced enough to build the Great Pyramid would likely have used its position to mark its own Prime Meridian. Then I counted 33 degrees to the west, to Morocco's Atlas Mountains, and established that the meridian that today runs north to south through a point 1° 52′ west of Greenwich would, to the pyramid builders, have marked their own 33rd meridian. So I then drew a horizontal line between the Great Pyramid and that point, and then another directly north along that ancient 33rd. Incredibly, my second line all but kissed four major English sacred sites on its way to the north—Stonehenge, Silbury Hill, Avebury, and Thornborough, the huge three-henge complex confirmed as "the world's first monument aligned to Orion's belt stars"—before nearing the border of Scotland at the Holy Isle of Lindisfarne, perhaps indicating that this ancient 33rd meridian may have once been as sacred and important as today's 33rd parallel, and possibly have been the Prime Meridian before Giza.

But that's when things got really interesting.

The four islands that had figured so mightily in my "Pyramids of Scotland" article—Orion's Belt Star islands and the Isle of May—lay in the rectangle formed between the ancient 33rd and 34th meridians and the 23rd to 23.5 degree parallels north of today's 33rd. Astonishingly, using the three most significant Freemasonic numbers, two of which relate to Earth's axial tilt, the geometry from the Great Pyramid's ancient Prime Meridian pointed the way to the North Berwick area; and, once there, those same numbers helped enclose the area of the North Sea wherein my belt-star islands and The May lay. Even more incredible, I discovered that the line I had drawn between Tara and The May, seven years ago, followed a 47° angle, as did a line drawn from the eastern edge of Lindisfarne and The May, creating a 47° pyramid with The May at its apex—perhaps, symbolically, the Great Pyramid's missing capstone. Due to the enormous distance involved, I have been unable to establish if the Lindisfarne line continues exactly to Giza, but I'd lay odds on it. And finally, I have calculated that the distance between the Great Pyramid and North Berwick equals one-tenth the circumpolar circumference of the Earth.

The Isle of May that my original Orion Correlation pointed to was an important site of Christian pilgrimage in the Middle Ages. Recent archaeological excavations, however, have shown that the site has been in use since at least the Bronze Age. Could it be that the Great Pyramid, thought by some to be built by the survivors of the cataclysm that destroyed Atlantis, built the Great Pyramid where they did in order to geodetically point the way back to their former homeland? Could it be that Princess Scota's people, when they left Egypt, were not heading to parts unknown, but were simply heading home?

That inhabited land once existed between Scotland and Scandinavia has been confirmed by Exeter University's Doggerland Project, named after the Dogger sandbank where prehistoric artifacts have been dredged up. Could the Isle of May have been anciently revered as the last remaining vestige of that sunken land yet remaining above the waves?

And could the Doggerland area have been just part of a much larger Atlantis?

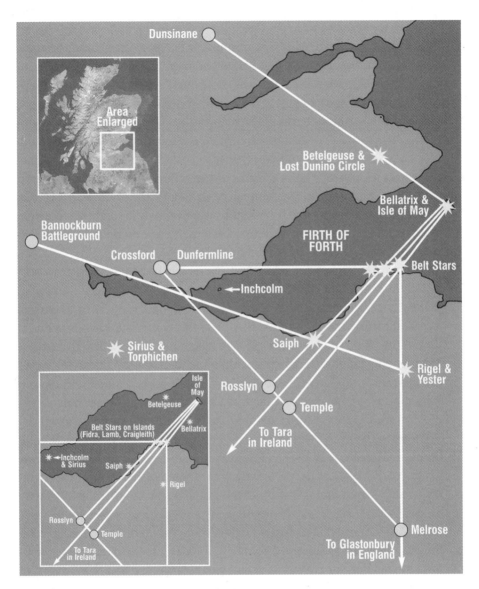

Chart of Orion and Sirius, enlargedd and pivoted on Craigleith Island (inset: Orion and Sirius with belt stars exactly over Fiora, The Lamb, and Craigleith).

Comyns Beaumont, in his 1946 *The Riddle of Prehistoric Britain*, specu-lates that Atlantis encompassed the entire British Isles, and that only some of it sank due to a comet strike that also tipped the Earth into its present day 23.5° angle. Moreover, he says, the center of Atlantis lay on the Isle of Mull, off the west coast of Scotland. I have calculated that Mull is now precisely 23.5 degrees north of the present day 33rd parallel and, if Beau-mont's comet-strike theory be given just a modicum of credence, would have then lain just a few miles to the west of the Straights of Gibraltar, the Pillars of Hercules in Plato's account of the sinking of Atlantis. Might not Plato have been hiding (yet ultimately revealing) the truth of things by couching his tale in geodesics? Might he not have just as surely been saying that Atlantis once lay just beyond where the Pillars of Hercules now lay, before it shifted 23.5 degrees to the north?

To sum up: There once was a land that sank beneath the sea due to a cat-aclysm that tilted the Earth's axis into its present day 23.5° angle—an event that was the source of all the world's far-flung flood legends. The survivors built—around the world—huge structures that fixed their new location in the cosmos, and built the Gizamids to establish a Prime Meridian that math-ematically memorialized an earlier Prime Meridian exactly 33° to the west, along which were built at least three of the best-known megalithic sites in Britain, thereby also encoding the location of their pre-deluvian homeland, 23.5° north of where it originally lay, and 33° south of today's North Pole. What are the chances that the Freemasonic numbers 23.5, 33, and 47 would lead us to a small patch of the globe containing three islands laid out in the pattern of Orion's Belt, near a very pyramidal hill just three feet shorter than the Great Pyramid, only 20 miles to the east of a Sphinx-shaped extinct vol-cano with Arthurian connections, in a city that is the acknowledged world capitol of Scottish Rite Freemasonry—all in a land with a much-decried Egyptian foundation legend? And finally, if we accept the dictum "form fol-lows function" as an architectural law, we might recognize in the immense size and shape of the pyramids the ideal physical mass and form necessary to defuse the power of yet another mighty wave? Flood shelters, anyone?

In the 19th-century words of Thomas H. Huxley, "The known is finite, the unknown is infinite; intellectually we stand on an islet in the midst of an illimitable ocean of inexplicability. Our business in every generation is to reclaim a little more land."

Ladies and gentlemen: Hail, Atlantis!

26

THE VINLAND MAP IS FOR REAL

New Study Makes the Case that the Vikings Were Here Before Columbus

BY FRANK JOSEPH

Scholars, convinced our continent was hermetically sealed off from the outside world before the arrival of Christopher Columbus, have been struck a heavy blow. A map long branded a hoax, because it indicates European awareness of America prior to 1492, has been found to be genuinely pre-Columbian.

Last July, world-class experts in document authentication at the Royal Danish Academy of Fine Arts presented the results of their study at Copenhagen's International Conference on the History of Cartography. According to Rene Larsen, director of the School of Conservation, "We have so far found no reason to believe that the Vinland Map is the result of a modern forgery. All the tests that we have done over the past five years—on the materials and other aspects —do not show any signs of fraud."

The document in question does far more than prove old-world Europeans beat Columbus across the Atlantic Ocean. Bound in a mid-15th century history of the Mongols, the so-called "Vinland Map" was re-drawn from a 200-year-older compilation of several, earlier maps indicating extensive knowledge of what is now the eastern United States going back a thousand years. The land mass portrayed farthest to the left, identified as Vinilanda Insula, encompasses an area from Maine in the north to the Carolinas in the south; from the Atlantic Seaboard to the Susquehanna River in central Pennsylvania.

Although compressed—directions, as well as some proportions, are skewered—details are less distorted than geographically correct. An overlay of the Vinland section forms a template for virtually every twist and turn of Maine's northern boundary at the Saint John River, just as the east coast down to Charleston, South Carolina, is clearly defined. Chesapeake

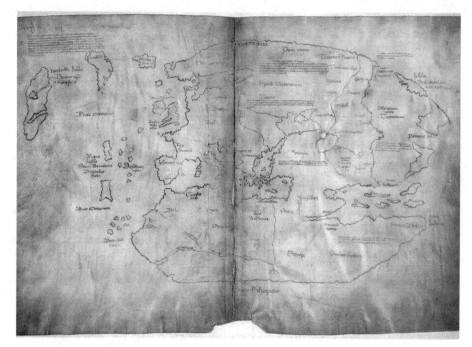

Vinland Map

Bay, undiscovered until 1586, and Lake Ontario, first visited by Jesuit missionaries 75 years later, are explicitly portrayed. The large region represented here must have been experienced by many Norse explorers over a protracted period of time. No single discoverer could have undertaken such extensive journeys during the course of one lifetime. Moreover, the strange combination of disproportion and accuracy does indeed suggest a later compilation of many maps made by different travelers on separate journeys over time. An anonymous medieval cartographer endeavored to combine them into a single map encompassing all areas of North America explored and known from AD 1000.

The creation of these individual maps also implies that relations between Scandinavian visitors and tribal native Americans must not have been as contentious as some Nordic sagas have portrayed them. History records that the Vikings were as adept at commerce as they were at war, and more commonly engaged in trade than pillage. The geographical information that went into the Vinland Map could only have resulted from far-flung travels that absolutely depended on the more or less consistent good will of the indigenous people. The overwhelmingly out-

MISSING CONNECTIONS

numbered Scandinavians must have sensibly bartered their way across North America.

But what exactly was Vinland? And where was it? The name had been coined by the famous Norseman, Leif Eriksson, in AD 1001. Seventy-five years later, the German geographer, Adam of Bremen, wrote of Eriksson in *Descriptio insularum Aquilonis* ("Description of the Northern Islands"), "he has also reported one island discovered by many in that ocean, which is called Vinland, for the reason that grapevines grow there by themselves, producing the best wine." Two later sources—the Icelandic sagas of Eric the Red and "Of the Greenlanders"—also told of Vinland. Its precise location was unclear until authentication of the Vinland Map, although the sagas already related that it lay south of Helluland ("Flatstone Land," most likely Baffin Island for its abundance of flagstone), and Markland ("Wood Land," an apparent reference to thickly forested Labrador, where, in fact, an early 11th century Viking settlement was discovered at L'Anse aux Meadows in 1960, two years after the Vinland Map came to light). "Vinland," then, was not confined to Maine, as some researchers have speculated, but only began there, and went on to encompass most of the eastern United States.

While preoccupied with the map's depiction of North America, inter-preters neglect its additionally provocative features. For example, the entire coastline of Greenland appears in details supposedly unknown until the late 19th century, when it was officially circumnavigated for the first time. More-over, Greenland is represented as an island, a fact likewise unappreciated until as recently as 1896, when it was thoroughly surveyed for the first time. No less surprisingly, the Vinland Map includes two other territories allegedly unknown and unexplored by the outside world in pre-Columbian times. Although their placement and size are only roughly correct, the Atlantic islands of Andros and Puerto Rico are unmistakably portrayed. Andros lies in the Bahamas between Cuba and Florida, about 130 miles southeast of Miami and some 260 miles northeast from Havana. The Vinland Map shows only the larger, northern half of Andros, upside-down. In fact, Andros con-sists of two islands separated by a twelve-mile gap. Beneath it, Puerto Rico appears in a more complete configuration but improperly oriented north to south from its true, east-west axis. Such topsy-turvy positioning occurred often during the early days of cartography, especially before the advent of latitude and longitude coordinates. The Vinland Map's authentication proves that Norse seafarers had not only explored much of the North American

Leif Eriksson

interior from its eastern seaboard, but had traveled to Andros and Puerto Rico and circumnavigated Greenland almost a thousand years before modern sailors duplicated the feat. While the utility of putting in at Puerto Rico can only be surmised, Andros is still valued for its abundance of fresh water deposits, making it a vital port-of-call for any transatlantic sailors, then or now.

The Vinland Map shows that its Viking makers, the earlier discoverers of America, traveled much further than anyone imagined in modern times. Tragically, all that remains of their extensive exploits are two, thin pieces of paper bound in a mid-15th century book, the *Hystoria Tartarorum*, or "Description of the Tartars" (sometimes referred to as "The Tartar Relation"), composed in 1445. The map of North America it contains was created for a church council at Basel, Switzerland, five years earlier.

The *Hystoria Tartarorum* was acquired in 1957 by Laurence C. Witten II, an antiquarian book dealer, and he offered it for sale to Yale University. Witten's asking price was higher than his alma mater could afford, but another Yale alumnus, the wealthy philanthropist, Paul Mellon, agreed to purchase the book for his school, but only if the map it contained could be authenticated by independent experts. For three years, it was secretly subjected to the ruthless scrutiny of two curators from London's British Museum and by Yale's own head librarian. In 1965, the outside world learned of the Vinland Map for the first time, when the examiners proclaimed its medieval authenticity, and Mellon purchased it for Yale, where it was insured for twenty-five million dollars, and is still preserved at the University library.

Notwithstanding Yale's academic prestige or the professional credentials of its examiners, America's archaeological establishment arose as one to savage the Vinland Map as a transparent fraud. Their unanimous, vituperative condemnation was based on little or no counter-evidence, but stemmed almost entirely from their unalterable supposition that the map was, *ipso facto*, a fake, because Columbus was the first and only discoverer of America. They had no less ruthlessly demeaned Helge Ingstad for daring to challenge their sacred paradigm, until the weight of physical evidence he unearthed at Labrador's L'Anse aux Meadows overcame their opposition, which they nonetheless down-played, qualifying his discovery as a botched Norse settlement of no real consequence. In fact, the site is now regarded—even by a growing number of mainstream researchers—as having been a jumping-off point for the further exploration of Vinland, as documented by the assailed map. If anything, Ingstad's discovery of the Viking settlement at L'Anse aux Meadows in 1960 tended to verify the authenticity of the Vinland Map, which had been disclosed for the first time three years before.

In answer to the critics, Yale University Press published *The Vinland Map and the Tartar Relation* by Dr. Raleigh Ashlin Skelton, Thomas E. Marston, and George Painter. Although favorably received by cartographers, historians, and document experts around the world, their book only elicited louder howls of outrage, minus any substantial argument, from U.S. archaeologists. A "Vinland Map Conference," sponsored by the Smithsonian Institution in 1967, stoked the flames of archaeological contempt when most scholars from a broad spectrum of scientific fields reaffirmed the map's medieval dating.

Five years later, even their majority conclusion was called into question, however, when chemical analysis found titanium dioxide, or anatase, in the map's ink. Micro-samples retrieved by forensic specialist, Walter McCrone and his team, were found in a rounded, crystalline form manufactured for use in pale pigments since the 1920s. The yellowing of ink on the map, he concluded, must, therefore, have been the result of deliberate forgery, not aging. Haters of the map promptly dismissed it as a proven hoax for the next fifteen years. But in 1987, another forensic team led by Dr. Thomas Cahill from the University of California at Davis employed particle-induced X-ray emission to find only trace amounts of titanium dioxide in the ink. The much higher concentrations McCrone found were due to his poor sample selection. McCrone returned to Yale to re-check his findings with new techniques, taking photo-micrographs at one-micrometer intervals through the thickness of the map's ink samples. To his surprise, application of Fourier transform spectroscopy identified the ink's binder as a gelatin, most likely from animal skin, sending the map's provenance yet again back into the Middle Ages.

The see-saw struggle over the Vinland Map's authenticity took another turn in mid-2002, when a new process (Raman spectroscopy) revealed high levels of 1920s-like anatase. The map's few remaining traces of black pigment consisted mostly of carbon, which should not have generated the map lines' yellowish residue, because only pre-modern, iron-based ink leaves such a color when it decays. Most of the map lines are yellow, while the rest of the *Hystoria Tartarorum* was produced entirely in iron-based ink.

In Raman spectroscopy, laser light interacts with phonons (vibrations occurring in a rigid crystal lattice, such as the atomic lattice of a solid), shifting their energy up or down to identify particular chemical bonds. While this process has been found effective in detecting hidden explosives at airport security checkpoints, or discovering counterfeit narcotics without opening their packaging, it is not entirely reliable under all other circumstances. Smithsonian Institution chemist Jacqueline Olin later reviewed the Raman spectroscopy examination to find it flawed and suggested the ink that went into illustrating the Vinland Map could have been produced during medieval times after all. Although her analysis was supported by many other chemists, skeptics pointed out that she herself did not replicate the supposedly medieval ink.

Beginning in early 2004, Dr. Rene Larsen and his colleagues at the Royal Danish Academy of Fine Arts initiated the longest, most in-depth and broad-based investigation of the Vinland Map so far undertaken. Chemists, cartographers, historians, conservators, and other scientists subjected the map to thorough investigation from every conceivable angle. They found that all previous tests of its ink were flawed and missed much of the chemical evidence. For example, the map's allegedly early 20th century anatase probably came from sand used to dry the wet ink, because sand was commonly used to dry ink prior to the introduction of blotter paper. "You often find remains of it in old books and manuscripts," Dr. Larsen said.

Kenneth Towe, a retired geologist from the Smithsonian National Museum of Natural History in Washington, DC, and a long-time opponent of claims for the Vinland Map's authenticity, categorized the Danes' five-year study as "bogus." He explained that "the problem is if the anatase came out of gneiss or any other natural source, it is going to have a totally different appearance than the anatase that appears on the Vinland

Map ink." According to Towe, the Vinland Map's ink has small, round, chemically-produced crystals; sand would have larger, fractured crystals that resulted from grinding, along with other minerals, such as quartz. But Dr. Larsen points out that the sand had been washed or cleaned to produce the smallest crystals. Moreover, anatase, even in relatively high levels, has since been found in many contemporaneous books from the 15th century and earlier. But chemical analysis formed only part of his multi-disciplined examination, which found, among other, complimentary discoveries, that wormholes in the *Hystoria Tartarorum* caused by wood-beetles were consistent with those in the Vinland Map.

Towe is virtually alone in his unremitting opposition to the exhaustive Danish investigation. A general consensus of scientific opinion applauds the lengthy, careful research conducted by Dr. Larsen and his team, who have proved that the Vikings discovered, explored, and mapped much of North America 500 years before Columbus. But with critics such as Kenneth Towe in charge of our country's educational system, don't look for a sweeping revision of American history books anytime soon.

27

ANCIENT EUROPEANS IN NORTH AMERICA

How Did A Thousand-Year-Old Byzantine Coin End Up in Wisconsin?

BY FRANK JOSEPH

During late October 2008, Brad Sutherland was overseeing excavation for a private home in the southern Wisconsin town of Twin Lakes. Just two or three miles north of the Illinois border—almost midway between the cities of Milwaukee and Chicago—the immediate vicinity was sparsely developed and under-populated, with something of the pristine and unexplored. As the site's rough-carpenter foreman, he was responsible for clearing the property and excavation prior to construction.

Sutherland was also something of a rock hound, and, after work, eagerly sifted through the mounds of freshly heaped earth for interesting specimens. Among the pieces of common quartz crystal, feldspar, and occasional fossil, a small, moderately different stone attracted his attention, particularly for its unusual, dark brown coloration. Tossed into a gathering pile of possible additions to his mineralogical collection, it was forgotten until the following February, when he got around to polishing and cleaning his latest finds. As water and brush were applied to the "brown stone," Brad was surprised to observe that it was actually a badly eroded, brass or bronze coin, and appeared to be very old. He could make out what appeared to be faint markings of some kind but was unable to discern the coin's age or nationality.

I was unaware of his discovery as I arrived at the Sci-Fi Café in Burlington, Wisconsin, the evening before a "New Age" conference on 2009's summer solstice. The meeting was organized by Brad's wife, Mary, renowned for connecting individuals otherwise unknown to one another for researching a common project. That talent was in evidence as soon as

Wisconsin Coin Front

Wisconsin Coin Back

Byzantine Coin

Brad showed me the coin he had found the previous fall. Under a powerful magnifying glass, I could make out the vague representation of a human figure but nothing more; until Robert Vlassic, who likewise arrived a day early for the conference, said it seemed to resemble Byzantine imagery. But without a better view of the coin, no one could be sure.

Just then, Lynn Baumgartner, a conference organizer, walked in on our impromptu investigation. Lynn just happened to be a specialist in photographing small, metal objects, and her digital camera was in the car. She took a dozen shots of Brad's find under various lighting conditions to profile every detail on both sides in various close-ups. They revealed the badly worn but nonetheless identifiable lineaments of a saint-like image on one face and the outlines of a kingly figure on the other.

Moving on Robert Vlassic's impression that the coin resembled the monetary style of Byzantium, Denise Markowsky got on the Sci-Fi Café's computer to cruise the Internet for a possible match with something from that ancient city. She, too, had arrived early for the conference, but her expertise, as a grammar school teacher familiar with tracking down a variety of sources on behalf of research education, was particularly valuable at the moment. Denise explored several websites devoted to ancient coins, until she yelled, "Bingo! There it is!" Everyone crowded around her monitor to see photographs of a coin exactly resembling Brad Sutherland's discovery.

It was described by Forum Ancient Coins (a numismatic dealer) as a "bronze follis" (a coin of fixed weight associated with late or post imperial times from the Eastern Roman Empire), minted in Constantinople, the former name of Istanbul, Turkey's most famous city. The website coin approximated Wisconsin's version in weight (8.418 grams) and maximum diameter: 28.0 millimeters. The Forum Ancient Coins' follis featured an identical "obverse bust of Christ facing, wearing nimbus cruciger (a sunburst halo), pallium (a large, woolen cloak worn by Greek philosophers and teachers), and colobium (a sleeveless shirt associated by the Romans with civilized attire), raising right (hand) in benediction, Gospels in left."

The front face of the coin represented "Constantine X bust facing, bearded, wearing crown and loros (a long scarf worn on festive occasions by an emperor), holding cross and akakia (a cylindrical, purple, silk roll containing dust, held by Byzantine emperors during official ceremonies, and symbolizing the mortal nature of all men)." [see http:// www.forumancientcoins.com/catalog/roman-and-greek-coins]

The historical figure portrayed on both the Forum Ancient Coins' specimen and Brad Sutherland's find is Constantine X, who was crowned Byzantine emperor in AD 1059. Born Constantine Doukas, he was the son of a nobleman, and became politically influential through his marriage to the niece of Byzantium's leading patriarch. As such, Constantine X was something of a Christian puppet, who undercut his country's armed forces' financial support in favor of the Church. Shortly thereafter, the Seljuk Turks threatened from the east, while Norman invaders menaced from the north.

Panicked, the Emperor raised taxes to make up for the damage he so recently inflicted upon the army. He initiated renewed recruitment drives, increased payroll salaries, and resupplied the army with new weapons and equipment. His measures came too late to prevent the Norman conquest of virtually the entire Italian peninsula, a loss compounded by defeats in the Balkans and throughout Asia Minor. Aged beyond his years by these unfortunate events, despised by his over-taxed citizens, and sick with some incurable illness, Constantine X died during his 61st year in 1067.

How was it possible for one of his coins to have found its way to southern Wisconsin? That it was not dropped as loose change by some careless numismatist strolling through the outback of Twin Lakes seems certain, as it was dug up from about nine or ten feet beneath the surface of the earth, indicating its pre-modern provenance. Mainstream archaeologists nonetheless dismiss Brad Sutherland's discovery, *ipso facto*, as insignificant and meriting no serious consideration because it was not made by an accredited, university-trained scholar under controlled, scientific conditions. In other words, *they* did not find it.

Even if they had, the coin would have been ignored as archaeologically worthless under the prevailing, conventional wisdom that since no overseas visitors arrived in North America before Columbus, the anomalous object can only be understood somehow within the context of the last five centuries. This Dark Age mentality to the contrary, the appearance of a self-evidently legitimate artifact minted more than 400 years before Christopher Columbus arrived in the New World demands a credible explanation.

But Constantine X's Byzantium was in no condition to undertake transatlantic voyages. The pre-Classical Greek city had been transformed in AD 337 into Constantinople, after the death of its namesake, Constantine I, who made it the Christian capital of the Roman Empire, which even before then had entered into its decline. The city remained known as Constantinople—the "City of Constantine"—until the advent of Turkish reforms imposed by Mustafa Kemal Atatürk in 1930.

By the time Constantine X took over as emperor, the long-extinct Roman Empire had been far less successfully supplanted by Byzantine imperialism, as politically decadent as it was culturally inferior and spiritually benighted. Roman civilization's precipitous descent was graphically spelled out in its own coinage, from the high works of art exemplified by the denarii of Caesar Augustus to the exceedingly crude workmanship evident in Constantine X's follis. Beset on all sides by military crises, the poor quality of his ships additionally contributed to the unlikelihood of far-flung expeditions to the other side of the world.

He did, however, have in his service a group of foreign mercenaries already well acquainted with the rigors of oceanic travel and in possession of vessels sturdy enough to successfully negotiate the seas that had barred others from long-distance voyages. These were the Varangians, Vikings from Sweden, who sailed southward down the Volga River through Russia to Constantinople as early as AD 842. In Old Norse, the name is Væring-jar, derived from *væringi* (literally, "a sworn person"), "a foreigner who has taken service with a new lord by a treaty of fealty to him, or protégé."

Big, fearless men, skilled in warfare, armed with immense battle-axes, renowned for their steadfast loyalty, and commanding the most seaworthy vessels afloat, they hired themselves out as the Varangian Guard. They formed an elite corps of warriors only thrown into combat when the fighting was most desperate because they fought to the last man, but more often they turned the tide of battle. As such, they were highly valued and richly rewarded by Byzantine emperors, who stationed them close by in barracks at the palace itself. In addition to their military role, the Varangians acted as a royal bodyguard responsible for palace security. Although guard membership and leaders were entirely Norse, its commanding officer, the akolouthos, was invariably a native-born Byzantine.

Swedish historian Lars Magnar Enoksen writes that, to the people of Constantinople, the "Scandinavians were frightening both in appearance and in equipment; they attacked with reckless rage, and neither cared about losing blood nor their wounds" (*Runor: historia, tydning, tolkning,* Historiska Media, Falun, 1998). These qualities so endeared them to Byzantine royalty that the Varangians were awarded extraordinary privileges, including *polutasvarf*, or "palace pillaging," that allowed them to carry away as much gold and jewels from the imperial treasury as they could pocket on the day each emperor died. Yet, polutasvarf was merely a "perk" to their more usual rewards. Accordingly, the Varangians were no strangers to wealth.

Iceland's *Laxdœla* saga tells of their early 11th century leader, Bolli Bollason, who, along with "all his followers, dressed in scarlet, and rode on gilt saddles … he had over all a scarlet cape; and he had Footbiter [the name he affectionately bestowed on his broadsword] girt on him, the hilt of which was bright with gold, and the grip woven with gold; he had a

Nicholas Roerich's vision of exploring Varangians

gilded helmet on his head, and a red shield on his flank, with a knight painted on it in gold ... and whenever they took quarters, the women paid heed to nothing but gazing at Bolli and his grandeur, and that of his followers."

The Varangians were extended other, unique privileges, including the right to worship their "pagan" gods in private, away from Constantinople's Christian population. They were also allowed to get drunk; again, only as long as they kept to themselves. By the 12th century, the Væringjar had built up a well-deserved reputation as "the Emperor's wine-bags." Most of them eventually returned to Sweden rich men. A few stayed on in the Byzantine world, but others, more true to Viking restlessness, sailed throughout the Mediterranean Sea and beyond in their incomparable long-ships. Some may have ventured as far as North America, a supposition suggested by the coin Brad Sutherland found in southern Wisconsin.

Its minting in the mid-11th century coincided not only with Varangians at war at the far western borders of the Byzantine Empire: The Vinland Map—a Viking representation of eastern North America from Maine to Virginia, as far inland as Lake Ontario—was composed during the same epoch (see chapter 26, page 207). The Norse were unquestionably exploring our continent one thousand years ago, according to a five-year investigation completed in spring 2009 by the Royal Danish Academy of Fine Arts, in Copenhagen. Scholars there authenticated the Vinland Map as a genuine, early 11th century document.

A Constantinople follis from that same period found deep beneath the surface of the ground in North America suggests the presence of visiting Varangians, because they were, after all, paid in Byzantine coin. That they actually arrived in southern Wisconsin is less probable. More likely, the coin Brad Sutherland discovered had been brought to Twin Lakes by an indigene, perhaps an ancestor of the Ho-Chunk, or "People of the Big Voice," who then, as now, reside in the area.

It was very possibly a trade item exchanged with another tribal Indian from the east, where the coin was originally received from the hand of a Varangian veteran in the service of Constantine X. As such, it is complimentary evidence for the contemporaneous Vinland Map and points to the Swedish Norse identity of that document's Viking creators.

28

THE DISCOVERY OF THE OLD WORLD
BY NATIVE AMERICANS

Before the White Man Came West,
Did the Red Man Go East?

BY STEVEN SORA

T he winter of 1534 was particularly cruel to the first French adven-
turers in the New World led by Jacques Cartier. In their camp on
the coast of the St. Lawrence River, near what would become Montreal, scurvy broke out.

The hideous disease had taken the lives of 25 men whose bodies were
piled under snowdrifts. The ground was too frozen to properly bury the
dead. Among the remaining 125, only ten men were healthy. Those ten
attempted to make enough noise to prevent the nearby Algonquin tribe from
finding out just how weak they were.

When their Native American neighbors did find out, it was just in
time to save their lives. The medicine man boiled the bark of a certain tree
to make a brew they called *annedda*, and had the men drink this strange
brew. To a man, all were saved, their scurvy cured by the concoction.

The British navy would not "discover" the cure for scurvy until 1795,
which was based on the same foundation the native seagoing peoples of
Canada had understood from centuries before.

The discussion of the ability of pre-Columbian North American peoples has never amounted to anything more than isolated accidents, in part
because of the need to paint a picture of American indigenous peoples as
savages. With ships as large or greater than that of Columbus, cities certainly
greater than those of Europe, and more exacting science of mathematics and
timekeeping, the Americas clearly transcended our previous understanding.

That the Native Americans had a cure for the greatest plight of long
distance sailors was not the last surprise for the French. What would

Traditional Micmac Wigwam. Non traditional garb. (1873)

grow to become Montreal was Hochlaga, a planned village with streets emanating from a central square. They were simply not the savages that they would become in the histories of the New World. Just as the Spanish would find the Aztec City of Tenochtitlan to be greater than their own great city of Seville, the Europeans would also encounter many surprises from the Native Americans of the North.

One of the greatest surprises was from a branch of Algonquin tribes called the Micmac. Upon entering the mouth of the St. Lawrence, the French met this tribe who surrounded their own ship with two separate fleets of 50 canoes each. The ability of the native population to mass a large number of people on the river was surprise enough, and the French were soon to discover they could navigate great distances as well, possibly making numerous voyages to Scotland and the northern isles.

Europeans would find that the native populations of the northeast actually did engage in a vast trade that brought both goods and knowledge from far flung corners of the continent. From Mexico came the ability to farm beans and corn. From the southeast came conch shells, from the northeast came obsidian, and from the Great Lakes came copper. Much of the trade was conducted by water routes.

MISSING CONNECTIONS

The ability to sail great distances by sea was made known to Columbus as well. We know that the Carib people who Columbus encountered had canoes, complete with masts, that held 25 to 70 people. Columbus seized a ship of the Putun Mayans larger than his own. It could hold as many or more sailors as his own ships held. The Maya had fleets of a hundred ships and more and built wharves in Tulum and on the island of Cozumel for trade. On the other side of the continent, the Kwakiutl in the Northwest had ocean-going "canoes" that held 70 to 100 individuals. Clearly trade was well established in the Americas before the Europeans arrived.

Could American Indians have crossed the Atlantic?

Actually, we know that they did cross the ocean, and long before Columbus. After Caesar had conquered Gaul, a canoe with three survivors landed in Germany. A chieftain of a Germanic frontier tribe handed the men over to the governor Quintus Meltellus, who recognized that they were not Europeans. The incident was recorded by the Roman historian Pliny. Other instances were mentioned in other works of the same period. Inuit people had been known to cross the icy North Atlantic in kayaks and one such kayak decorated the cathedral at Nidaros in Norway.

When Columbus was still a map-maker he sailed to Galway in Ireland. Here a powerful current reaches the British Isles all the way from the Gulf of Mexico. When Columbus was there it washed ashore with two brown skinned, flat-faced individuals who Columbus assumed were "Indians," that is, from India. The incident helped convince him of his mission to reach Asia via the Atlantic.

Stranger still than these accidental visits, Native Americans had crossed the Atlantic, hundreds of years before, and "discovered" Europe and may have colonized Scotland.

They were the seagoing tribe that Cartier would meet, the Micmac. Historians confine these people to an area of Newfoundland and Nova Scotia, although part of the tribe was not the taller Algonquin stock but a shorter, darker people who adorned themselves in blue ink.

Tattoos and faces dyed in blue earned them the name "blue noses," a moniker that still exists on hundreds of fishing boats from Newfoundland to Maine. It is even a nickname for the coastal residents of the Northeast.

Micmacs wore loincloths, but they kept warm with a liberal coating of animal fat rubbed into the skin. This coat kept out the freezing weather and enabled them to sail the icy Atlantic.

When they landed in Scotland, the taller Celtic peoples called them "pixies," a name that still exists in the folklore of the British Isles. The Romans called them Picts.

The Micmac/Picts stayed apart from the Celts, living in the Highlands and keeping their own customs and language. In AD 81, hostilities with their neighbors in the south led to war, and the Picts laid waste to one-third of Briton. Two Roman historians, Nennius and Gildas, record these ancient hostilities.

Gildas said that they came from across the sea. He had no understanding of just where "over the sea" meant. Because he would have understood the closer locations such as France or Scandinavia, the implication is that it was elsewhere. Nennius described the war that followed. Rome could not defeat the Micmac/Picts. At best they could keep them confined to the Highlands despite the two walls that were built across the island. Here in the North they ruled until AD 844, when they united with the Scotti, a tribe that migrated from Ireland, a shorter over-the-sea distance.

The Algonquin speaking American Indians had a name for the ocean, *Katai* or *Katai-ikan* meaning "great ocean." Such a word might have led Europeans, including Columbus, to believe survivors of the Atlantic current might have come from "Cathay" or China.

The Aberlemno Serpent Stone is attributed to the Picts

It must be said that historians would find a relationship between a North American people and a Northern European people remote at best, yet there are some "coincidences" that are not easily explained away.

Both the Micmacs and the Picts wore loincloths. Unlike the practice of other tribes the loincloth of the Micmac described his clan. He was easily recognized by the insignias on his cloth. The loincloth of the Picts, and of course the later Highlanders, was the "kilt," an article of clothing that still in the 21st century allows the wearer to distinguish himself as a part of a clan. Early kilts carried the animal names of the clans along with the color chosen—the Red Deer Clan, the White Dog Clan, etc.

The Picts also painted their faces and tattooed their skin. Like the Micmacs, they wore little clothing, because they did not want to cover their artwork.

Feathered headdresses existed among the Micmac peoples, with rank determined by the number of feathers worn. This custom was also exhibited among the Picts, the only European people to denote rank by this method.

Both Micmac and Pict were matriarchal. This meant that individuals traced their family through the mother. The Celts were patriarchal. Families of both Picts and Micmacs were extended into the clan system. While the family was the first loyalty, clan was very important. The Clan Chattan, which means the Clan of the Cat, was the largest in Scotland.

In making decisions among the clan, women sat on the councils of the Picts and Micmacs as well as the fierce Iroquois. The women would determine which man would be the chieftain of the people.

As a form of celebration, the dances of the American Indian are well known. Among the lands in the British Isles, it is the Scots and Irish who are known for their dancing. The Highlanders are known for an annual Gathering of the Clans as practiced among wider tribal units of American Indians.

Racial characteristics are also shared among the Picts and Micmacs. Both are shorter than their neighbors, and both had darker complexions. The Celts, in comparison, were more likely to be taller, red or blond haired; the blue-eyed inhabitants of the later British Isles. The expression "dark Irish" or "Black Irish" survives today to distinguish them from the Celtic cousins. Anthropologists claim a Mediterranean melding, or even African, although there is no proof.

Other links are found in language. The prefix "maqq" is found in the Pictish language. It means "son of" but is not followed by a name. Dr. John Fraser, an Oxford professor of Celtic languages, said it is because the Picts placed no importance on an immediate father but a great deal of importance on their clan. They were sons of a wider clan group. It resembles the fosterage custom found in the Isles. In many cases, sons left their families and went to train as warriors. The teachers might be female or male. Prop-

A stone room at Skara Brae, Orkney Islands. The inhabitants would have been very small.

erty was owned by the woman and inherited often by the first daughter. A Pictish wife would not leave her family to live with her husband until she bore a child.

Finally, when Pict and Celt united, it was Celtic influence that made the father more important. "Maqq" or "Mac" was followed by a proper name.

Historian Charles Seaholm pioneered the concept of the Pict/Native American connection. He developed his theory by comparing Scottish surnames with place names found in New England.

Pennycook was a Pictish settlement that only became a surname much later when the Normans brought the use of surnames to the British Isles. Penacook was a settlement in New England that would later become Concord (New Hampshire) when Europeans settled there. It was a Native American word meaning "sloping down place." Other places were found using that same description to dub the place Pennacook. In Scotland, the Pennacook Clan took their name from a place with a similar description.

Hossack, in the rocky lands around Inverness, also lent its name to a family name. In New England, *hoosac* means "stone place," and as such there are several in those states.

Kinbuck, in Scotland, is a word that combines *kin* with the *-uck* ending, which is generally Pictish. *Kin* and *ken* can often signify a relation to water. In New England, Kennebunkport, Kennebec, and Kennebago are all places with water meanings in the name.

The late Harvard professor Barry Fell produced a large list of Algonquin and Scot-Irish names as well. Merrimack, a New Hampshire River, in the Algonquin language means "deep fishing." In Gaelic *merrio-mack* means "of great depth."

Monad in Algonquin is "mountain," in Gaelic, *monadh* means the same. *Nock* is an Algonquin word meaning "hill" and it corresponds to the Gaelic *cnoc*, meaning the same.

Seaholm's and Fell's work on place names produced scores of words that have the same or similar meanings on both sides of the Atlantic—words that mostly describe features of geography from hills, to rivers, to arable land. Neither agree with just who brought these commonly shared words to whom. Fell insists the Celts carried them west, while Seaholm thinks the Picts went east.

On both sides of the Atlantic, there are places where it appears the inhabitants were very small people. In New Hampshire there is the "Stonehenge of the Americas" where rooms created from rock exist in a stone village complete with astronomically oriented stones. At Skara Brae, in the Orkney Islands, are very similar stone rooms, near astronomically oriented monuments. Inhabitants of both places would have had to be very small.

Similarly, homes dug into the earth with only the top portion above ground in Scotland were called *wee gammes*, little houses. The homes of American Indians in some places were similarly called *wigwams*.

When Cartier, the man who would be rescued by a more knowledgeable primitive people, came to North America, he met a chief and recorded the chief's name as Donnacana. He said the name was a title, sort of related to "royal king." He believed that all the high chiefs would take this title.

In Scotland, the Duncan Clan received its name originally from Donnacaidh, who was their high chief. The word itself was also a title this time meaning "Brown Warrior." Similarly, Verranzano would encounter a chief with the name Magnus.

The reality of pre-Columbian ocean crossings would one day be discounted by nationalism and in the attempt to legitimize land grabbing by the Europeans. Clearly the evidence of voyages of discovery made from both directions presents us with a different picture.

29

ANCIENT CITIES IN THE FOREST

Shining New Light on Old Legends

BY WILLIAM B. STOECKER

It has been said that we might not even recognize an alien life form should we encounter one, nor the ruins of an alien civilization (at least not on Mars, if NASA and the Jet Propulsion Laboratory have their way). But how about ancient ruins here on Earth? Are we often looking in the wrong places and overlooking evidence of cultures that do not fit our preconceived notions? Can we even define "civilization"? There is reason to believe that the ruins of ice age "Atlantean" cultures may lie under water on the continental shelves, and the remnants of cultures that flourished during the Holocene Optimum may yet be found in areas that are today very arid or very cold.

If we are to become new explorers of the previously unseen, if we are to open our eyes to the possibility of unknown, or lost, or even alien cultures, we first need to reexamine our preconceived notions about how we perceive civilization at all.

Archaeologists always assumed that civilization began about 5,500 to 6,000 BP (before the present). People first developed agriculture, and then woven fabrics and fired ceramics, and began building towns of adobe brick or stone. Writing followed soon after. Aside from the fact that agriculture was developed by 12,000 BP at the latest, and the fact that the origins of the alphabet are a complete mystery, recent finds cast serious doubt on all of our assumptions.

Hunter-gatherers in Central Europe made woven fabrics and fired ceramics by 28,000 BP. Other hunter-gatherers at the Gobekli Tepe site in what is now Turkey built large monuments of cut stone bearing at least some resemblance to Stonehenge and other stone circles, monuments which possible indicate some knowledge of mathematics and astronomy. Our assumption that fabrics, ceramics, and shaped stone structures followed the invention of farming is clearly mistaken.

We know of five ways for a people to obtain food. There are hunter-gatherers, fishermen (a variant of hunting), herdsmen, farmers (like many North American Indians a few centuries ago) who hunted for their animal protein, and farmers who also keep domestic livestock. It is now obvious that any of these food obtaining systems—not just agriculture—can allow a civilization to develop; fishing during the last ice age could have supported quite a large population of seafarers.

Early Spanish explorers searched for lost cities like El Dorado in the rain forests of the vast Amazon river system. In 1541, Francisco de Orellana and Friar Gaspar de Carvajal went down the Amazon tributaries from the west and claimed to have seen huge walled cities, gleaming white, and roads up to 60 feet wide. But European diseases decimated the native population in what may have been the greatest epidemic in history, and later explorers and settlers found only "primitive" farmers in small villages, who hunted for their meat, rather like many of the Indians of North America. Yet the legends persisted.

Percy Fawcett, a colonel in the Royal Artillery and a veteran of World War I, was born in 1867 in Devon, England, to a rather adventurous fam-

El Dorado [*Atlantis Rising* art]

ily. His father was a Fellow in the Royal Geographic Society, and his brother Edward was a mountain climber. A man with intellectual interests (some would say obsessions), he believed that the ruins of Atlantis, or at least one of its colonies, might be found in the Brazilian rainforest. He made several expeditions and, in 1925, he and his oldest son Jack went into the (then largely unexplored) Matto Grosso region in search of a lost city he called "Z." They vanished off the face of the Earth and were apparently never seen again. They may have been murdered and robbed by the Kalapalos Indians, who admitted being the last to see them and who had some of their possessions, or by Indians further along on their route, such as the Arunas, Suyas, or Xavantes. The Kalapalos claimed to have seen Fawcett's nightly campfire smoke further in the distance each day for five days. This is certainly possible, as travel in dense jungle can be painfully slow. Supposedly, one member of the Kalapalos tribe admitted that they had murdered and robbed the Fawcett's; and it is a fact that the tribe captured and robbed the members of an expedition in 1996, but they released them unharmed. There are other rumors that Fawcett and his son were captured by Indians and lived among them for years, even marrying into the tribe, but there is no evidence of this.

Whatever happened to Fawcett and his son, we know that he was looking for a stone city in a region where there was little stone to be found, and practically none suitable for building. In the humid and rainy Amazon, structures of wood and thatch decay and adobe is washed away; whatever remains becomes covered by the forest. Blinded by his own assumptions, Fawcett could have walked directly over the remains of an advanced culture and never seen or recognized it. Actually, in at least one part of the Amazon there is an ancient stone structure, the so-called "Amazon Stonehenge" in Brazil near the border with French Guiana, discovered by Brazil's Amapa Institute of Scientific and Technological Research. It consists of 127 blocks of granite, many of them ten feet tall, and there is a hole in one that aligns with the sun at the time of the winter solstice. Ceramics nearby have been dated as early as 2,000 BP. In the Andean foothills of southeast Peru, there are oddly symmetrical structures that may be the remains of cities and of pyramids rivaling in size those at Giza. Or they may be natural formations ... no one yet is willing to finance an excavation in this relatively inaccessible area.

Regarding the "Stonehenge" and its associated pottery, there is no way to be certain that the circle and the ceramics were made by the same cul-

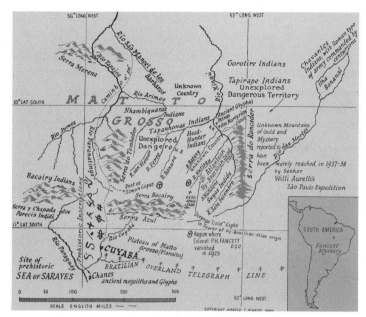

Harold T. Wilkens' 1949 map of Col. Percy Fawcett's ill-fated expedition

ture or at the same time, although it seems likely. There is really no way to date stone blocks. Ceramics and stones used in hearths and heated to a high enough temperature can be dated by thermoluminescence. Electrons are trapped in the crystal lattice of ceramics and are driven out when they are fired. Over the centuries, new electrons seep back in and can be measured by the dim light they emit when the material is heated during testing. Supposedly, the older the material is the brighter the light, as there has been time for more electrons to be trapped, and the dating method can be used for artifacts up to several hundred thousand years old. In practice, there are many uncontrollable variables that reduce the accuracy, and the older something is the less accurate the dating. The method is pretty good for artifacts dating from about 300-10,000 BP. Charcoal from cooking fires and other organic material can be dated using carbon-14, a radioactive isotope caused by ordinary carbon's exposure to cosmic rays. Once the carbon is trapped by plants using atmospheric carbon dioxide for photosynthesis, the radiation begins to decrease as the carbon-14 decays back into ordinary carbon-12. Carbon-14 has a half life of 5,700 years, meaning that it is only half as radioactive after that time; so the older the material the less accurate the dating, with the maximum being about 60,000 years. There are numerous other problems, including the possibility of contamination of samples, but carbon-14 dating, within the last few tens of thousands of years, is usually fairly accurate.

A number of years ago there were reports in the media of the discovery in the Amazon basin of the ruins of ancient towns, roads, canals, and huge, earthen mounds. There were claims that some of the ruins might date back as far as 7,000 BP and that the Indians, presumably, had even dug canals connecting different rivers with one another. More recently, articles have been published with photographs and detailed information on this culture, but all references to canals actually connecting rivers have been dropped; and all accounts now claim that the culture dates back only to about 1,800 BP at the most and that it survived until about 700 BP. Dozens of sites, ironically exposed by deforestation, have been discovered. There are huge, geometric earthworks with canals (none of which, it is now claimed, connect rivers to one another), and mounds upon which towns were built. Other towns were surrounded by earthen walls and moats and housed up to 2,500-5,000 people each. The towns were built on high ground between rivers, usually near springs, and the moats were up to 36 feet wide and 3 feet deep. The walls around the towns were low, about 3 feet tall, so their real function is a mystery; clearly they would not be effective for defense. The houses were presumably like those used by more modern Indians, constructed of wood and thatch (many of the contemporary ones are quite large, well engineered, and beautifully built). Of course, such structures would not survive long in the rainforest. The ancient Indians used fired ceramics, but, so far, there is no evidence of metals.

There is no evidence of domestic livestock, so presumably they hunted and fished for animal protein. Their agriculture was quite advanced, and archaeologists are only beginning to understand it. One of the developments, if it can be fully understood, could have important benefits for modern inhabitants of the area. The soil in much of the Amazon is actually quite poor and is particularly deficient in many minerals, so when land is cleared for farming and ranching, often, after only a few growing seasons, it becomes infertile and a wasteland is created. But the ancient Indians in these towns seem to have practiced a peculiar variant of slash and burn agriculture, somehow managing to control the burning so as to create large amounts of charcoal, which was then pulverized and worked into the soil. The tiny and highly absorptive charcoal grains hosted fungi and bacteria, which seem to aid in capturing and retaining soil nutrients.

The resulting black soil is now called "terra preta," and if the technology can be relearned, the region may become fertile farmland again.

Some archaeologists also suspect that the ancient Indians modified the surrounding forests, planting more useful trees. Since this was not the kind of monoculture we practice today (with huge fields or orchards devoted to one crop), and since the trees were probably not planted in rows, we would not recognize such an area as being anything special. Note that North American Indians also modified the natural environment, sometimes burning wooded areas to create more grassland for deer and other game animals. This would be a kind of intermediate step between hunting and animal husbandry, and the planting of useful trees would be intermediate between gathering and farming. A lot of our assumptions about early cultures are proving to be incorrect.

But what of early accounts of canals connecting rivers and of the culture dating back many thousands of years? Was this just a mistake, an exaggeration, or are archaeologists now covering something up or being overly conservative? This has been known to happen. The massive Amazon system drains into the Atlantic Ocean, and the Orinoco system empties into the Caribbean. It is, to say the least, highly unusual for river systems going in different directions to connect with one another naturally. For example, the Tigris and Euphrates, which flow almost parallel to one another through Iraq and whose deltas combine before reaching the Persian Gulf, are not connected at all in the mountains that are their source. A tributary of the Tigris will drain one way, and a tributary of the Euphrates, on the other side of a narrow ridge, will drain another way. But the Guarina River, a tributary of the Rio Negro, which flows into the Amazon, is connected by the 300 kilometer long Casiquiare River (if it is a river) to the upper Orinoco. This connection was, of course, always known to the local Indians, but the first Europeans to travel its entire length were the great German explorer and naturalist, Alexander von Humboldt and his French comrade, Aime Bonpland. Now it is (just barely) possible to imagine a way such a connection might be formed naturally. If the two drainages were once separated by high ground and then the river basins silted up until they were as high as the divide, and if there was a flood in one system but not the other, maybe, somehow, this could form without human intervention. But it looks like an incredibly long canal.

30

THE SECRET SEARCH FOR THE
MISSING MAP OF COLUMBUS

Did Charles Hapgood Enlist President Eisenhower
in a Wild Goose Chase or Was It Something
Much More Astonishing?

BY RAND & ROSE FLEM-ATH

A 1960 Memo to President Eisenhower revived a centuries-old quest: locating the "Lost World Map of Columbus." Here, verbatim, is the message which Charles Hapgood sent to President Eisenhower:

To: President Dwight D. Eisenhower

From: Charles H. Hapgood Professor of History

Re: THE PIRI REIS WORLD MAP OF 1513 AND
THE LOST MAP OF COLUMBUS

Memorandum

For several centuries scholars have been searching for the lost map of Christopher Columbus. The map is referred to by Columbus' contemporaries, and by the historian Las Casas, as one he used to navigate by to the New World.

In 1929 a map was discovered in the former Imperial Palace (The Seraglio) in Constantinople, authored by a Turkish admiral of the 16th century, Piri Reis. In the inscriptions written on this map the author states that the western part, showing the American coasts, was copied from a map that had been in the possession of Christopher Columbus, but which had fallen into the hands of Piri Reis with the booty seized from eight Spanish ships captured by him in a battle off the coast of Valencia in 1501 or 1508.

The Piri Reis map (a copy of which accompanies this memorandum) attracted the attention of President Kemal Ataturk, and of the American Secretary of State, Henry Stimson, who, in 1932, asked the Turkish Government for a color facsimile of the map, and for a search of Turkish archives and collections to see if the lost map of Columbus might not be found. The facsimile of the map now hangs in the Map Division of the Library of Congress, but the original Piri Reis worked from— Columbus' own map (or a copy of it)—was never found.

We now have excellent reason to believe that the original map still exists, and in the Spanish archives! The reason that this map has remained so long undiscovered appears to be, simply, that it is very different from the other contemporary maps and is not at all what scholars would expect to find in a map of Columbus. It is not a map Columbus himself made, but one he found in the Old World. It should resemble the western side of the Piri Reis map, if it can be found. Evidence of its present whereabouts came to me through my old friend and scientific collaborator, James H. Campbell, who, together with his father, a professional geographer, actually saw this map in 1893. I am enclosing a separate account of this incident in Mr. Campbell's own words. It seems that in 1893, at the time of the Columbian Exposition at Chicago, the Spanish Government built and sent to America replicas of Columbus' three ships. The caravels were sailed across the Atlantic, and through the Great Lakes to Chicago. It was there that Mr. Campbell and his father were invited, as he describes in detail, to see Columbus' own map in the chart room of the Santa Maria!

In addition to the important purpose of clearing up many mysteries relating to the Discovery of America, we have another purpose in asking that a search be made for the map now. Studies of the map by various scholars have shown that it contains many details that were not known to geographers in 1513. These indicate that the map must descend from maps made in very ancient times, and that navigators (possibly of Phoenician origin) discovered and explored the coasts or Americas perhaps a millennium before the Christian era. This, of course, tends to give support to the tradition that Columbus brought a map from the Old World. It seems that Columbus left the Old World with quite a good map of America in his pocket!

The most remarkable detail of the Piri Reis map indicating its enormous age was pointed out by Captain Arlington H. Mallery some years ago. He stated that the lower part of this map showed the sub-glacial topography of Queen Maud Land, Antarctica, and the Palmer Peninsula. After four years of study of the map we came to recognize that Captain Mallery's statement was correct, but, desiring the most authoritative checking of our conclusions, we submitted the data to the cartographic staff of the Strategic Air Command. I attach a letter from Col. Harold Z. Ohlmeyer, Commander of the 8th Reconnaissance Technical Squadron, SAC, in confirmation. Needless to say this is a matter of enormous importance for cartography and for history. The Antarctic ice cap is at present one mile thick over the areas shown on the Piri Reis Map. Consultations with geological specialists have indicated beyond question the truth that the data on the map is many thousands of years old. It seems that the Antarctic ice cap covered the queen Maud Land coast not later than 6,000 years ago. The map information must have been obtained earlier, either by the Phoenicians or by some earlier (and unknown) people.

If the Columbus map can now be found we shall learn whether it contained the Antarctic data, or whether Piri Reis used another source map. If the Columbus map did contain the data, then we will know he found the map in Europe, and that therefore he had a good idea of where he was going.

We have found, in our long study of the Piri Reis map, a number of errors which explain, in our opinion, Columbus' confusion as to whether Cuba was the mainland, and his underestimate of the distance to America.

The most important step at the present time is to push the search in Spain for the map that was on the replica of the Santa Maria during the summer of 1893. Success in this search will make it possible to rewrite, in a fundamental way, the history of the Discovery of America.

Very sincerely yours,

Charles H. Hapgood
Keene Teachers College

PROFESSOR CHARLES HAPGOOD'S MEMO got the President's attention. He instructed the American Ambassador to Spain to use his influence to find the ancient map that Columbus had on board during his historic 1492 voyage across the Atlantic.

Hapgood was seeking the holy grail of ancient maps, the so-called *mappa mundus* thought to be the original map of the world. He believed the Piri Reis map was but a fragment of this much older complete and accurate document that predated the Age of European Discovery.

In November 1929, Halil Edhem, the Director of Turkey's National Museum, was hunched over his solitary task of classifying documents. He pulled toward him a map drawn on Roe deer skin. As Halil opened the chart to its full dimensions (2 feet by 3 feet wide, or 60 X 90 cm) he was surprised by how much of the New World was depicted on a map dated 1513.

The document was the legacy of a pirate turned Turkish Admiral, Piri Reis (circa 1470-1554). He was born in Gallipoli, a naval base on the Marmara Sea and was the nephew of Kemal Reis, a pirate who had reinvented himself as a Turkish Admiral adventurer who made his name in naval warfare. Piri Reis sailed with his famous uncle from 1487 to 1493. It was during these voyages that he was introduced to the lucrative spoils of piracy. The fleet fought pirates and captured and plundered enemy ships. In 1495, Kemal Reis' skill in the art of battle earned him

Christopher Columbus (Painting by Carl von Piloty)

an invitation to join the Imperial Turkish Fleet. His nephew accompanied him to his new assignment.

The pirates had transformed into respectable Admirals.

After Kemal was killed during a naval battle in 1502, Piri Reis turned his back on the seafaring life and began a second career as a map maker. A perfectionist, Piri Reis would not tolerate the slightest error in his drawings. In 1513 he created his famous map. He relied on older source maps, including charts captured from Christopher Columbus when the Turks raided one of his ships before the crew had a chance to throw the charts overboard.

A COLUMBUS CONTROVERSY

The general public first learned of the map's existence in the February 27, 1932 issue of the *Illustrated London News*. The article, entitled, "A Columbus Controversy: America—And Two Atlantic Charts," noted that Columbus got little further than the mouth of the Orinoco, in Venezuela, in his voyage along the coast of South America in 1498, so that the stretches of the South American coast given in the Piri Reis's chart must have been copied from other sources.

In the July 23 edition of the magazine, Akcura Yusuf, President of the Turkish Historical Research Society, wrote a more detailed account.

"Piri Reis himself explains, in one of the marginal notes on his map, how he prepared it:

> This section explains the way the map was prepared. It is the only chart of its kind existing now. I, personally, drew and prepared it. In preparing the map I used about twenty old charts and eight Mappa Monde [i.e. the charts called Jaferiye by the Arabs, and prepared at the time of Alexander the Great, in which the whole inhabited world is shown]; the charts of the West Indies; and the new maps made by four Portuguese, showing the Sind, Indian, and Chinese Seas geometrically represented. I also studied the chart that Christopher Columbus drew for the West. By reducing all these charts to a single scale, I compiled the present map. My map is as correct and reliable for the seven seas as are the charts that represent the seas of our countries.

The author pointed out a significant fact: "...the map in our possession is a fragment." If the other fragments had not been lost, we should have had in our possession a Turkish chart drawn in 1513 representing the Old and New Worlds together.

Hapgood enlisted the help of the Cartographic staff of the Strategic Air Command (SAC) in studying the map. The U.S. Air Force investigation determined that the southern part of the map did accurately depict portions of subglacial Antarctica. This conclusion flew in the face of conventional wisdom which dictated that the island continent hadn't been discovered until 1818.

USAF Lt. Colonel Harold Z. Ohlmeyer wrote to Hapgood on July 6, 1960. This letter from Lt. Colonel Ohlmeyer was included in Hapgood's 1960 Memo to the President.

SOURCES FOR PIRI REIS: HOW OLD?

Hapgood and his students found, to their surprise, that this ancient map, which should have been full of errors, was remarkably accurate. It possessed a standard of technical excellence beyond what Europeans could have achieved in 1513.

Determining longitude at sea wasn't even possible until the 1730s, when John Harrison invented and perfected the marine chronometer, a highly sophisticated mechanical clock. The incredible mechanical obstacles that the chronometer's inventor had to overcome are documented in Dava Sobel's *Longitude* (2007).

One of the oddities about the Piri Reis map was that it had been drawn using an extremely sophisticated projection. An "equidistant projection" depicts the features of the earth from a single point on its surface. This projection can be calculated from any spot on the globe.

Perhaps the most familiar equidistant projection is the blue and white flag of the United Nations, centered on the North Pole. To draft a map using this method requires advanced mathematics, instrumentation, and knowledge unrealized by the Europeans of 1513.

The equidistant projection was one that was very familiar to the cartographic staff of the Strategic Air Command at Westover Air Force Base in Massachusetts. It was used to target Soviet military and economic assets. For example, a map drawn using Moscow as its center allowed the military to calculate the quickest delivery time for a missile to travel from any NATO base to the Soviet capital.

The Piri Reis Map of 1513

Charles Hapgood explained to Arch C. Gerlach (Chief of the Map Division at the Library of Congress) that the Piri Reis map "required more astronomy than was known in the Renaissance. The mathematics require that whoever constructed it had to know the linear distance from Syene to the North Pole to within a degree of accuracy. Piri Reis did not know that, neither did Columbus…"

Hapgood, as well as the Air Force experts, had become convinced by their exhaustive studies that the Piri Reis map offered compelling evidence that an unknown, ancient civilization possessed advanced astronomical and geodesic knowledge.

SYENE OR THE TROPIC OF CANCER?

Hapgood and his students spent months trying to determine the exact center of the Piri Reis Map. At first, Hapgood was convinced that it was the city of Syene where Eratosthenes (3rd century BC), the librarian and father of geography, had made his famous calculations about the circumference of the Earth. Hapgood submitted this suggestion to the cartographic crew at Westover Air Force Base. Captain Burroughs concurred. He wrote, "Piri Reis' use of the portolano projection (centered on Syene, Egypt) was an excellent choice..."

THE PIRI REIS MAP'S PROJECTION

The 1513 Piri Reis projection is but a fragment of the secret map that Columbus may have possessed. When the lost map is found it will depict the entire globe using an equidistance projection centered on the ancient Egyptian city of Syene.

We see to the right how the complete map must have looked based on the same projection used by Piri Reis in 1513. The chart Christopher Columbus carried on his voyage would have resembled this projection.

Despite the fact that professionals had verified Syene as the center of the map, Hapgood remained skeptical. He thought that the ancients would have been more likely to use the Tropic of Cancer, which divides the tropical from the temperate climatic zones. Hapgood was certain that such an important global marker would have been highly significant to the ancient navigators.

Syene World

Today, the Tropic of Cancer lies near Syene but not precisely over it. The difference in distance is small, but Hapgood and his students wanted to be exact in their calculations. There was considerable debate whether or not to use the measurement from the ancient city or from the climatic marker. Hapgood mistakenly assumed that it had to be an either/or choice between Syene or the Tropic of Cancer. It was a false choice.

There was a time when the Tropic of Cancer lay directly over Syene. We believe that a clue to that synchronicity of time and place lies within the very projection of the Piri Reis Map. When did the Tropic of Cancer and Syene share exactly the same latitude?

By calculating the difference in distance from the latitude of today's Tropic of Cancer (23°27'N) to that of Syene (24°05'30"N), we discover the answer—about 5,775 years ago—that is, circa 3767 BC.

The projection of the Piri Reis points like an arrow at a pivotal turning point in human history: Egyptian civilization dawned circa 3800 BC.

THE SECOND SANTA MARIA

Hapgood feared that the Spanish authorities would not take up the President's challenge to locate the source maps that Columbus had used to chart his trip to the New World. After all, they had no motive to re-write history since they were content with its outcome—Spain had discovered America. To overcome this problem Hapgood drafted a letter for President Eisenhower to send to Franco, Spain's fascist leader.

Included with the letter was James Hunter Campbell's (1873–1962) account of his sighting of the elusive map. Campbell was only 19 years old in the summer of 1893 when he accompanied his father to see the replica of the Santa Maria while it was docked in Toronto on its way to the World's Columbian Exposition (the Chicago World's Fair), held to celebrate the 400th anniversary of Christopher Columbus' arrival in America.

The mention of the chart being "four feet square" intrigued Hapgood since the Piri Reis map was about "two by three feet." Might the map that Campbell saw actually depict the entire world and not just the Piri Reis fragment?

Hapgood was also curious about the senior Campbell's reaction to the map. Campbell's father was no ordinary examiner of the old document; he had written geography texts. The fact that he "poured over the chart with his nose almost touching the paper" was suggestive. We know that the senior Campbell was not puzzled by the inscriptions since he was a "Spanish scholar." So what was it that fascinated him? We suggest it was the unusual equidistant projection—uncommon in 1893.

THE WHITE HOUSE ACTS

We discovered through President Eisenhower's Archives that the U.S. State Department, upon orders from Eisenhower, directed the American

Ambassador to Spain, John David Lodge, to pursue the matter of Hapgood's memorandum.

Ambassador Lodge's younger brother, Henry Cabot Lodge (1902–1985), was Richard Nixon's running mate during the 1960 campaign. Despite the obvious distractions, Lodge followed through on the presidential order. The Spanish authorities came up empty handed.

WE TAKE UP THE HUNT

As librarians, we were challenged by the problem of finding this critical document. We began by contacting a friend in Toronto, Shawn Montgomery, to see if he could follow up on Campbell's suggestion that the Royal Canadian Yacht Club might have log entries concerning the visit of the Santa Maria replica.

The logs from 1893 no longer existed.

We then turned to the Chicago side of the mystery and contacted Ray Grasse, an author and friend living in Chicago. Ray suggested that we contact the Chicago Historical Society. The Librarian at the society, Emily Clark, told us that the Captain who sailed the replica of the Santa Maria in 1893 was named V. M. Concas.

Ms. Clark turned our request over to Cynthia Matthews who worked in the Archives. She hit on the mother lode and sent us an account of the trip written by the Captain himself. From this we discovered that Hapgood's logical assumption that the "lost Columbus map" was housed in the Spanish Archives was incorrect. In fact, according to Captain Concas, the Columbus maps were located in an entirely different location:

"She [Spain] had sent also the original charts of America, but the difficulties attending the proper custody in the Convent of Rabida of this valuable collection of charts, where are also the original documents connected with the discovery of America (also belonging to Spain), has resulted in their being examined by a very limited number of persons."

Could the "lost map of Columbus" be found within the sand-colored walls of the modest La Rábida Monastery?

The Monastery was originally built by the Knights Templar in 1261. After they fell from power in 1307, the Franciscans chose the Monastery as one of their Spanish bases.

In 1485, Christopher Columbus began lobbying European royalty to finance an unprecedented voyage to India and China. He would sail west across the Atlantic, something that had never been done before. Until then all voyages to India and China had sailed south, hugging the coast of Africa before traveling east.

Frustrated in his attempts to enlist a patron to support his "westward" route to Asia, Columbus decided to join the rich pilgrims who regularly journeyed across Europe. His hope was that one of them would finance his venture or use their influence to obtain an audience for him with one of the royal families.

In 1490 he arrived at La Rábida. Fortunately for Columbus, the Prior of La Rábida took a liking to him and intervened on Columbus' behalf with King Ferdinand and Queen Isabella. The great explorer was at the Monastery when he received the exciting news that his ambitious voyage had been approved. It would not be surprising that he left his most valuable maps to the Prior who made his dream possible.

Is the lost map still lying in the shadows on a dusty shelf in a quiet Spanish monastery?

What could we discover from it if we could see its ancient face?

How would our concept of history be changed if Hapgood and Campbell were right?

CONTRIBUTING AUTHORS

HERBERT BANGS, M.Arch., deceased in 2010, was a professional architect, a designer for R. R. Buckminster Fuller's architectural firm, Geodesics, Inc., and was the Baltimore County architect and principal master planner. He is author of *The Return of Sacred Architecture: The Golden Ratio and the End of Modernism*, which includes a foreword by John Anthony West.

PETER BROS has long challenged the current, splintered concepts of empirical science and has spent his life studying the nature of physical reality and humanity's place in the universe. He is the author of the 9 volume *Copernican Series*.

DAVID HATCHER CHILDRESS, known to his many fans as the real-life Indiana Jones, is author or coauthor of over 20 books. He has appeared on Fox-TV's *Sightings and Encounters*, two NBC-TV specials, *The Conspiracy Zone*, and segments for the Discovery Channel, A&E, The Sci-Fi Channel, The Travel Channel and others. (*adventuresunlimitedpress.com*)

PHILIP COPPENS, deceased in 2012, was an author and investigative journalist, reporting on subjects from the world of politics to ancient history and mystery. He lectured extensively and appeared on numerous television and DVD documentaries, including *Ancient Aliens: The Series* (The History Channel). He is the author of several books, including *The Stone Puzzle of Rosslyn Chapel*, *The Canopus Revelation*, *Land of the Gods*. (*philipcoppens.com*)

RALPH ELLIS has been researching biblical and Egyptian history for more than 30 years. Being independent from theological and educational establishments allows Ralph to tread where others do not dare, which has allowed him to bring to light so many new biblical and historical truths. He is the author of *Mary Magdalene: Princess of Orange* and *Jesus: Last of the Great Pharaohs*, among many other books. (*edfu-books.com*)

RAND AND ROSE FLEM-ATH are authors of *When the Sky Fell, The Atlantis Blueprint*, and *Field of Thunder*. To learn the latest on the search for Columbus' lost world map visit their website. (*flem-ath.com*)

WILLIAM HENRY is an author, investigative mythologist, regular guest presenter on *Ancient Aliens*, and star of Arcanum TV. He is the author of *The Secret of Sion, Mary Magdalene the Illuminator: The Woman Who Enlightened Christ, Cloak of the Illuminati*, among many others.(*williamhenry.net*)

FRANK JOSEPH is a leading scholar on ancient mysteries, and the editor-in-chief of *Ancient American* magazine. He is the author of many books, including *Atlantis and 2012, The Destruction of Atlantis, The Lost Civilization of Lemuria, Survivors of Atlantis*, and *The Lost Treasure of King Juba*. He lives in Minnesota. (*ancientamerican.com*)

LEN KASTEN has written numerous articles for *Atlantis Rising*. While in the Air Force, Kasten experienced a UFO encounter that transformed his life. Since then, he has been deeply involved in UFO research, life after death, sacred geometry, Atlantis, and related subjects. He brings his extensive metaphysical background to he writing of *The Secret History of Extraterrestrials*, which provides the reader with a depth of understanding of UFO phenomena not otherwise readily available. (*et-secrethistory.com*)

JOHN KETTLER is a former military aerospace intelligence analyst with a life-long interest in the "black world" of covert and special ops, government secrets and coverups, world-wide conspiracies, UFOs, ETs, secret technology and much more. He spent years working on defense projects for Hughes Aircraft and Rockwell. Kettler was a frequent contributor to *Atlantis Rising* magazine for more than a decade. (*johnkettler.com*)

CYNTHIA LOGAN has been a freelance writer and editor for over 20 years. Her articles have appeared in *Atlantis Rising* magazine, as well as numerous regional, national, and international publications.

JEFF NISBET, while researching his family's Scottish roots, discovered that one of the historical luminaries of the Nisbet clan, Lord Nisbet of Dirleton, had been an early Grand Master of Scottish Freemasonry. Nisbet's research into Scottish history, the Freemasons, and the Knights Templar has led to his writing numerous articles for *Atlantis Rising* as well as other publications. (*mythomorph.com*)

ROBERT M. SCHOCH, a full-time faculty member at Boston University, earned his Ph.D. in geology and geophysics at Yale University. He is best known for his re-dating of the Great Sphinx of Egypt featured in the Emmy Award-winning NBC production *The Mystery of the Sphinx*. He is a frequent guest on many top-rated talk shows. His latest book is *The Parapsychology Revolution*. (*robertschoch.com*)

MARK AMARU PINKHAM is the author of *Guardians of the Holy Grail: The Knights Templar, John the Baptist and The Water of Life*. Mark currently serves as the North American Grand Prior of the International Order of Gnostic Templars, a division of the Scottish Knights Templar dedicated to reviving the Goddess and Gnostic rites and wisdom of the original Knights Templar. (*gnostictemplars.org*)

STEVEN SORA lives on Long Island. In 1999 he published the widely read and frequently quoted *Lost Treasure of the Knights Templar*. He is the author of many books dealing with esoteric history and over 100 articles. He is a frequent guest in documentaries dealing with ancient mysteries and lost history.

WILLIAM ("BEN") STOECKER, former Air Force Intelligence Officer, was driven to seek the truth through a lifetime of thought and study. As a result, he can effectively challenge orthodoxy in many fields, including science, history, astronomy, and more. He is author of *The Atlantis Conspiracy*. His articles appear regularly on *UnexplainedMysteries.com*.

About the Editor

J. DOUGLAS KENYON is the editor and publisher of *Atlantis Rising* magazine. He is also the editor of *Paradigm Busters, Missing Connections, Forbidden History, Forbidden Science*, and *Forbidden Religion*. (*atlantisrising.com*)

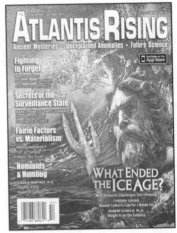